SAMS
Teach Yourself

D1621570

Microsoft®

SQL Server™
2005 Express

in **24** Hours

Alison Balter

SAMS   800 East 96th Street, Indianapolis, Indiana, 46240 USA

Sams Teach Yourself Microsoft® SQL Server 2005 Express in 24 Hours

International Standard Book Number: 0-672-32741-4

Library of Congress Catalog Card Number: 00-109716

Printed in the United States of America

Second Printing: October 2006

Trademarks

Warning and Disclaimer

Publisher
Paul Boger

Managing Editor
Gina Kanouse

Acquisitions Editor
Loretta Yates

Development Editor
Mark Renfrow

Project Editor
George Nedeff

Copy Editor
Margo Catts

Indexer
Ken Johnson

Proofreader
Heather Waye Arle

Technical Editor
Todd Meister

Team Coordinator
Cindy Teeters

Book Designer
Gary Adair

Layout Technician
Nonie Ratcliff

Contents at a Glance

Part III: Security and Administration

Table of Contents

Sams Teach Yourself Microsoft SQL Server 2005 Express in 24 Hours

About the Author

Alison Balter is the president of InfoTechnology Partners, Inc., a computer consulting firm based in the rural Santa Rosa Valley Area, close to Camarillo, California. Alison is a highly experienced independent trainer and consultant specializing in Windows applications training and development. During her 23 years in the computer industry, she has trained and consulted with many corporations and government agencies. Since Alison founded InfoTechnology Partners, Inc. (formerly Marina Consulting Group) in 1990, its client base has expanded to include major corporations and government agencies such as Shell Oil, Accenture, Northrop, the U.S. Drug Enforcement Administration, Prudential Insurance, Transamerica Insurance, Fox Broadcasting, the U.S. Navy, and others.

InfoTechnology Partners, Inc., is a Microsoft Certified Partner, and Alison is a Microsoft Certified Professional. Alison was one of the first professionals in the computer industry to become a Microsoft Certified Solutions Developer.

Alison is a partner in the multimedia training company Blast Through Learning, Inc., and is the author of more than 300 internationally marketed computer training videos and CD-ROMs, including 18 Access 2000 videos, 35 Access 2002 videos, and 15 Access 2003 videos. These videos and CD-ROMs are available by contacting Alison's company, InfoTechnology Partners, Inc. Alison travels throughout North America, giving training seminars on Microsoft Access, Visual Studio .NET, Microsoft SQL Server, Visual Basic, and Visual Basic for Applications. She is also featured in several live satellite television broadcasts for National Technological University.

Alison is a regular contributing columnist for *Access/Office/VB Advisor*, as well as other computer publications. She is also a regular on the Access, Visual Studio .NET, SQL Server, and Visual Basic national speaker circuits. She was one of four speakers on the Visual Basic 4.0 and 5.0 World Tours seminar series co-sponsored by Application Developers Training Company and Microsoft.

Alison is also the author of eight other books published by Sams Publishing: *Alison Balter's Mastering Access 95 Development*, *Alison Balter's Mastering Access 97 Development*, *Alison Balter's Mastering Access 2000 Development*, *Alison Balter's Mastering Access 2002 Desktop Development*, *Alison Balter's Mastering Access 2002 Enterprise Development*, *Mastering Microsoft Office Access 2003*, *Microsoft Office Access 2003 in a Snap*, and *Learning Office Access 2003 in 24 Hours*. Alison is a coauthor of three Access books published by Sams Publishing: *Essential Access 95*, *Access 95 Unleashed*, and *Access 97 Unleashed*.

An active participant in many user groups and other organizations, Alison is a past president of the Independent Computer Consultants Association of Los Angeles and of the Los Angeles Clipper Users' Group.

On a personal note, Alison keeps herself busy horseback riding, skiing, ice skating, running, lifting weights, hiking, traveling, and dancing. She most enjoys spending time with her husband, Dan, their daughter, Alexis, their son, Brendan, and their golden retriever, Brandy.

Alison's firm, InfoTechnology Partners, Inc., is available for consulting work and on-site training in Microsoft Access, Visual Studio .NET, Visual Basic, and SQL Server, as well as for Windows Server 2003, Windows 2000, Windows NT, Windows 98, Windows XP, PC networking, and Microsoft Exchange Server. You can contact Alison by email at Alison@ InfoTech-Partners.com, or visit the InfoTechnology Partners Web site at http://www. InfoTech-Partners.com.

Dedication

I dedicate this book to my husband, Dan, my daughter, Alexis, my son, Brendan, my parents, Charlotte and Bob, and my real father, Herman. Dan, you are my partner in life and the wind beneath my wings. You are a true partner in every sense of the word. I am so lucky to be traveling the path of life with such a spectacular person. Alexis, you are the sweet little girl that I always dreamed of. You are everything that I could have ever wanted and so very much more. You make every one of my days a happy one! Brendan, you are the one who keeps me on my toes. There is never a dull moment with you around. I wish I had just a small portion of your energy. I thank you for the endless laughter that you bring to our family and for reminding me about all the important things in life. Mom and Dad, without all that you do to help out with life's chores, the completion of this book could never have been possible. Words cannot express my gratitude!

Herman, I credit my ability to soar in such a technical field to you. I hope that I inherited just a small part of your intelligence, wit, and fortitude. I am sorry that you did not live to see this accomplishment. I hope that you can see my work and that you are proud of it. I also hope that in some way you share in the joy that Dan, Alexis, and Brendan bring to me.

Finally, I want to thank God for giving me the gift of gab, a wonderful career, an incredible husband, two beautiful children, a spectacular area to live in, a very special home, and an awesome life. Through your grace, I am truly blessed.

Acknowledgments

Writing a book is a monumental task. Without the support and understanding of those close to me, my dreams for this book would have never come to fruition. Special thanks go to the following special people who helped to make this book possible and more important-ly, who give my life meaning:

Dan Balter (my incredible husband), for his ongoing support, love, encouragement, friend-ship, and, as usual, being patient with me while I wrote this book. Dan, words cannot ade-quately express the love and appreciation that I feel for all that you are and all that you do for me. You treat me like a princess! Thank you for being the phenomenal person you are, and thank you for loving me for who I am. I enjoy sharing not only our career successes, but even more I enjoy sharing the life of our beautiful children, Alexis and Brendan. I look forward to continuing to reach highs we never dreamed of. There is no one I'd rather spend forever with than you.

Alexis Balter (my precious daughter and awesome ice skater), for giving life a special mean-ing. Your intelligence, compassion, caring, and perceptiveness are far beyond your years. Alexis, you make all my hard work worth it. No matter how bad my day, when I look at you, sunshine fills my life. You are the most special gift that anyone has ever given me.

Brendan Balter (my adorable son and little powerhouse), for showing me the power of per-sistence. Brendan, you are small, but, boy, are you mighty! I have never seen such tenacity and fortitude in such a little person. Your imagination and creativity are amazing! Thank you for your sweetness, your sensitivity, and your unconditional love. Most of all, thank you for reminding me how important it is to have a sense of humor.

Charlotte and Bob Roman (Mom and Dad), for believing in me and sharing in both the good times and the bad. Mom and Dad, without your special love and support, I never would have become who I am today. Without all your help, I could never get everything done. Words can never express how much I appreciate all that you do!

Al Ludington, for helping me to slow down and experience the shades of gray in the world. You somehow walk the fine line between being there and setting limits, between comforting me and confronting me. Words cannot express how much your unconditional love means to me. Thanks for showing me that a beautiful mind is not such a bad thing after all.

Sue Lopez, for being the most wonderful best friend anyone could possibly have. You inspire me with your music, your love, your friendship, and your faith in God. Whenever I am hav-ing a bad day, I picture you singing "Dear God" or "Make Me Whole," and suddenly my day gets better. Thank you for the gift of friendship.

Anne Weidenweber, for being my other wonderful best friend. I love our walks and the time we spend together. You are an inspiring, uplifting, and motivating influence in my life. I know that someday we will both reach our dreams as MK nationals. Meanwhile we'll enjoy the journey to the top together!

Roz, Ron, and Charlie Carriere, for supporting my endeavors and for encouraging me to pursue my writing. It means a lot to know that you guys are proud of me for what I do. I enjoy our times together as a family. Charlie, we are so proud of how you are doing at Yale.

Steven Chait, for being a special brother. I want you to know how much you mean to me. When I was a little girl, I was told about your gift to write. You may not know this, but my desire to write started as a little girl, wanting to be like her big brother. Now as adults, I see how many ways we truly are alike.

Greggory Peck from Blast Through Learning, for your contribution to my success in this industry. I believe that the opportunities you gave me early on have helped me reach a level in this industry that would have been much more difficult for me to reach on my own. Most of all, Greggory, thanks for your love and friendship. I love you bro!

Nicole Phelps, for being the best office manager anyone could ever have. You are awesome at everything that you do! I also enjoy your company and your friendship. Thanks for making my day-to-day work life easier.

Scott Barker, for helping me to keep all of my clients happy while I am writing. You are an awesome programmer, but more importantly, an incredible friend! I love spending time with you and your wonderful family, and consider them like part of our family.

Kim Lohman, for keeping me in shape. As I wrote this book you kept me from being a couch potato by cracking the whip and making sure that I worked out every day. I really enjoy our long walks, and most of all our friendship.

Diane Dennis, Shell Forman, Bob Hess, Ron Henderson, Norbert Foigelman, Karen Stakes, Chris Sabihon, and all the other wonderful friends that I have in my life. Diane, you have been my soul mate in life since we were four! Shell, my special "sister," I am lucky to have such a special friend as you. Bob, you are always there when we need you, and somehow manage to keep a smile on your face. Ron, you started out as a client but have a *very* special place in my heart. Norbert, you are a very special friend to me and to my family. Karen, you always brighten up my day. I feel so lucky to work with you and greatly appreciate all that you do for me. Chris, not only are you a special friend, but you have had an important impact on my spiritual path in life!

Acknowledgments

My friends at the Archdiocese of Los Angeles, Ellen McCrea, Tim Wade, Glenn Berger, Steve Flint, Chuck Hinkle, Eric Grimmius, and all the other special clients and work associates that I have in my life. Although all of you started out as work associates, I feel that our relationship goes much deeper than that. I am *very* lucky to have people in my work life like you. Thank you all for your patience with my schedule as I wrote this book.

Loretta Yates, Mark Renfrow, and George Nedeff for making my experience with Sams a positive one. I know that you all worked very hard to ensure that this book came out on time and with the best quality possible. Without you, this book wouldn't have happened. I have *really* enjoyed working with *all* of you over these past several months. I appreciate your thoughtfulness and your sensitivity to my schedule and commitments outside this book. It is nice to work with people who appreciate me as a person, not just as an author.

Tell Us What You Think!

As the reader of this book, *you* are our most important critic and commentator. We value your opinion and want to know what we're doing right, what we could do better, what areas you'd like to see us publish in, and any other words of wisdom you're willing to pass our way.

As Publisher for Sams Publishing, I welcome your comments. You can fax, email, or write me directly to let me know what you did or didn't like about this book—as well as what we can do to make our books stronger.

Please note that I cannot help you with technical problems related to the topic of this book, and that due to the high volume of mail I receive, I might not be able to reply to every message.

When you write, please be sure to include this book's title and author as well as your name and phone or fax number. I will carefully review your comments and share them with the author and editors who worked on the book.

Email: feedback@samspublishing.com

Mail: Greg Wiegand
            Associate Publisher
            Que & Sams Publishing
            800 East 96th Street
            Indianapolis, IN 46240

Introduction

Many excellent books about SQL Server 2005 Express are available, so how is this one different? In talking to the many people I meet in my travels around the country, I have heard one common complaint. Instead of the host of wonderful books available to expert Database Administrators (DBAs), my students yearn for a book targeted toward the beginning-to-intermediate DBA or developer. They yearn for a book that starts at the beginning, ensures that they have no gaps in their knowledge, and takes them through some of the more advanced aspects of SQL Server 2005 Express. Along the way, they want to acquire volumes of practical knowledge that they can easily port into their own applications. I wrote *Sams Teach Yourself Microsoft SQL Server 2005 Express in 24 Hours* with those requests in mind.

This book begins by providing you with an introduction to basic relational database design. It is mandatory that you understand database design principals before moving on to the other hours, so this hour is a must. During the hour you'll get a summary of all the components that we will be covering through the remainder of the book.

Hour 2 teaches you the basics of working with SQL Server Express. You learn about the versions of SQL Server 2005 available. You then learn how to set up SQL Server Express and how to get started with SQL Server Management Studio Express.

Hour 3 is one of the most important hours. During hour three you learn the ins and outs of working with SQL Server Management Studio. It is in this tool that you will be spending most of your time. During this hour you will also learn how to create a new SQL Server database.

Hours 4 through 20 cover tables, relationships, views, and stored procedures. These objects are at the heart of every SQL Server database. During hour 4 you learn how to work with tables. Then you move on to hour 5 where you learn how to work with table relationships.

Knowledge of the T-SQL language is an important aspect of SQL Server 2005 Express. Probably the most used keyword used in T-SQL is SELECT. Hour 6 delves into the SELECT statement in quite a bit of detail. Hour 7 expands on hour 6 by showing you how you can build T-SQL statements based on data from multiple tables. Not only can you use T-SQL to retrieve data, you can also use it to modify data. Hour 8 shows you how to modify data with action queries. Hour 9 introduces you to many of the built-in T-SQL functions such as DataAdd, DateDiff, and Upper. These built-in functions prove invaluable for building database applications.

Another important SQL Server 2005 Express object is the view. Hour 10 shows you how to build and work with views. During hour 10 the topics become more and more complex until you move to Hour 11, "More About Views." Hour 11 covers topics such as subqueries, outer joins, and using views to secure data.

Hours 12, 13, and 14 show you how to use T-SQL to design SQL Server stored procedures. You learn topics such as the basics, how to control the flow, the use of built-in functions, updating data, and transaction handling. Hour 15 teaches you about ADO.NET. Armed with the basics of ADO.NET, you are ready to design your stored procedures in Visual Basic .NET or C#. Hours 16 through 19 show you how to build your stored procedures in Visual Basic .NET and C# respectively. During the hour you'll learn why you may decide to take advantage of this new technology.

Without the ability to effectively debug, almost any programmer will be lost. Hour 20 covers the powerful debugger available when building stored procedures in Visual Basic .NET or C#.

The last three hours cover security and administration. You learn about SQL Server authentication and permissions validation and how you can take advantage of both to properly secure your databases. You'll also learn how to configure, maintain, and tune the SQL Servers that you manage. Without proper care, even the fastest hardware could run a database that is abysmally slow!

Finally, several of the chapters in the book use a database called NorthWind. Appendix A includes the steps necessary to attach to the NorthWind database so that you can follow along with those chapters.

SQL Server 2005 Express is powerful and exciting. With the keys to deliver all that it offers, you can produce applications that provide much satisfaction as well as many financial rewards. After poring over this hands-on guide and keeping it nearby for handy reference, you too can become masterful at working with SQL Server 2005 Express. This book is dedicated to demonstrating how you can fulfill the promise of making SQL Server 2005 Express perform up to its lofty capabilities. As you will see, you have the ability to really make SQL Server 2005 Express shine in the everyday world!

Conventions Used in This Book

The people at Sams Publishing have spent many years developing and publishing computer books designed for ease of use and containing the most up-to-date information available. With that experience, we've learned what features help you the most. Look for these features throughout the book to help enhance your learning experience and get the most out of HTML.

- ▶ Screen messages, code listings, and command samples appear in monospace type.

- ▶ Terms that are defined in the text appear in italics. *Italics* are sometimes used for emphasis, too.

- ▶ In code lines, placeholders for variables are indicated by `italic monospace type`.

Tip

Tips give you advice on quick or overlooked procedures, including shortcuts.

Did you Know?

Note

Notes present useful or interesting information that isn't necessarily essential to the current discussion, but might augment your understanding with background material or advice relating to the topic.

By the Way

Caution

Cautions warn you about potential problems a procedure might cause, unexpected results, or mistakes that could prove costly.

Watch Out!

PART I

Introduction to SQL Server

HOUR 1

Basic Relational Database Design

Before you learn about SQL Server Express 2005, it is important that you understand the basics of server databases and of relational database design. In this hour you'll learn:

- ▶ Database basics
- ▶ The difference between system and user objects
- ▶ Table basics
- ▶ Relational Database Design Concepts
- ▶ The basics of database diagrams, views, stored procedures, user-defined functions, and triggers
- ▶ What SQL Server stored procedures are, versus Transact-SQL statements stored on a user's machine

Database Basics

A client-server system is made up of two components: an application that is used to present the application's data, and a database system that is used to store it. An application may be designed in Visual Studio 2005, Microsoft Access, or some other graphical user interface. For the purpose of this course, a database is a collection of objects stored on a SQL Server. This collection of objects includes all the tables, views, stored procedures, functions, and other objects necessary to build a database system. If tables relate to one another, they should generally be in the same database. Fortunately, SQL Server allows a very large number of objects within a database, so don't be concerned that you are adding too many tables to a database. As long as they are part of the overall system, they should be within the same database.

System Versus User Objects

System databases include Master, Model, MSDB, Resource, TempDB, and Distribution. SQL Server creates these databases during the installation process. As their name implies, they are part of the system, and most of them are required for the server to run properly. In addition to system databases, there are also system tables, stored procedures, functions, and other system objects (see Figure 1.1).

By the Way

Resource is a hidden, system database that contains all system objects included with SQL Server 2005 Express.

FIGURE 1.1
System objects include databases, tables, stored procedures, functions, and other types of system objects.

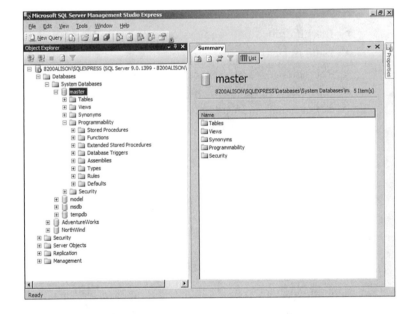

Whereas system objects are part of the SQL Server system, you create user objects. User objects include the databases, stored procedures, functions, and other database objects that you build (see Figure 1.2). You can add and drop user objects as necessary. This book is dedicated to showing you how to create and work with user objects, as well as how to administer your SQL Server.

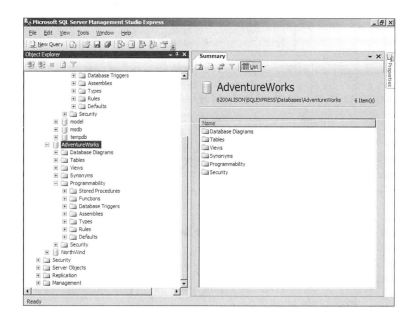

FIGURE 1.2
You build the user objects that make up your database system.

Table Basics

Tables are generally the first thing that you add to a SQL Server database. Tables contain the data in your SQL Server Express database. Each table contains information about a subject. For example, one table may contain information about customers, whereas another table may contain information about orders. Each table in a database must have a unique name. A table is made up of rows and columns. We refer to the columns as *fields*. Each field has a unique name and contains a specific piece of information about the row. For example, within the Customers table, the fields included may be the CustomerID, CompanyName, ContactFirstName, ContactLastName, and so on. Each row contains an individual occurrence of the subject modeled by the table. For example, each row in the Customer table contains information about a specific customer.

Relational Database Design Concepts

Many people believe that database tools are so easy to use that database design is something that they don't need to worry about. I couldn't disagree more! Just as a house without a foundation will collapse, a database with poorly designed tables and relationships will fail to meet the needs of the users. Therefore, before you learn how to create a SQL Server database, you will benefit from learning database design principles.

The History of Relational Database Design

Dr. E.F. Codd first introduced formal relational database design in 1969 while he was at IBM. He based it on set theory and predicate logic. Relational theory applies to both databases and database applications. Codd developed 12 rules that determine how well an application and its data adhere to the relational model. Since Codd first conceived these 12 rules, the number of rules has expanded into the hundreds!

Goals of Relational Database Design

The number one goal of relational database design is to, as closely as possible, develop a database that models some real-world system. This involves breaking the real-world system into tables and fields and determining how the tables relate to each other. Although on the surface this might appear to be a trivial task, it can be an extremely cumbersome process to translate a real-world system into tables and fields.

A properly designed database has many benefits. It greatly facilitates the process of adding, editing, deleting, and retrieving table data. Reports are easy to build. Most important, the database becomes easy to modify and maintain.

Rules of Relational Database Design

You must follow certain rules if you want to adhere to the relational model. These rules determine what is stored in a table and how the tables are related.

The Rules of Tables

Each table in a system must store data about a single entity. An entity usually represents a real-life object or event. Examples of objects are customers, employees, and inventory items. Examples of events include orders, appointments, and doctor visits.

The Rules of Uniqueness and Keys

Tables are composed of rows and columns. To adhere to the relational model, each table must contain a unique identifier. Without a unique identifier, it becomes programmatically impossible to address a row uniquely. You guarantee uniqueness in a table by designating a *primary key*, which is a single column or a set of columns that uniquely identifies each row in a table.

Each column or set of columns in a table that contains unique values is considered a *candidate key*. One candidate key becomes the *primary key*. The remaining candidate keys become *alternate keys*. A primary key made up of one column is considered a simple key. A primary key comprising multiple columns is considered a *composite key*.

It is generally a good idea to pick a primary key that is

- ▶ Minimal (has as few columns as possible)
- ▶ Stable (rarely changes)
- ▶ Simple (is familiar to the user)

Following these rules greatly improves the performance and maintainability of your database application, particularly if you are dealing with large volumes of data.

Consider the example of an employee table. An employee table is generally composed of employee-related fields such as Social Security number, first name, last name, hire date, salary, and so on. You could consider the combination of the first name and last name fields a primary key. This choice might work until the company hires two employees with the same name. Although you could combine the first and last names with additional fields to constitute uniqueness (for example, hire date), this would violate the rule of keeping the primary key minimal. Furthermore, an employee might get married and change her last name.

Using a name as the primary key violates the principle of stability. The Social Security number might be a valid choice, but a foreign employee might not have a Social Security number. This is a case where a derived rather than natural primary key is appropriate. A derived key is an artificial key that you create. A natural key is one that is already part of the database.

I suggest adding an EmployeeID as an Identity field. Although the field would violate the rule of simplicity (because an employee number is meaningless to the user), it is both small and stable. Because it is numeric, it is also efficient to process. In fact, I use Identity fields as primary keys for most of the tables that I build.

By the Way

Foreign Keys and Domains

A *foreign key* in a table is the field that relates to the primary key in a second table. For example, the CustomerID is the primary key in the Customers table. It is the foreign key in the Orders table.

A *domain* is a pool of values from which columns are drawn. A simple example of a domain is the specific data range of employee hire dates. In the case of the Order table, the domain of the CustomerID column is the range of values for the CustomerID in the Customers table.

Normalization and Normal Forms

One of the most difficult decisions that you face as a developer is what tables to create and what fields to place in each table, as well as how to relate the tables that you create. *Normalization* is the process of applying a series of rules to ensure that your database achieves optimal structure. Normal forms are a progression of these rules. Each successive normal form achieves a better database design than the previous form did. Although there are several levels of normal forms, it is generally sufficient to apply only the first three levels of normal forms. The following sections describe the first three levels of normal forms.

First Normal Form

To achieve first normal form, all columns in a table must be atomic. This means, for example, that you cannot store the first name and last name in the same field. The reason for this rule is that data becomes very difficult to manipulate and retrieve if multiple values are stored in a single field. Using the full name as an example, it would become impossible to sort by first name or last name independently if both values are stored in the same field. Furthermore, you must perform extra work to extract just the first name or the last name from the field.

Another requirement for first normal form is that the table must not contain repeating values. An example of repeating values is a scenario in which Item1, Quantity1, Item2, Quantity2, Item3, and Quantity3 fields are all found within the Orders table (see Figure 1.3). This design introduces several problems. What if the user wants to add a fourth item to the order? Furthermore, finding the total ordered for a product requires searching several columns. In fact, all numeric and statistical calculations on the table become extremely cumbersome. The alternative, shown in Figure 1.4, achieves first normal form. Notice that each item ordered is located in a separate row.

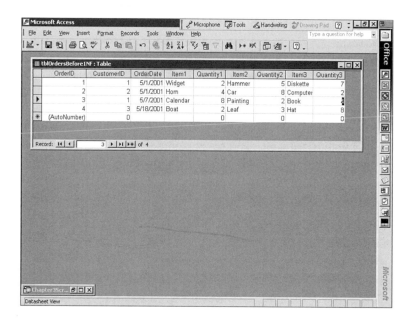

FIGURE 1.3
This table contains repeating groups. Repeating groups make it difficult to summarize and manipulate table data.

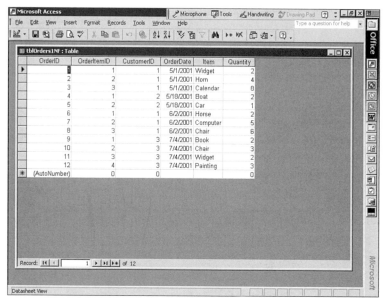

FIGURE 1.4
This table achieves first normal form. Notice that all fields are atomic and that the table contains no repeating groups.

Second Normal Form

To achieve second normal form, all nonkey columns must be fully dependent on the primary key. In other words, each table must store data about only one subject.

Notice the table shown in Figure 1.4. It includes information about the order (OrderID, CustomerID, and OrderDate) and information about the items that the customer is ordering (Item and Quantity). To achieve second normal form, this data must be broken into two tables: an orders table and an order detail table. The process of breaking the data into two tables is called *decomposition*. It is considered to be *nonloss* decomposition because no data is lost during the decomposition process. After the data is broken into two tables, you can easily bring the data back together by joining the two tables in a query. Figure 1.5 shows the data broken up into two tables. These two tables achieve second normal form.

FIGURE 1.5
These tables achieve second normal form. The fields in each table pertain to the primary key of the table.

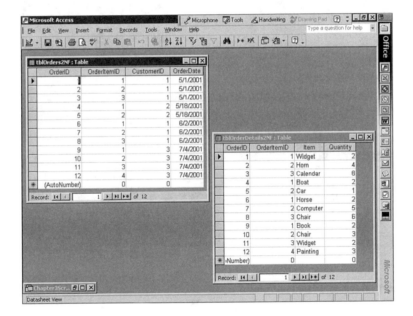

Third Normal Form

To attain third normal form, a table must meet all the requirements for first and second normal form, and all nonkey columns must be mutually independent. This means that you must eliminate any calculations, and you must break out data into lookup tables.

An example of a calculation stored in a table is the product of price multiplied by quantity. Rather than storing the result of this calculation in the table, you would generate the calculation in a query, or in the control source of a control on a form or a report.

The example in Figure 1.5 does not achieve third normal form because the description of the inventory items is stored in the order details table. If the description changes, the user needs to modify all rows with that inventory item. The order detail table, shown in Figure 1.6, shows the item descriptions broken into an inventory table. This design achieves third normal form. All fields are mutually independent. The user can modify the description of an inventory item in one place.

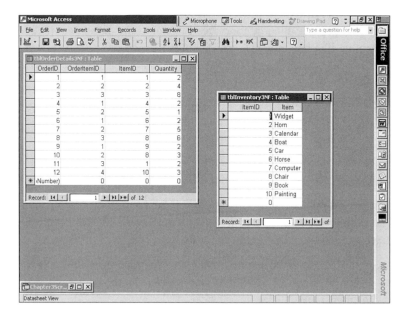

FIGURE 1.6
This table achieves third normal form.

Denormalization—Purposely Violating the Rules

Although the developer's goal is normalization, many times it makes sense to deviate from normal forms. We refer to this process as *denormalization*. The primary reason for applying denormalization is to enhance performance.

An example of when denormalization might be the preferred tactic could involve an open invoices table and a summarized accounting table. It might be impractical to calculate summarized accounting information for a customer when the user needs it. The system maintains summary calculations in a summarized accounting table so that the system can easily retrieve them as needed. Although the upside of this scenario is improved performance, the downside is that the system must update the summary table whenever changes are made to the open invoices. This imposes a definite trade-off between performance and maintainability. You must decide whether the trade-off is worth it.

If you decide to denormalize, document your decision. Make sure that you make the necessary application adjustments to ensure that the system properly maintains denormalized fields. Finally, test to ensure that performance is actually improved by the denormalization process.

Integrity Rules

Although integrity rules are not part of normal forms, they are definitely part of the database design process. Integrity rules are broken into two categories. They include overall integrity rules and database-specific integrity rules.

Overall Rules

The two types of overall integrity rules are referential integrity rules and entity integrity rules. Referential integrity rules dictate that a database does not contain any orphan foreign key values. This means that

▶ Child rows cannot be added for parent rows that do not exist. In other words, an order cannot be added for a nonexistent customer.

▶ A primary key value cannot be modified if the value is used as a foreign key in a child table. This means that a CustomerID cannot be changed if the orders table contains rows with that CustomerID.

▶ A parent row cannot be deleted if child rows are found with that foreign key value. For example, a customer cannot be deleted if the customer has orders in the orders table.

By the Way

SQL Server Express has two wonderful features. One is called Cascade Update, and the other is called Cascade Delete. These features make it easier for you to work with data, while ensuring that referential integrity is maintained. With the Cascade Update feature, SQL Server Express automatically updates the foreign key field on the child rows when the primary key of the parent is modified. This allows the system to modify a primary key while maintaining referential integrity. Likewise, the Cascade Delete feature deletes the associated child rows when the parent rows are deleted, once again maintaining referential integrity.

Entity integrity dictates that the primary key value cannot be null. This rule applies not only to single-column primary keys, but also to multicolumn primary keys. In fact, in a multicolumn primary key, no field in the primary key can be null. This makes sense because if any part of the primary key can be null, the primary key can no longer act as a unique identifier for the row. Fortunately, SQL Server does not allow a field in a primary key to be null.

Database-Specific Rules

The other set of rules applied to a database are not applicable to all databases, but, instead, are dictated by business rules that apply to a specific application. Database-specific rules are as important as overall integrity rules. They ensure that the user enters only valid data into a database. An example of a database-specific integrity rule is that the delivery date for an order must fall after the order date.

Database Diagram Basics

A database diagram graphically shows the structure of the database (see Figure 1.7). It shows how one table is related to another within the database. Using a database diagram, you can modify the tables, columns, relationships, keys, indexes, and con-straints that make up the database. For more about database diagrams, see Hour 5, "Working with Table Relationships." As you will see in Hour 5, database diagrams are very powerful!

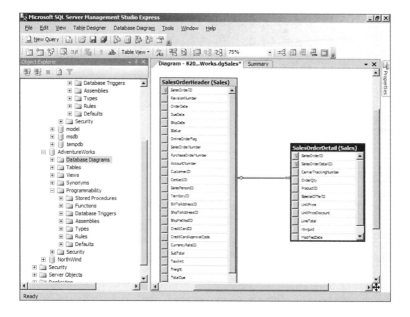

FIGURE 1.7
A database dia-gram graphically shows the structure of the database.

View Basics

A *view* is a virtual table. Its contents are based on a query. Like a table, a view is composed of rows and columns. Except in the case of a special type of view called an indexed view, views exist only in memory. The data in a view comes from one or more tables in the database (see Figure 1.8). It can also come from other views, and even from data in other databases. Whenever you reference a view, SQL Server dynamically retrieves the rows and columns contained in it. There are no restrictions on querying and only a few restrictions on modifying via views. For more information about views see Hour 10, "Working with SQL Server Views," and Hour 11, "More About Views."

FIGURE 1.8
The View Designer included in SQL Server Management Studio helps you when designing a view.

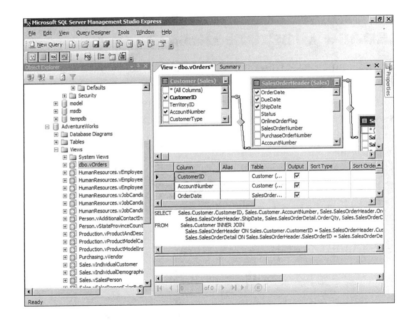

Stored Procedure Basics

A *stored procedure* is a piece of programming code that can accept input parameters and can return one or more output parameters to the calling procedure or batch (see Figure 1.9). Stored procedures generally perform operations on the database, including the process of calling other stored procedures. They can also return status information to the calling procedure to indicate whether they succeeded or failed.

SQL Server stored procedures have many benefits over their alternative, which is to execute Transact-SQL programs stored locally on client computers. SQL Server stored procedures provide *excellent* security for your database. You can grant rights to the stored procedure without granting rights to the underlying objects. For example, you can write a stored procedure that updates employee information without even granting the user SELECT rights to the Employee table! Stored procedures also allow for modular programming by providing a means for you to create a procedure once and call it from any application. If you need to modify the procedure, you modify it in one place. Finally, stored procedures reduce network traffic—for two reasons. The first is that with stored procedures, it is not necessary for hundreds of lines of complex T-SQL code to travel over the network. Instead, just a single line (calling the stored procedure) travels over the network. The other reason that stored procedures reduce network traffic is that they limit data with WHERE clauses. They help to ensure that your application sends just the necessary data over the network wire. For more information about stored procedures, see Hour 12, "Using T-SQL to Design SQL Server Stored Procedures," Hour 13, "Important Stored Procedure Techniques," and Hour 14, "Stored Procedure Special Topics."

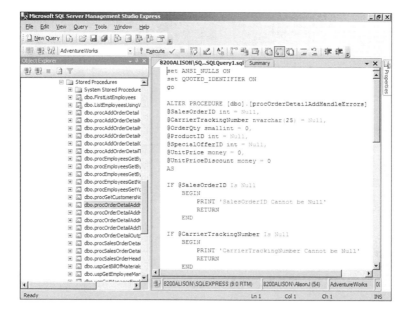

FIGURE 1.9
You can easily create a stored procedure from within the SQL Server Management Studio.

User-Defined Function Basics

User-defined functions are procedures that accept parameters, perform some sort of action, and return the result of that action as a value (see Figure 1.10). The return value can be either a single scalar value or a result set. A single scalar value is a simple value such as a number. A result set refers to something such as an ADO.NET recordset.

User-defined functions have many benefits. Like stored procedures, they allow modular programming, meaning that you can call them from anywhere in your program. If you need to modify the function, you can do so in one place. User-defined functions also allow for faster execution. SQL Server caches them in memory so that they execute faster after the first execution. Finally, user-defined functions reduce network traffic. They can limit data with a WHERE clause, reducing the data returned to the client. For more about user-defined functions see Hour 14, "Stored Procedure Special Topics."

FIGURE 1.10
User-defined functions are procedures that accept parameters, perform some sort of action, and return the result of that action as a value.

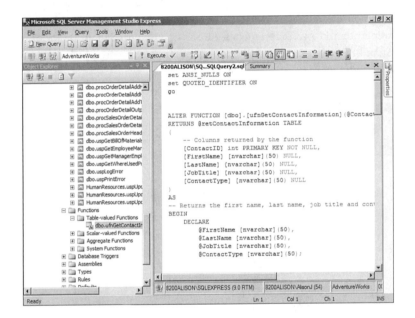

Trigger Basics

A trigger is a special type of stored procedure that executes when a language event executes. There are two kinds of triggers: DML triggers and DDL triggers. Microsoft introduced DDL triggers with SQL Server 2005. They execute when changes are made to the structure of the database. An example is when someone tries to remove a field from a table. You can write a DDL trigger that prevents the removal of the field if the field contains any data. You can also use a DDL trigger to audit changes made to the structure of a database. For example, you can write a record to an audit table each time someone deletes a table.

DML triggers are invoked when a data manipulation language (DML) event takes place in the database. DML events include INSERT, UPDATE, and DELETE statements that occur when data is modified in a table or view. DML triggers have several uses. They can protect your database against incorrect INSERT, UPDATE, and DELETE statements, enforcing restrictions more complex than those available with CHECK constraints. Furthermore, whereas CHECK constraints can reference data in only one table, triggers can reference data in multiple tables. For example, a trigger can evaluate a value in another table and perform or prohibit an insert, update, or delete to the current table based on that value. You can also use triggers to compare table values before and after an update, taking action based on those differences. Finally, you can include multiple DML triggers of the same type on a table. This causes different actions to take place in response to the same modification statement. For more about triggers see Hour 14, "Stored Procedure Special Topics."

SQL Server Stored Procedures Versus Transact-SQL Statements Stored on Local Computers

SQL Server stored procedures are compiled code stored *and* executed on the server. You can execute them from just about any client (Visual Basic .NET, Microsoft Access, Visual FoxPro, Visual Basic, Microsoft Word, and so on). If you need to modify a stored procedure, you modify it on the server. The changes that you make impact all the clients that call the stored procedure.

Contrast that to SQL statements stored on a local computer. These are statements embedded within programming code. For example, you can write ADO .NET code in a Visual Basic .NET application to update data that meets a specific condition. You can write similar code in your Microsoft Access and Microsoft Word applications. If you make a change to your business logic, you must modify your application code everywhere that it appears.

Summary

A database is similar to a house. Without the proper foundation it will fall apart. In this hour you learned the basics of relational database design. You reviewed the various system objects, getting a sense of what each object does along the way. Finally, we talked about the difference between SQL Server stored procedures and Transact-SQL stored on a user's machine.

Q&A

Q. *Explain the difference between system objects and user objects.*

A. SQL Server creates system objects during the installation process. They are part of the system, and most of them are necessary for SQL Server to function properly. Whereas system objects are part of the SQL Server system, you create user objects. User objects include the databases, stored procedures, functions, and other system objects that you build.

Q. *Describe normalization.*

A. Normalization is the process of applying a series of rules to ensure that your database achieves optimal structure. Normal forms are a progression of these rules. Each successive level of normal form achieves a better database design than the previous one. It is generally sufficient to apply the first three levels of normal forms to your data.

Q. *What is the difference between a DDL trigger and a DML trigger?*

A. A DDL trigger executes in response to a change to the structure of a database (for example, CREATE, ALTER, DROP). A DML trigger executes in response to a change in data (INSERT, UPDATE, DELETE).

Workshop

Quiz

1. Name three attributes of a good primary key.

2. What is a foreign key?

3. Name two things that can be returned by a user-defined function.

4. Name the SQL Server 2005 system databases.

5. What is the number one goal of relational database design?

6. Antinormalization is a term used to describe the process of violating the rules of normalization (true/false).

7. Name two types of overall integrity rules.

Quiz Answers

1. Short (Minimal), Stable, and Simple.

2. A foreign key in a table is the field that relates to the primary key in a second table.

3. A single scalar value or a result set.

4. Master, Model, MSDB, Resource, TempDB, and Distribution.

5. To develop a database that as closely as possible models some real-world system.

6. False. It is called denormalization.

7. Referential integrity and entity integrity.

Activities

Practice designing a system. Begin with a real-world scenario such as a church tithing system. Determine all the tables necessary for the system and what each table will do. Make sure that the tables meet the rules of first, second, and third normal forms. Finally determine the relationships between the tables in the database.

HOUR 2

SQL Server Basics

You should know some basics when getting started with SQL Server 2005 Express. Knowledge of these basics will help you to make decisions about whether the product is right for you, and will help you with the installation process. In this hour you'll learn:

▶ The versions of SQL Server 2005 that are available
▶ How to install SQL Server Express
▶ How to get started with the SQL Server Management Studio Express

Versions of SQL Server 2005 Available

Microsoft recognizes that there is a plethora of database users with disparate needs. They therefore have released the following six versions of SQL Server 2005:

▶ SQL Server 2005 Express Edition
▶ SQL Server 2005 Workgroup Edition
▶ SQL Server 2005 Developer Edition
▶ SQL Server 2005 Standard Edition
▶ SQL Server 2005 Enterprise Edition
▶ SQL Server 2005 Mobile Edition

SQL Server 2005 Express Edition

SQL Server 2005 Express provides a great means of getting started with SQL Server. It offers a robust, reliable, stable environment that is free and easy to use. It provides the same protection and information management provided by the more sophisticated versions of SQL Server. Other advantages of SQL Server Express include

- ► Easy installation

- ► Lightweight management and query editing tool

- ► Support for Windows authentication

- ► "Secure by Default" settings

- ► Royalty-free distribution

- ► Rich database functionality, including triggers, stored procedures, functions, extended indexes, and Transact-SQL support

- ► XML Support

- ► Deep integration with Visual Studio 2005

SQL Server 2005 Express has a few disadvantages that make it unusable in many situations. These include

- ► Support for only one gigabyte of RAM

- ► Support for a four-gigabyte maximum database size

- ► Support for only one CPU

- ► Absence of the SQL Agent Job Scheduling Service

- ► Absence of the Database Tuning Advisor

SQL Server 2005 Workgroup Edition

SQL Server Workgroup Edition provides a great solution for small organizations or workgroups within larger entities. It includes a rich feature set, but is affordable and simple to work with. Other valuable features include the fact that there is no limit on database size and that it supports the SQL Agent Job Scheduling Service. The disadvantages of SQL Server 2005 Workgroup Edition include

- ► Support for only three gigabytes of RAM

- ► Support for only two CPUs

- ► Absence of the Database Tuning Advisor

SQL Server 2005 Developer Edition

SQL Server 2005 Developer Edition is designed specifically for developers who are building SQL Server 2005 applications. It includes *all* functionality of SQL Server

2005 Enterprise Edition, but with a special license that limits its use to development and testing. Its license specifies that you cannot use it for production development. For more details about the features of SQL Server 2005 Developer Edition, see the section "SQL Server 2005 Enterprise Edition" later in this section.

SQL Server 2005 Standard Edition

SQL Server Standard Edition provides an affordable option for small- and medium-sized businesses. It includes all functionality required for non-critical e-commerce, data warehousing, and line-of-business solutions. The advantages of SQL Server 2005 Standard Edition include

▶ RAM limited solely by operating system RAM

▶ No limit for database size

▶ Full 64-bit support

▶ Database mirroring

▶ Failover clustering

▶ Inclusion of the Database Tuning Advisor

▶ Inclusion of the full-featured Management Studio

▶ Inclusion of the Profiler

▶ Inclusion of the SQL Agent Job Scheduling Service

The disadvantages of SQL Server 2005 Standard Edition include

▶ Support for only four CPUs

▶ No support for online indexing

▶ No support online restore

▶ No support for fast recovery

SQL Server 2005 Enterprise Edition

SQL Server 2005 Enterprise Edition includes all the tools that you need to manage an enterprise database management system. It offers a complete set of enterprise management and business intelligence features, and provides the highest levels of scalability and availability of all the SQL Server 2005 editions. It supports an unlimited number of CPUs and provides all the features unavailable in the other versions of SQL Server 2005.

SQL Server 2005 Mobile Edition

SQL Server 2005 Mobile Edition enables you to easily port corporate applications over to mobile devices. SQL Server 2005 Mobile Edition offers many advantages. They include

▶ Inclusion of SQL Workbench (a tool that replaces SQL Server 2005 Management Studio)

▶ Full integration with SQL Server 2005

▶ Inclusion of synchronization functionality

▶ Excellent reliability and performance due to a revamped storage engine and an improved query processor

▶ Multi-user support via multi-user synchronization and row-level locking

▶ Full integration with Visual Studio 2005

▶ Increased device support

Installing SQL Server Express

Although installing SQL Server Express is a fairly simple process, you are asked a few questions during the installation process that might need some clarification. The text that follows walks you through the process of installing the SQL Server 2005 Express database engine, and provides an explanation of the various options available to you. Follow these steps:

1. When you launch the setup program, an end-user license agreement appears (see Figure 2.1). You must accept the agreement before proceeding. After clicking to accept the agreement, click Next. The Installing Prerequisites step of the installation process runs (see Figure 2.2).

2. After verifying that all the required components were installed successfully, click Next. The Microsoft SQL Server 2005 Setup welcome screen appears (see Figure 2.3).

3. Click Next. SQL Server 2005 Setup performs a System Configuration Check. The results appear as in Figure 2.4).

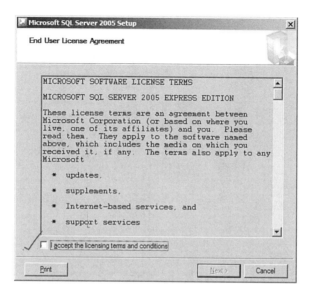

FIGURE 2.1
You must accept the end-user license agreement before installing SQL Server 2005 Express.

FIGURE 2.2
The Installing Prerequisites step of the installation process verifies that all the required components were installed successfully.

FIGURE 2.3
The Microsoft
SQL Server
2005 Setup
welcome screen
commences the
actual installa-
tion process.

FIGURE 2.4
It is important
to note the
results of
the System
Configuration
Check.

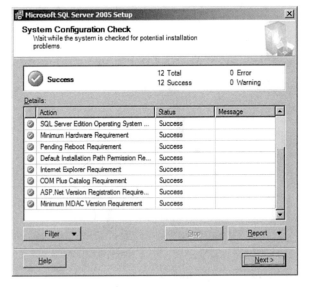

4. Click Next to proceed to the next step of the wizard. The Registration
   Information step of the installation process appears (see Figure 2.5).

FIGURE 2.5
You must provide registration information as part of the installation process.

5. Fill in the required information and click Next. The Feature Selection step of the wizard appears (see Figure 2.6). The wizard helps you select what features are installed on your computer and how the setup process will install them.

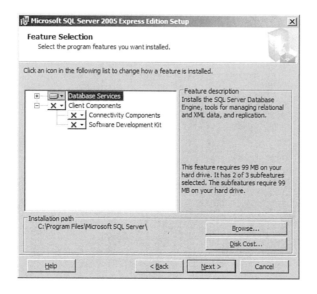

FIGURE 2.6
The Feature Selection step of the wizard enables you to determine what features are installed on your computer.

6. If desired, click Disk Cost to view the space available on each drive. The Disk Cost step of the wizard appears (see Figure 2.7).

FIGURE 2.7
The Disk Cost dialog shows you the space available on each disk drive.

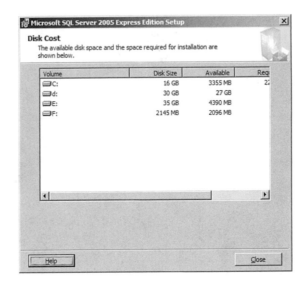

7. Click Close to close the Disk Cost dialog and then Next to proceed with the wizard. The Authentication Mode step of the wizard appears (see Figure 2.8). Here you must determine whether your server will accept only Windows logins, or whether it will also support SQL Server logins. For more information on this topic, see Hour 21, "SQL Server Authentication."

FIGURE 2.8
The Authentication Mode step enables you to determine the type of authentication you want to accept.

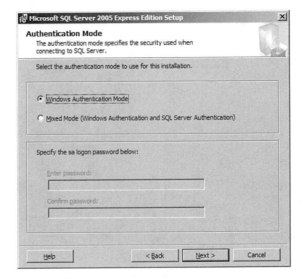

8. After making your selection, click Next to proceed to the next step. The Error and Usage Report Settings dialog appears (see Figure 2.9). Here you determine

what happens when an error occurs (where SQL Server will send error reports), and whether you want Microsoft to receive information automatically about your feature usage.

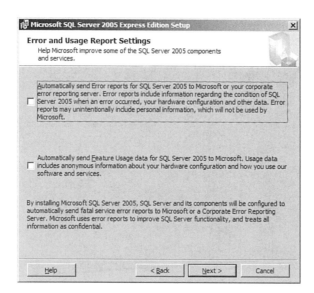

FIGURE 2.9
The Error and Usage Report Settings dialog enables you to determine what happens when an error occurs.

9. Click the appropriate check boxes and click Next. The Ready to Install step of the wizard appears. The dialog shows you what components the SQL Server 2005 Express Edition Setup will install (see Figure 2.10).

FIGURE 2.10
The Install step of the wizard shows you what components will be installed.

10. Click Install to complete the process. After a moment the Setup Progress dialog appears (see Figure 2.11).

FIGURE 2.11
The Setup
Progress dialog
shows you what
is happening
during the setup
process.

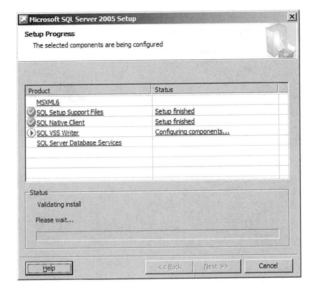

11. Click Next when setup is finished. The Completing Microsoft SQL Server 2005 Setup step of the wizard appears (see Figure 2.12).

FIGURE 2.12
The Completing
Microsoft SQL
Server 2005
Setup step of
the wizard
provides a sum-
mary of what
happened dur-
ing the setup
process.

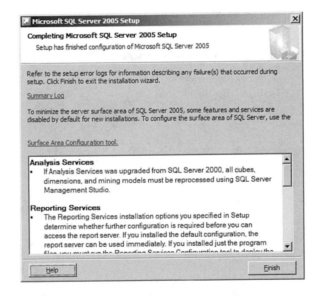

Installing the database engine is generally not enough. You will have no way to manage the server and its objects. This is where SQL Server Management Studio Express fits in. Microsoft provides a separate installation program for SQL Server Management Studio Express. To run it, follow these steps:

1. After the installation wizard launches, a welcome screen appears (see Figure 2.13).

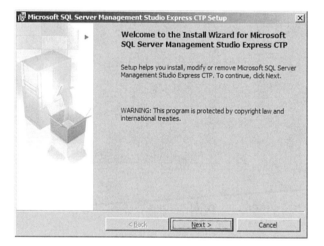

FIGURE 2.13
The SQL Server Management Studio Express installation program begins with a welcome screen.

2. Click Next. The License Agreement step of the wizard appears (see Figure 2.14).

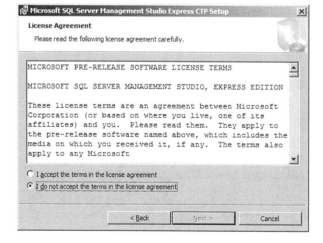

FIGURE 2.14
You must complete the License Agreement step of the wizard before proceeding.

3. Click to accept the license agreement.

4. Click Next. The Registration Information dialog appears (see Figure 2.15).

FIGURE 2.15
The Registration
Information step
of the wizard
enables you
to enter user
and company
information.

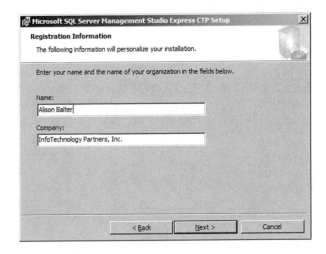

5. Fill in the registration information and click Next. The Feature Selection step
   of the wizard appears (see Figure 2.16).

FIGURE 2.16
The Feature
Selection step
of the wizard
enables you to
determine what
features will be
installed.

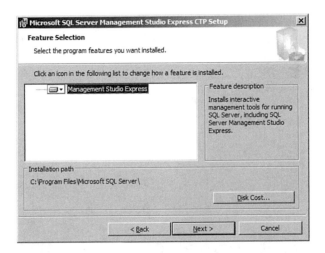

6. Select the desired features and click Next.

7. The Ready to Install the Program step of the wizard appears. Click Install to
   complete the process.

8. When the installation process is complete, the Completing the Microsoft SQL Server Management Studio Express Setup step of the wizard appears. Click Finish.

Getting Started with the SQL Server Management Studio Express

SQL Server Management Studio Express is the tool that you use to manage your SQL Server and its objects. Using this tool, you can create and work with databases, tables, stored procedures, indexes, and much more! Hour 3, "Getting to Know the SQL Server Object Explorer," will go into quite a bit of detail about the workings of SQL Server Management Studio Express. In fact, I will use this very powerful tool throughout the course.

Here are some basics that you should know before proceeding with the hours that follow. To get started with SQL Server Management Studio Express, follow these steps:

1. When you launch SQL Server Management Studio Express, the Connect to Server dialog appears (see Figure 2.17). Here you provide login information.

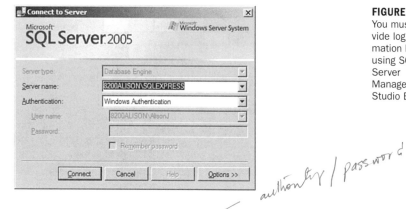

FIGURE 2.17
You must provide login information before using SQL Server Management Studio Express.

2. Provide the server name and the type of authentication and then click Connect. If you are successful, you are placed in SQL Server Management Studio Express (see Figure 2.18).

FIGURE 2.18
SQL Server
Management
Studio Express
enables you to
manage all
aspects of SQL
Server.

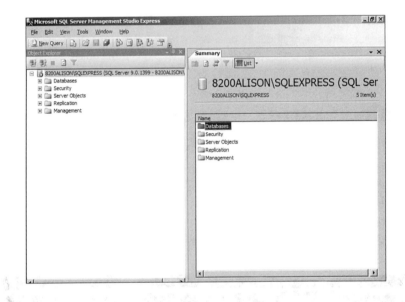

When selecting a server name, you select the name of the server, along with
\SQLEXPRESS. For example, in Figure 2.17 8200ALISON\SQLEXPRESS is selected.
You then select the type of authentication. For more information about authentica-
tion, see Hour 21.

> **3.** Notice that you can use the Object Explorer to expand and contract nodes,
> enabling you to focus on what you want to work on (see Figure 2.19).

FIGURE 2.19
You can expand
and contract
nodes within
the Object
Explorer.

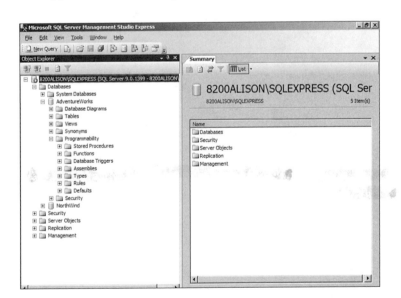

4. If you click to select an object in the Object Explorer, summary information about that object appears in the Summary pane (see Figure 2.20). This pane differs quite a bit depending upon what you select in the object explorer.

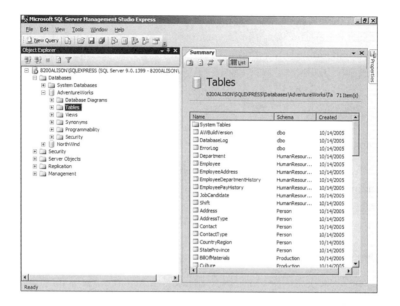

FIGURE 2.20
The Summary pane provides information about the object selected in the Object Explorer.

5. When you are modifying an object, such as a table, the Properties window becomes active, enabling you to modify object properties (see Figure 2.21) .

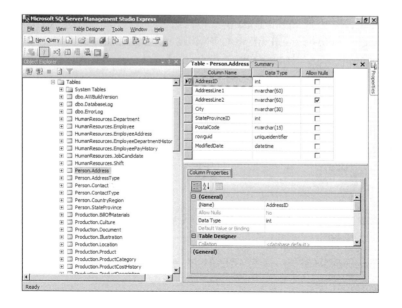

FIGURE 2.21
The Properties window enables you to modify object properties.

Summary

It is always important to learn the basics of a product before forging on to more advanced techniques. This hour began by describing the versions of SQL Server 2005 available so that you are better equipped to make the decision as to which version of the product is right for you. You then learned how to install SQL Server 2005 Express Edition. Finally, you got a brief overview of SQL Server Management Studio Express.

Q&A

Q. *Discuss the advantages of SQL Server 2005 Express.*

A. SQL Server 2005 Express is free and is easy to use. It provides the same protection and information management provided by more sophisticated versions of SQL Server. It is easy to install, provides rich database functionality, and sports deep integration with Visual Studio 2005.

Q. *Name some limitations of SQL Server 2005 Express.*

A. SQL Server 2005 Express limits you to one gigabyte of RAM, a four-gigabyte maximum database size, and support for only one CPU. Furthermore, it does not come with either a job scheduling server or a database tuning advisor.

Q. *Name some advantages of SQL Server 2005 Mobile Edition.*

A. SQL Server 2005 Mobile Edition enables you to port applications to mobile devices. It provides full integration with SQL Server 2005, and even includes synchronization functionality. It offers excellent reliability and performance, as well as multi-user support. Finally, it provides full integration with Visual Studio 2005 and increased device support.

Workshop

Quiz

1. Name the version of SQL Server 2005 designed for small businesses or departments in larger enterprises.

2. What version of SQL Server 2005 supports four CPUs?

3. SQL Server 2005 Developer Edition enables you to create databases of any size (true/false).

4. Name the management tool available for SQL Server 2005 Mobile Edition.

5. You are prompted for authentication model during the installation of the SQL Server 2005 Express database engine (true/false).

6. Name the management tool you use to manage SQL Server 2005 Express databases.

7. Name the tree view that enables you to view the objects managed by your SQL Server.

Quiz Answers

1. SQL Server 2005 Workgroup Edition.

2. SQL Server 2005 Standard Edition.

3. True. It is exactly like Enterprise edition except for licensing.

4. SQL Workbench.

5. True.

6. SQL Server 2005 Express Manager.

7. Object Explorer.

Activities

Download SQL Server 2005 Express Edition. Install both the database engine and SQL Server 2005 Express Management Studio. Launch Management Studio and practice expanding and contracting the nodes of the Object Explorer. Select different nodes, and view the summary information.

HOUR 3

Getting to Know the SQL Server Management Studio

The Microsoft SQL Server Management Studio Express is the new interface that Microsoft has provided for management of your SQL Server database. It is the main tool that you will use when maintaining your databases and the objects they contain. In this hour you'll learn:

▶ The system databases that ship with SQL Server 2005 Express
▶ What is available under the Security node of the Management Studio
▶ The types of server objects that are available
▶ What is available under the Replication mode of Management Studio
▶ What is available under the Management node of the Management Studio
▶ How to create or attach to a SQL Server database

Microsoft SQL Server Management Studio Express

Management Studio has replaced its predecessor, Enterprise Manager. Not only is Management Studio easier to use, it provides more functionality than Enterprise Manager. It combines Enterprise Manager and Query Analyzer into one powerful tool. In the sections that follow, you will explore the various nodes available in Management Studio and learn what is available under each node.

The Databases Node

The Databases node is the first node in SQL Server Management Studio. Within the Databases node are one or more subnodes. The first subnode is System Databases. There are additional subnodes for each database contained on the server (see Figure 3.1). The sections that follow cover each of the system databases found under the System Databases subnode.

FIGURE 3.1
Within the Databases node are one or more subnodes.

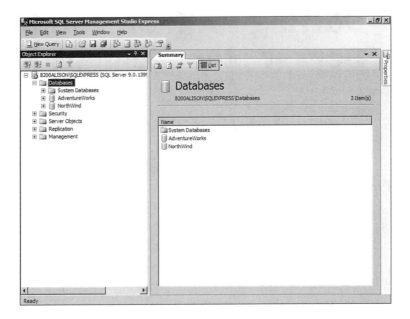

The Master Database

The master database is the "database of all databases." It keeps track of logon accounts, linked servers, system configuration settings, and more. It also contains initialization settings for SQL Server. Prior to SQL Server 2005, Master also contained tables that stored information about all the other system objects (databases, tables, views, stored procedures, triggers, functions, and more). SQL Server 2005 stores these tables in a database called Resource. Resource contains tables that track of all the objects that are associated with the SQL Server. The Resource database is hidden and should be accessed only by a Microsoft Customer Support Services (CSS) specialist to provide troubleshooting and support services to customers.

The Model Database

Model is a very special database. Anything that you place in model is automatically propagated to all the databases that you create thereafter. This means that, for example, you can add a State table to Model. That State table then appears in all the new databases that you build. You work with Model just as you work with any other database. You can include almost any object in Model. This means that you easily can propagate tables, views, stored procedures, triggers, functions, and more.

This not only provides you with standardization between databases, but provides you with a great jump start on creating the databases you need. If you modify Model, you do not affect any existing databases. All new databases will be affected by your changes.

The MSDB Database

The MSDB (Microsoft Database) database is used by SQL Server, SQL Server Management Studio, and SQL Server Agent. All three of them use it to store data, including scheduling information and backup and restore history information. For example, SQL Server maintains a complete backup and restore history in MSDB. There are several ways that you can add to or modify information stored in the MSDB database. They include

- ► Scheduling tasks

- ► Maintaining online backup and restore history

- ► Replication

The TempDB Database

TempDB is a system database that acts as a resource to all users working with a particular instance of SQL Server. TempDB holds the following objects:

- ► Temporary user objects such as temporary tables, temporary stored procedures, temporary table variables, or cursors

- ► Internal objects used by the database engine to perform tasks such as sorting

- ► Row versions that are generated in data modification transactions

The Security Node

As its name implies, the Security Node enables you to manage SQL Server security. Using the Security Node, you can work with logins, add to and remove people from server roles, and create credentials. This chapter provides an introduction to security. For more information, see Hour 21, "SQL Server Authentication," and Hour 22, "SQL Server Permissions Validation."

The Logins Node

Logins represent the users and roles that have access to your system. Note in Figure 3.2 that two types of icons appear under the Logins node. One is granting a role access to the database, and the other is granting a user access to the database.

FIGURE 3.2
Notice that
Administrators
is a role, and sa
is a user.

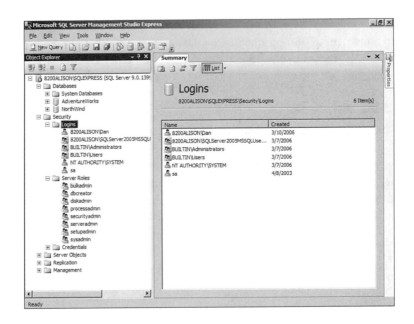

The Server Roles Node

Server Roles are predefined roles, supplied by SQL Server. Each Server Role possesses a pre-defined set of rights. Figure 3.3 shows the available Server Roles. You cannot add or remove Server Roles.

FIGURE 3.3
Each Server
Role possesses
a pre-defined
set of rights.

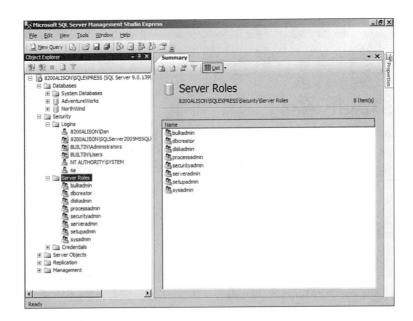

The Credentials Node

Credentials are new to SQL Server 2005. A credential is a record that contains the authentication information required for SQL Server to connect to an outside resource. Most credentials are made up of a Windows login and password.

Server Objects

Server Objects refer to a set of objects used at the server level (not at the database level). These objects include Backup Devices, Linked Servers, and Server Triggers.

Backup Devices

Backup devices include the tapes and disks that you use to back up or restore your SQL Server. When creating a backup, you must designate the backup device that you want to use (see Figure 3.4). You select from a list of backup devices that you have created.

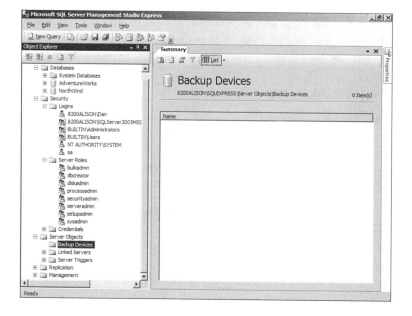

FIGURE 3.4
When creating a backup, you must first designate the backup device you want to use.

Linked Servers

Linked servers enable you to work with other SQL Servers, as well as databases other than SQL Server databases, right from within Management Studio. This offers a few advantages:

▶ The capability to get remote server access

▶ The capability to issue distributed queries, updates, commands, and transactions on heterogeneous data sources across the enterprise

▶ The capability to address diverse data sources in a similar manner

Server Triggers

Server triggers are DDL (Data Definition Language) triggers. They execute in response to changes being made to the structure of the database. They are great for both auditing and regulating database operations. For example, if SQL Server determined that there were more than a specified number of records in a table, it would not allow users to remove fields from the table.

The Replication Node

Data replication is the capability of a system to make copies of its data and application objects automatically in remote locations. You easily can propagate any changes to the original or data changes to the copies to all the other copies. Data replication enables users to make changes to data offline at remote locations. SQL Express synchronizes changes to either the original or the remote data with other instances of the database.

The original database is referred to as the *design master*. You can make changes to definitions of tables or other application objects only at the design master. You use the design master to make special copies called *replicas*. Although there is only one design master, replicas can make other replicas. The process of the design master and replicas sharing changes is referred to as *synchronization*.

To see an example of data replication at work, imagine that you have a team of salespeople who are out on the road all day. At the end of the day, each salesperson logs on to one of the company's servers through Terminal Services. The replication process sends each salesperson's transactions to the server. If necessary, the process sends any changes to the server data to the salesperson.

Management

The Management node contains tools that help you to manage your SQL Server. These tools include the capability to view both the SQL Server Logs and the Activity Monitor.

SQL Server Logs

SQL Server Express 2005 adds entries for certain system events to the SQL Server Error Log and to the Microsoft Windows application log. You can use these logs to identify the sources of problems. Using the SQL Server Management Studio Log File Viewer, you can integrate SQL Server, SQL Server Agent, and the Windows logs into a single list, making it easy to review all related events.

Activity Monitor

You use the Activity Monitor component of SQL Server Management Studio to get information about users' connections to the database engine and the locks that they hold. The Activity Monitor has three pages. The Process Info page contains information about the connections. The Locks by Process page sorts the locks by the connection. The Locks by Object page sorts the locks by the object name.

Creating a SQL Server Database

Before you can build tables, views, stored procedures, triggers, functions, and other objects, you must create the database in which they will reside. A database is a collection of objects that relate to one another. An example would be all the tables and other objects necessary to build a sales order system. To create a SQL Server database, follow these steps:

1. Right-click the Databases node and select New Database. The New Database dialog appears (see Figure 3.5).

2. Enter a name for the database.

3. Enter a path for the database (see Figure 3.6).

4. Click to select the Options page and change any options as desired (see Figure 3.7).

5. Click OK to close the New Database dialog and save the new database. The database now appears under the list of databases (see Figure 3.8) under the Databases node of SQL Server Management Studio. If the database does not appear, right-click the Databases node and select Refresh.

FIGURE 3.5
The New Database dialog enables you to create a new database.

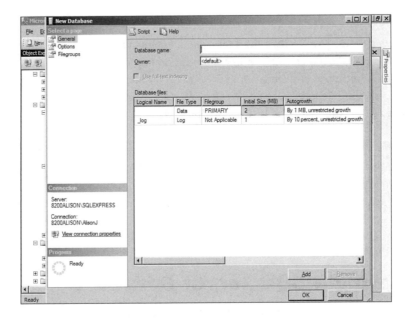

FIGURE 3.6
You can opt to accept the default path, or you can designate a path for the database.

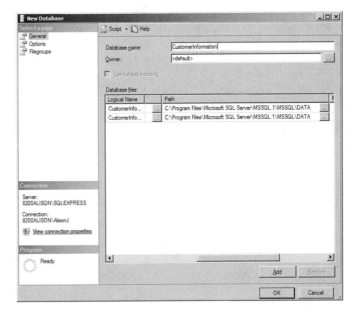

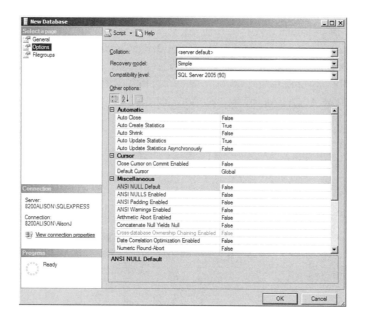

FIGURE 3.7
The Options page of the New Database dialog enables you to set custom options for the database.

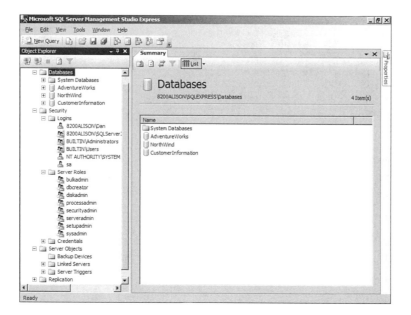

FIGURE 3.8
The new database appears under the list of databases in the Databases node.

Files

In the previous section you created a new SQL Server database. You accepted all the default options available on the General page of the New Database dialog. Many important options are available on the General page. They include the Logical Name, File Type, Filegroup, Initial Size, Autogrowth, Path, and File Name (see Figure 3.9).

FIGURE 3.9
Several important features are available on the General page of the New Database dialog.

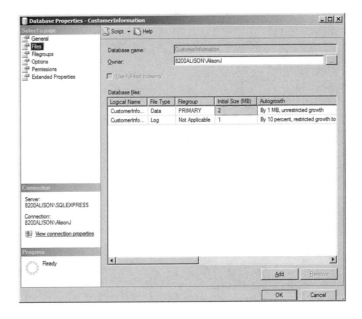

The logical name is the name that SQL Server will use to refer to the database. It is also the name that you will use to refer to the database when writing programming code that accesses it.

The File Type is Data or Log. As its name implies, SQL Server stores data in data files. The file type of Log indicates that the file is a transaction log file.

The initial size is *very* important. You use it to designate the amount of space you will allocate initially to the database.

By the Way

> I like to set this number to the largest size that I ever expect the data database and log file to reach. Whereas disk space is very cheap, performance is affected every time that SQL Server needs to resize the database.

Related to the initial size is the Autogrowth option. When you click the Build button (ellipse) to the right of the currently selected autogrowth option, the Change Autogrowth dialog appears (see Figure 3.10).

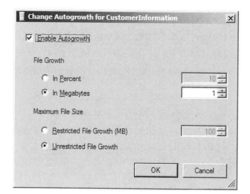

FIGURE 3.10
The Change Autogrowth dialog enables you to designate options that affect how the database file grows.

The first question is whether you want to support autogrowth at all. Some database designers initially make their databases larger than they ever think they should be and then set autogrowth to false. They want an error to occur so that they will be notified when the database exceeds the allocated size. The idea is that they want to check things out to make sure that everything is okay before allowing the database to grow to a larger size.

The second question is whether you want to grow the file in percentage or in megabytes. For example, you can opt to grow the file 10% at a time. This means that if the database reaches the limit of 5,000 megabytes, then 10% growth would grow the file by 500 megabytes. If instead the file growth was fixed at 1,000 megabytes, the file would grow by that amount regardless of the original size of the file.

The final question is whether you want to restrict the amount of growth that occurs. If you opt to restrict file growth, you designate the restriction in megabytes. Like the Support Autogrowth feature, when you restrict the file size, you essentially assert that you want to be notified if the file exceeds that size. With unrestricted file size, the only limit to file size is the amount of available disk space on the server.

File Groups

One great feature of SQL Server is that you can span a database's objects over several files, all located on separate devices. By doing this you improve the performance of the database because multiple hardware devices can access the data simultaneously.

The Transaction Log

SQL Server uses the transaction log to record *every* change that is made to the database. In the case of a system crash, you use the transaction log, along with the most recent backup file, to restore the system to the most recent data available. The transaction log supports the recovery of individual transactions, the recovery of all incomplete transactions when SQL Server is once again started, and the rolling back of a restored database, file, filegroup, or page forward to the point of failure. Specifying information about the transaction log is very similar to doing so for a database. Follow these steps:

1. While creating a new database, notice that you can also enter information about the log file (see Figure 3.11). To begin, enter a logical name for the database. I recommend that you use the logical name of the database along with the suffix _log.

FIGURE 3.11
While creating a new database, you can also enter information about the log file.

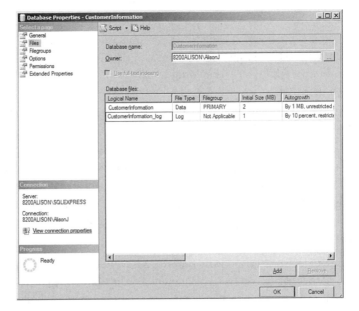

2. Specify the initial size of the log file.

3. Indicate how you want the log file to grow.

4. Designate the path within which you wish to store the database.

5. Continue the process of creating the database file.

> Do not move or delete the transaction log unless you are fully aware of all the possible ramifications of doing so.

Watch Out!

Attaching to an Existing Database

There are times when someone will provide you with a database that you want to work with on your own server. That database may be a SQL Server 2005 database, or might even be a SQL Server 2000 database. To work with an existing database, all you have to do is attach to it. Here's the process:

1. Right-click the Databases node and select Attach. The Attach Databases dialog appears (see Figure 3.12).

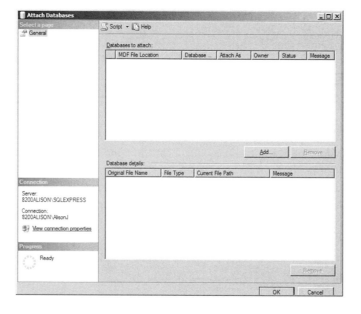

FIGURE 3.12
The Attach Databases dialog enables you to attach to existing .mdf database files.

2. Click Add. The Locate Database Files dialog appears (see Figure 3.13).

3. Locate and select the .mdf to which you want to attach.

4. Click OK to close the Locate Database Files dialog.

5. Click OK to close the Attach Databases dialog. The database appears in the list of user databases under the Databases node of SQL Server Management Studio.

FIGURE 3.13
The Locate Database Files dialog enables you to select the database to which you want to attach.

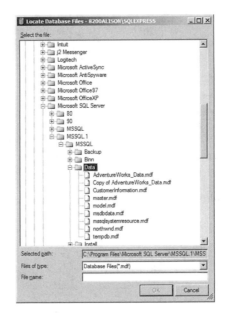

Summary

It is important that you are comfortable with the SQL Server Management Studio Express. It is the tool that you will use the most when managing SQL Server databases. In this hour you learned about the various nodes available within SQL Server Management Studio Express and what functions you can perform under each node. Finally, you learned how to create and attach to a SQL Server database.

Q&A

Q. *Explain what the Master database is used for.*

A. The Master database is the database of all databases. It keeps track of all the login accounts, linked servers, system configuration settings, and more. It also contains initialization settings for SQL Server.

Q. *Explain how you utilize the Model database.*

A. Model is a very special database. Any objects that you place in Model propagate automatically to any new databases that you create. This provides standardization as well as rapid application development.

Q. *Describe MSDB and what it does.*

A. MDSB stores data, including scheduling information and backup and restore history information.

Workshop

Quiz

1. What is a linked server?

2. What is a DDL trigger?

3. TempDB is one of the system databases (true/false).

4. It is always okay to delete a log file (true/false).

5. What is a Server Role?

6. Credentials are made up of what?

7. Name two types of backup devices.

Quiz Answers

1. A linked server enables you to work with other SQL Servers as well as databases other than SQL Server databases, right from within Management Studio.

2. A DDL trigger executes in response to changes made to the structure of the database.

3. True.

4. False.

5. A server role is pre-defined by SQL Server. It possesses a pre-defined set of rights.

6. Credentials are made up of a login and a password.

7. Tape and disk.

Activities

Create a new SQL Server database. View it in the Object Explorer. Expand the Security Node. View the existing logins. Expand the Server Roles node and take a look at the list of Server Roles. Expand the Server Objects Node. Explore the Backup Devices, Linked Servers, and Server Triggers nodes. Expand the Management node. Take a look at both the SQL Server Logs and at the Activity Monitor.

PART II

Working with Tables, Views, and Stored Procedures

HOUR 4

SQL Server Tables

After you have created a database, you are ready to add other objects to it. Generally, the first objects that you add to a database are the tables that it contains. In this hour you'll learn:

- ▶ How to create SQL Server tables
- ▶ How to create constraints
- ▶ How to work with identity columns
- ▶ How to work with computed columns
- ▶ How to work with user-defined data types
- ▶ How to add and modify indexes

Creating SQL Server Tables

Tables are made up of rows and columns. We refer to columns as *fields*. Each field has a unique name and contains a specific piece of information about the row. Each table in a SQL Server database must have a unique name.

To create a table, follow these steps:

1. Within Management Studio, right-click the Tables node of the database to which you want to add a table and select New Table. The Table Designer appears (see Figure 4.1).

2. Enter the column names, data types, and length for each field in the table.

3. Designate whether each field allows nulls.

4. Enter the other properties for the table.

FIGURE 4.1
The Table
Designer
enables you to
enter the col-
umn names,
data types,
length, and
other properties
for each field in
the table.

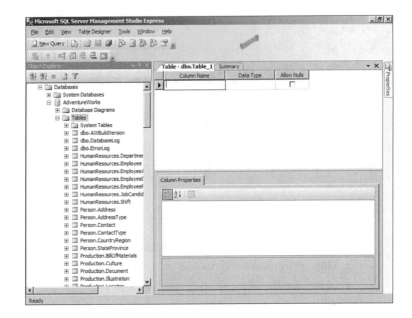

One of the most important properties of a column in a table is the data type. If you do not select the correct data type for a field, the rest of your design efforts will be futile. The data type determines what data you can store in the field. Table 4.1 out-lines the available field types and the type of information that each data type can contain.

TABLE 4.1   Field Types and Appropriate Uses

Field Type	Description	Storage
Bigint	New to SQL Server 2000. Can hold numbers ranging from -2^{63} to 2^{63}.	8 bytes.
Binary	Holds from 1 to 8,000 bytes of fixed-length binary data.	Whatever is in the column, plus 4 addition-al bytes.
Bit	Can hold a value of either 1 or 0. Nulls not allowed.	8-bit fields take up 1 byte of data.
Char	Holds from 1 to 8,000 bytes of fixed-length non-Unicode characters.	The number of bytes corresponds to the length of the field (regardless of what is stored in it).
DateTime	Holds valid dates from January 1, 1753 to December 31, 9999.	4 bytes.

TABLE 4.1 CONTINUED

Field Type	Description	Storage
Decimal	Used for numbers with fixed precision and scale. When maximum precision is used, values can range from 10^{38} -1 to 10^{38} 1. Scale must be less than or equal to the precision.	Depends on the precision.
Float	Can hold positive and negative numbers from $-1.79E + 308$ to $1.79E + 308$. It offers binary precision up to 15 digits.	8 bytes.
Image	Consists of linked data pages of binary data. It can contain up to 2,147,483,647 bytes of binary data.	Depends on what is stored in it.
Int	Can store *whole* numbers from, $-2,147,483,648$ to $2,147,483,647$.	4 bytes.
Money	Can store decimal data ranging from -2^{63} to 2^{63}, scaled to four digits of precision. It offers accuracy to 1/10,000 of a monetary unit.	8 bytes.
NChar	Can contain from 1 to 4,000 Unicode characters.	Twice the amount of bytes of Char. Corresponds to the length of the field (regardless of what is stored in it).
NText	Can hold data up to 1,073,741,823 Unicode characters.	Each character takes 2 bytes of storage.
Numeric	Used for numbers with fixed precision and scale. When maximum precision Values can range from -10^{38} to 1 to 10^{38} $+1$.	Depends on the precision.
NVarChar	Can contain from 1 to 4,000 Unicode characters.	2 bytes per character stored.
NVarChar(MAX)		
Real	A smaller version of `float`. Contains a single-precision floating-point number from $-3.40E + 38$ to $3.40E + 38$.	4 bytes.
SmallDateTime	Consists of two 2-byte integers. Can store dates only between 1/1/1900 and 6/6/2079.	4 bytes.

TABLE 4.1   Continued

Field Type	Description	Storage
SmallInt	A smaller version of int. Can store values between –32,768 and 32,767.	2 bytes.
SmallMoney	A smaller version of money. Can store decimal data scaled to four digits of precision. Can store values from –214,748.3648 to +214,748.3647.	4 bytes.
SQL_Variant	New to SQL 2000. Can store int, binary, and char values. Is a very inefficient data type.	Varies.
Text	Stores up to 2,147,483,647 characters of non-Unicode data.	1 byte for each character of storage.
TimeStamp	Generates a unique binary value that SQL Server automatically creates when a row is inserted and that SQL Server updates every time that the row is edited.	8 bytes.
TinyInt	Stores whole numbers from 0 to 255.	1 byte.
UniqueIdentifier	A globally unique identifier (GUID) that is automatically generated when the NEWID() function is used.	16 bytes.
VarBinary	Can hold variable-length binary data from 1 to 8000 bytes.	Varies from 1 to 8000 bytes.
VarBinary(MAX)		
VarChar	A variable-length string that can hold 1 to 8,000 non-Unicode characters.	1 byte per character stored.
VarChar(MAX)		
XML		

Working with Constraints

Constraints limit or control the types of data that the user can enter into your tables. There are seven main categories of constraints. They include primary key constraints, foreign key constraints, default constraints, not null constraints, check constraints, rules, and unique constraints. The text that follows covers each of these constraint types in detail.

Primary Key Constraints

A primary key constraint is a column or a set of columns that uniquely identify a row in the table. Although you can designate more than one field as the primary key, each table can have only one primary key.

Every table in your database should have a primary key constraint. Furthermore, it is best if your primary key meets the following criteria:

- Short
- Stable
- Simple

Short means that it should be composed of as few fields as possible and the smaller the field type is, the better. In fact, the optimal primary key is a single int field. *Stable* means that the data within the field never changes. A great candidate for a primary key is an identity column. The "Identity Columns" section of this hour covers identity columns in detail. *Simple* means that it is easy to remember and deal with. For example, an int field is simple, whereas a char field containing a long string of complex characters is not.

To add a primary key to a table, follow these steps:

1. Use the gray selectors on the left side of the Table Designer to select the fields that compose the primary key (see Figure 4.2).

2. Click the Set Primary Key tool on the toolbar. The columns appear with a Key icon on the record selector (see Figure 4.3).

Foreign Key Constraints

A foreign key constraint consists of a column or of a set of columns that participates in a relationship with a primary key table. The primary key is on the *one side* of the relationship, whereas the foreign key is on the *many side* of the relationship. A table can have only one primary key, but it can have multiple foreign keys. Each foreign key relates to a different primary key in a separate table. SQL Server looks up the foreign key value in the primary key table to ensure that only valid data is included in the table. Hour 5, "Working with Table Relationships," covers foreign key constraints in additional detail.

FIGURE 4.2
Use the gray selectors on the left side of the Table Designer to select the fields that compose the primary key.

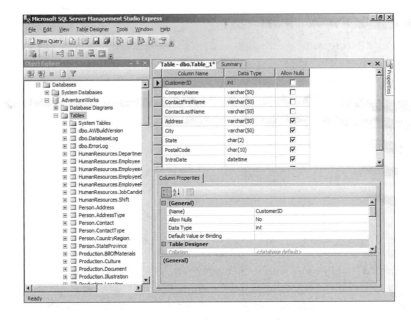

FIGURE 4.3
The columns included in the primary key appear with a Key icon on the record selector.

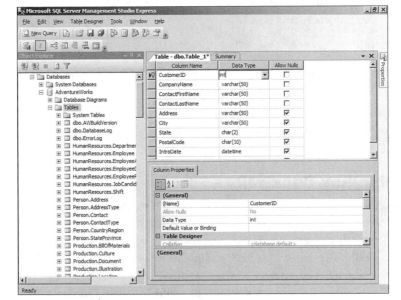

Default Constraints

A default constraint is a value that SQL Server automatically places in a particular field in a table. A default value can be a constant, Null, or a function. All fields except identity and time stamp fields can contain default values. Each column can have one default constraint. You enter the default constraint in the properties for the desired field (see Figure 4.4).

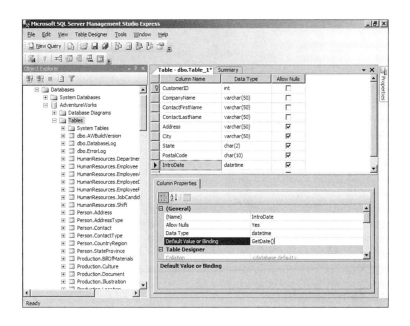

FIGURE 4.4
You enter the default constraint in the properties for the desired field.

Table 4.2 shows examples of default constraints.

TABLE 4.2 **Examples of Default Constraints**

Expression	Result
GetDate()	Sets the default value to the current date
Null	Sets the default value to Null
7	Sets the default value to the number 7
'Hello'	Sets the default value to the string "Hello"

Not Null Constraints

In certain situations, you may want to require the user to enter data into a field. The Not Null constraint enables you to accomplish this task. To set a Not Null constraint, ensure that you uncheck the Allow Nulls check box (see Figure 4.5).

FIGURE 4.5
To set a Not
Null constraint,
ensure that the
Allow Nulls
check box is
unchecked.

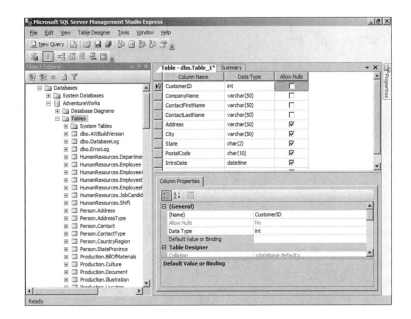

Check Constraints

Check constraints limit the range of values that a user can enter into a column. You can enter as many check constraints as you want for a particular column. SQL Server evaluates the check constraints in the order in which you entered them. To enter a check constraint, follow these steps:

1. Click the Manage Check Constraints tool on the toolbar. The Check Constraints dialog box appears.

2. Click Add to add a new constraint.

3. Provide a constraint name and a constraint expression.

4. Designate other options as necessary. The completed dialog appears as in Figure 4.6.

5. Click Close to close the dialog box and add the constraint.

Table 4.3 shows examples of Check constraints.

TABLE 4.3   Examples of Check Constraints

Expression	Result
@State In('CA', 'AZ', 'UT', 'CO')	Limits the value entered to CA, AZ, UT, and CO

TABLE 4.3   Continued

Expression	Result
`DateEntered <= GetDate()`	Limits the value entered to a date on or before the current date
`CreditLimit Between 0 and 10000`	Limits the value entered to a value between 0 and 10,000

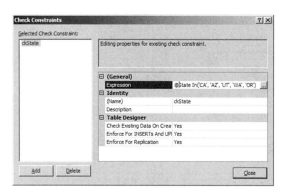

FIGURE 4.6
The Properties dialog box enables you to enter Check constraints for the table.

Rules

Whereas Check constraints apply only to the table for which you enter them, you can apply rules to multiple tables. Microsoft is phasing out support for rules. You are therefore not allowed to create new rules. Instead of using rules, you should use check constraints and triggers.

Unique Constraints

A unique constraint requires that each entry in a particular column be unique. Each table can have 249 unique constraints. You create a unique constraint by creating a unique index.

Identity Columns

Identity columns provide an autoincrementing value for a table. You should use an identity column as the primary key field for any table that has no natural primary key that is short, stable, and simple. Identity columns are often of the int data type. You use the properties of the field to designate a column as an identity column (see Figure 4.7). Notice that after you designate a column as an identity column, you can designate both the identity seed and the identity increment. The *identity seed* is the starting value for the field. The *identity increment* is the value by which each automatically assigned value is incremented. For example, an identity field with an identity seed of 100 and an identity increment of 5 assigns the values 100, 105, 110, and so on.

FIGURE 4.7
You use the
field's proper-
ties to desig-
nate a column
as an identity
column.

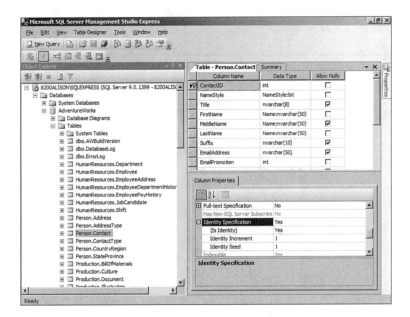

Working with Computed Columns

With computed columns, you can create a column that is based on data in other columns. SQL Server automatically updates the computed column when the columns on which it depends are updated. An example is an extended total that you base on the product of the price and quantity columns. To create a computed column, enter the desired formula into the (Formula) property under the Computed Column Specification key of the column (see Figure 4.8).

Table 4.4 shows examples of computed columns.

TABLE 4.4   Examples of Computed Columns

Expression	Result
Price * Quantity	Calculates the product of the price times the quantity
(Price * Quantity) * (1 - Discount)	Calculates the discounted price
FirstName + ' ' + LastName	Combines the contents of the first and last name fields, and separates them with a space

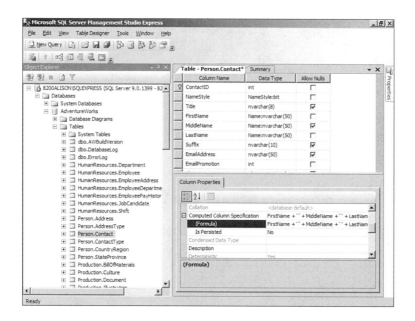

FIGURE 4.8
To create a computed column, enter the formula into the *(Formula)* property under the Computed Column Specification key of the column.

Working with User-Defined Data Types

User-defined data types enable you to further refine the data types provided by SQL Server. A user-defined data type is a combination of a data type, length, null constraint, default value, and rule. After you define a user-defined data type, you can use it in any tables that you build. To create a user-defined data type, follow these steps:

1. Expand the Programmability node for the database.

2. Expand the Types node under Programmability.

3. Right-click the User-Defined Data Types node and select New User-Defined Data Type. The New User-Defined Data Type dialog box appears (see Figure 4.9).

4. Enter the required information, such as the name, data type, default, and rule associated with the user-defined type and click OK.

To apply a user-defined data type to a field, follow these steps:

1. Go into the design of the table to whose field you want to apply the data type.

2. Open the Data Type drop-down for the field to which you want to apply the data type (see Figure 4.10).

3. Select the user-defined data type.

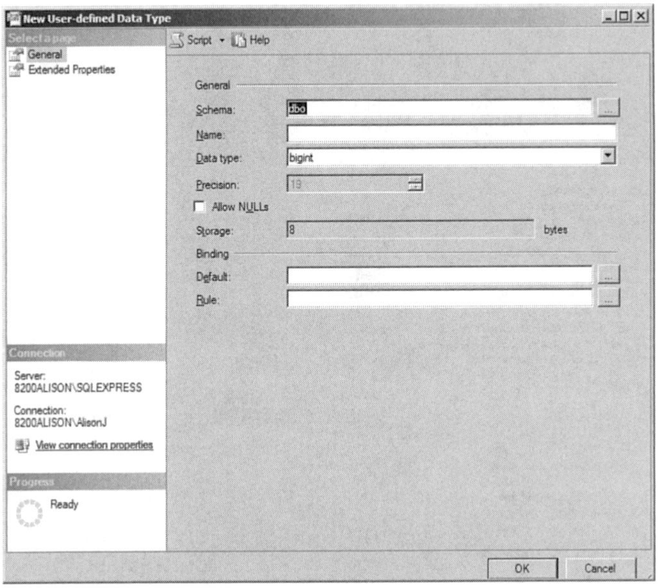

FIGURE 4.9
The User-Defined Data Type Properties dialog box enables you to create or modify a user-defined data type.

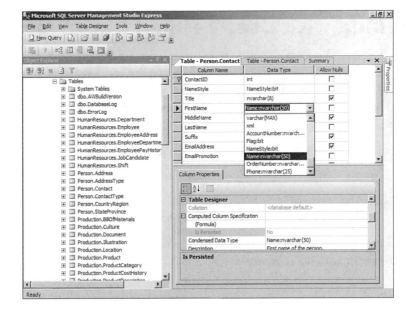

FIGURE 4.10
You can select a user-defined data type as the data type for a field.

As mentioned previously, you can include a rule as part of a user-defined data type. By doing so, you can easily apply the rule to many of the fields that you create. You must first create the rule. You can then select it from the Rule drop-down list in the User-Defined Data Type Properties dialog box.

Adding and Modifying Indexes

You use indexes to improve performance when the user searches a field. Although it's generally best to include too many indexes rather than too few, indexes do have downsides. Indexes speed up searching, sorting, and grouping data. The downside is that they take up hard disk space and slow the process of editing, adding, and deleting data. Although the benefits of indexing outweigh the detriments in most cases, you should not index every field in each table. Create indexes only for fields or combinations of fields by which the user will search, sort, or group. Do not create indexes for fields that contain highly repetitive data. A general rule is to provide indexes for all fields regularly used in searching and sorting, and as criteria for queries.

To create and modify indexes, follow these steps:

1. Modify the design of the table.

2. Click to expand the list of tables in the database to which you want to add the index.

3. Click to expand the options under the table to which you want to add the index.

4. Right-click Indexes and select New Index (see Figure 4.11). The New Index dialog appears (see Figure 4.12).

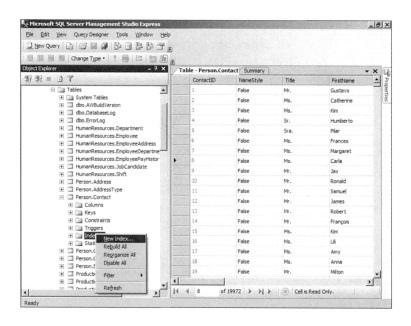

FIGURE 4.11
Right-click Indexes and select New Index to open the New Index dialog.

FIGURE 4.12
The New Index dialog enables you to determine the properties of the index..

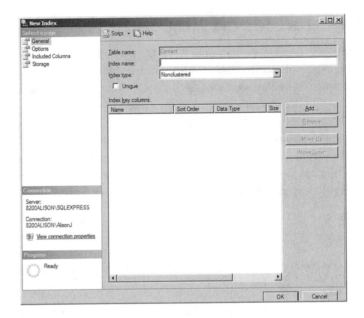

5. Enter a name for the index.

6. Select the type of index you want to create. Select Clustered to designate the index as clustered. You can have only one clustered index per table. The data is stored physically based on the order of the clustered index.

7. Click Add. The Select Columns dialog appears (see Figure 4.13).

FIGURE 4.13
The Select Columns dialog enables you to select the field or fields on which you want to base the index.

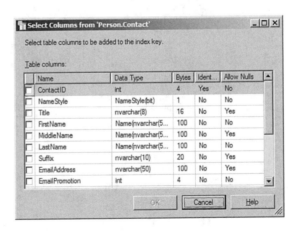

8. Click to select the field or fields on which you want to base the index.

9. Click OK to close the dialog.

10. Designate whether each field is included in ascending or descending order in the index.

11. If desired, click Create Unique to designate the index as a unique constraint.

12. The completed New Index dialog appears as in Figure 4.14. Click OK to close the dialog and create the index.

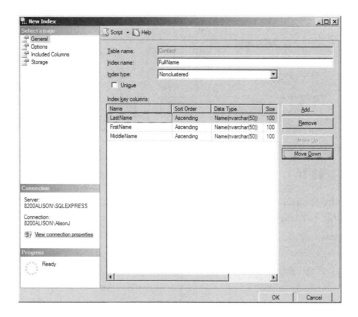

FIGURE 4.14
The Properties window enables you to manage table indexes.

To view all indexes associated with a table, follow these steps:

1. Click to expand the Indexes node for a table (see Figure 4.15).

2. Right-click the index you want to modify and click Properties. The Index Properties dialog appears.

3. Make the desired changes to the index.

4. Click OK when you are finished.

FIGURE 4.15
The Manage
Indexes dialog
enables you to
manage table
indexes.

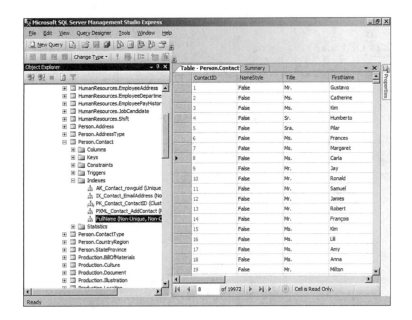

Summary

Tables and the relationships between them are the foundation for any application that you build. It is therefore important that you set up your tables with all the necessary properties and then establish the proper relationships between them. This hour began by covering all the important aspects of designing database tables. You then learned about important topics such as constraints, identity columns, and indexes. Now that you have explored the various ways that you can refine the tables that you build, in the next hour you will learn how to use database diagrams to relate the tables in your database.

Q&A

Q. *What is the difference between a check constraint and a rule?*

A. Both check constraints and rules limit the range of values that a user can enter into a column. Whereas check constraints apply only to the table for which you enter them, you can apply rules to multiple tables.

Q. *Explain what a primary key is, and describe the ideal criteria for a primary key.*

A. A primary key is a column or a set of columns that uniquely identify a row in a table. A primary key should be short, stable, and simple.

Q. *Describe a foreign key and indicate how many foreign keys each table can contain.*

A. A foreign key constraint consists of a column or a set of columns that participate in a relationship with a primary key table. The primary key is on the one side of the relationship, whereas the foreign key is on the many side of the relationship. A table can have multiple foreign keys.

Workshop

Quiz

1. What is a default constraint?

2. What is a Not Null constraint?

3. Provide an example of a computed column.

4. A column can have only one check constraint (true/false).

5. Why is the data type that you select for a field important?

6. What is an identity column?

7. What is the best use of an identity column?

Quiz Answers

1. A default constraint is a value that SQL Server automatically places in a particular field in a table.

2. A Not Null constraint enables you to require that the user enter data into a field.

3. An extended price that is equal to the price times the quantity.

4. False.

5. The data type determines what data you can store in a field.

6. Identity columns provide an autoincrementing value for a table.

7. The best use of an identity column is as the primary key for a table. This is because it is short, stable, and simple.

Activities

Create a table that will store customer information. Add a field called CustomerID that will be the primary key of the table. Make it an identity field. Add a field called CompanyName. Make it VarChar(40). Add a Not Null constraint to the field. Add a field called Address and another field called City. Make them both VarChar(35). Add a field called State. Make it Char(2). Add a check constraint to ensure that the state is CA, UT, AZ, WY, OR, or WA. Give it a default value of CA. Add a field called IntroDate. Make it a DateTime field and give it a default value of today's date. Add a check constraint to ensure that the date entered is on or after today's date. Finally, add a field called CreditLimit. Make it a Money field. Give it a default value of $5,000. Add a Check constraint to ensure that the amount entered is between zero and $10,000. Save the table and try entering data into it. Test the various defaults and constraints that you added to the table's structure.

HOUR 5

Working with Table Relationships

After you add the tables to your database, you establish relationships between them. This helps to ensure the integrity of the data that users enter into the system. In this hour you'll learn:

- ▶ What relationships are and why you would want to use them
- ▶ How to work with database diagrams
- ▶ How to work with table relationships
- ▶ How to designate table and column specifications
- ▶ How to add a relationship name and description
- ▶ How to determine when foreign key relationships constrain the data entered in a column
- ▶ How to designate INSERT and UPDATE specifications

An Introduction to Relationships

Three types of relationships can exist between tables in a database: one-to-many, one-to-one, and many-to-many. Setting up the proper type of relationship between two tables in your database is imperative. The right type of relationship between two tables ensures

- ▶ Data integrity
- ▶ Optimal performance
- ▶ Ease of use in designing system objects

This hour discusses many reasons for these benefits. Before you can understand the benefits of relationships, though, you must understand the types of relationships available.

One-to-Many

A one-to-many relationship is by far the most common type of relationship. In a *one-to-many relationship*, a record in one table can have many related records in another table. A common example is a relationship set up between a Customers table and an Orders table. For each customer in the Customers table, you want to have more than one order in the Orders table. On the other hand, each order in the Orders table can belong to only one customer. The Customers table is on the *one side* of the relationship, and the Orders table is on the *many side*. For this relationship to be implemented, the field joining the two tables on the one side of the relationship must be unique.

In the Customers and Orders tables example, the CustomerID field that joins the two tables must be unique within the Customers table. If more than one customer in the Customers table has the same customer ID, it is not clear which customer belongs to an order in the Orders table. For this reason, the field that joins the two tables on the one side of the one-to-many relationship must be a primary key or must have a unique index. In almost all cases, the field relating the two tables is the primary key of the table on the one side of the relationship. The field relating the two tables on the many side of the relationship is called a *foreign key*.

One-to-One

In a one-to-one relationship, each record in the table on the one side of the relationship can have only one matching record in the table on the other side of the relationship. This relationship is not common and is used only in special circumstances. Usually, if you have set up a one-to-one relationship, you should have combined the fields from both tables into one table. The following are the most common reasons why you should create a one-to-one relationship:

▶ The number of fields required for a table exceeds the number of fields allowed in a SQL Server table.

▶ Certain fields that are included in a table need to be much more secure than other fields included in the same table.

▶ Several fields in a table are required for only a subset of records in the table.

The maximum number of fields allowed in a SQL Server table is 1024. There are very few reasons (if any) why a table should ever have more than 1024 fields. In fact, before you even get close to 1024 fields, you should take a close look at the design of your system. On the *very* rare occasion when having more than 1024 fields is appropriate, you can simulate a single table by moving some of the fields to a second table and creating a one-to-one relationship between the two tables.

The second reason to separate data that logically would belong in the same table into two tables involves security. An example is a table containing employee information. Many users of the system might need to access certain information, such as employee name, address, city, state, ZIP code, home phone, and office extension. Other fields, including the hire date, salary, birth date, and salary level, might be highly confidential. Although you can easily solve this problem with views, in which you create a view with only those fields that all the users can see, you may opt instead to store the secure fields in a table separate from the less-secure fields.

The last situation in which you would want to define one-to-one relationships occurs when certain fields in a table will be used for only a relatively small subset of records. An example is an Employee table and a Vesting table. Certain fields are required only for vested employees. If only a small percentage of a company's employees are vested, it is not efficient in terms of performance or disk space to place all the fields containing information about vesting in the Employee table. This is especially true if the vesting information requires a large volume of fields. By breaking the information into two tables and creating a one-to-one relationship between them, you can reduce disk-space requirements and improve performance. This improvement is particularly pronounced if the Employee table is large.

Many-to-Many

In a *many-to-many relationship*, records in both tables have matching records in the other table. You cannot directly define a many-to-many relationship; you must develop this type of relationship by adding a table called a *junction table*. You relate the junction table to each of the two tables in one-to-many relationships. An example is an Orders table and a Products table. Each order probably contains multiple products, and each product is found on many different orders. The solution is to create a third table called Order Details. You relate the Order Details table to the Orders table in a one-to-many relationship based on the OrderID field. You relate the Order Details table to the Products table in a one-to-many relationship based on the ProductID field.

Working with Database Diagrams

One way that you can establish and maintain relationships between SQL Server tables is to create a database diagram. It is important to understand how to create a database diagram, add tables to it, edit the diagram, and remove tables from the diagram. The sections that follow cover these topics.

Creating a Database Diagram

To create a database diagram:

1. Right-click the Database Diagrams node and select New Database Diagram. The dialog in Figure 5.1 will appear.

FIGURE 5.1
If you haven't yet created any database diagrams for a database, you will be prompted as to whether you want to create one.

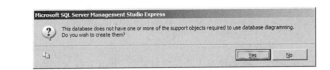

2. Click Yes to proceed.

3. Right-click the Database Diagrams node again and select New Database diagram. The Add Table dialog appears (see Figure 5.2).

FIGURE 5.2
The Add Table dialog allows you to select the tables that you want to include in the database diagram.

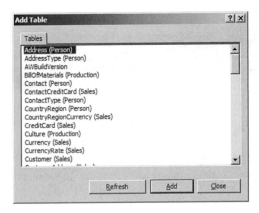

4. Designate the tables that you want to add to the database diagram and click Add. Click Close. The diagram appears as in Figure 5.3.

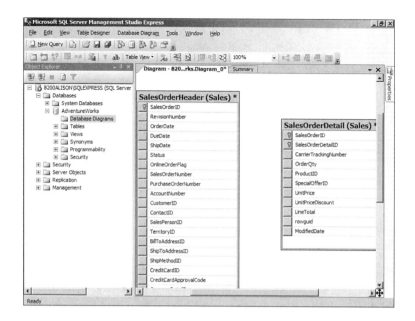

FIGURE 5.3
After adding tables to the database diagram, they appear in the Database Diagram window.

5. Click and drag from the field(s) in the Primary Key table that you want to relate to the field(s) in the Foreign Key table. The Tables and Columns dialog box appears (see Figure 5.4) .

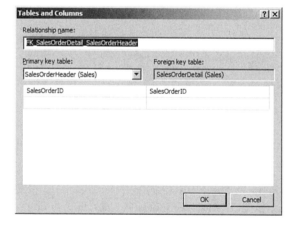

FIGURE 5.4
The Tables and Columns dialog box allows you to you to designate what tables and columns will participate in the relationship.

6. Provide a relationship name and verify that the desired relationship has been established. Click OK to close the dialog. The Foreign Key Relationship dialog appears (see Figure 5.5).

FIGURE 5.5
The Foreign Key relationships dialog allows you to designate properties for the relationship.

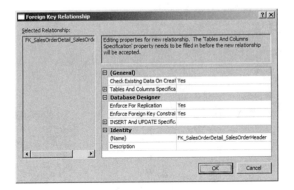

7. Designate any properties for the relationship and click OK. You are returned to the database diagram.

8. When you close the database diagram, SQL Server first prompts you as to whether you want to save the changes that you made (see Figure 5.6). Click Yes to commit the changes to the underlying tables. The Choose Name dialog appears.

FIGURE 5.6
SQL Server prompts you as to whether you want to save changes to the underlying tables.

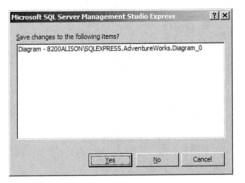

9. Enter a name for the database diagram and click OK. The Save dialog appears letting you know what tables you will affect (see Figure 5.7). Click Yes to proceed and update the designated tables. The database diagram should now appear under the Database Diagrams node of SQL Server Management Studio.

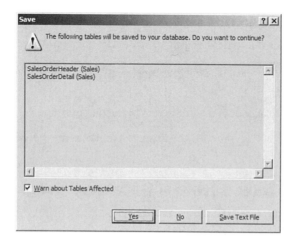

FIGURE 5.7
The Save dialog
lets you know
what tables your
changes will
affect.

Editing a Database Diagram

To edit the relationship between two tables in a database diagram:

1. Right-click any table in the database diagram and select Relationships. The Foreign Key Relationships dialog appears (see Figure 5.8).

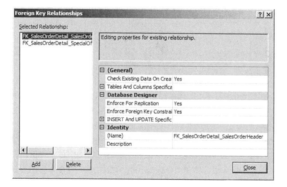

FIGURE 5.8
The Foreign Key
Relationships
dialog allows
you to indicate
the relationship
that you wish
to modify.

2. Click to select the relationship you wish to modify.

3. Modify any of the desired properties (the remaining sections in this hour will cover these properties in additional detail).

4. Click Close.

Adding Tables to a Database Diagram

To add tables to the database diagram:

1. Right-click anywhere in the Relationships window and select Add Table. The Add Table dialog box appears.

2. Select the tables that you want to add to the diagram and click Add.

3. Click Close. SQL Server adds the requested tables to the diagram.

Removing Tables from a Database Diagram

To remove tables from the database diagram:

1. Right-click the table that you want to remove and select Remove from Diagram.

2. It is important to note that SQL Server removes the table from the diagram but does not remove the relationship from the database.

By the Way

> **Note**
>
> It is important to understand the correlation between the database diagram and the actual relationships that you have established within the database. A database can contain multiple database diagrams. Each database diagram lets you view and modify the existing relationships. When you establish relationships, SQL Server creates the actual relationship between the tables. You can delete the tables from the database diagram (by right-clicking and selecting Remove Table from Diagram), but the relationships still will exist (permanently removing relationships is covered in the section "Using the Properties Window to Delete a Relationship," later in this hour). The Database Diagram window provides a visual blueprint of the relationships that you have established. If you modify the layout of the diagram by moving around tables, adding tables to the diagram, or removing tables from the diagram without changing any relationships, SQL Server *still* prompts you to save the changes to the diagram when you close the diagram window. In that case, SQL Server is not asking whether you want to save the relationships that you have established; it is simply asking whether you want to save the visual layout of the window.

Working with Table Relationships

It is easy to view all the foreign key relationships in which a table is participating. Follow these steps:

1. Right-click the table and select Modify. The design of the table appears (see Figure 5.9).

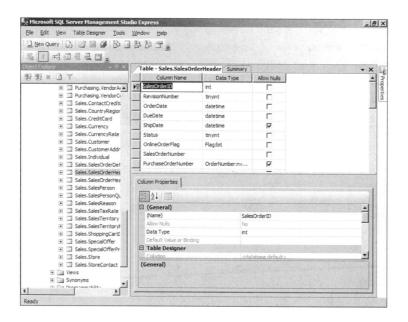

FIGURE 5.9
While the design of the table is visible, you are able to select the Relationships tool on the toolbar.

2. Click the Relationships tool on the toolbar. The Foreign Key Relationships dialog appears (see Figure 5.10).

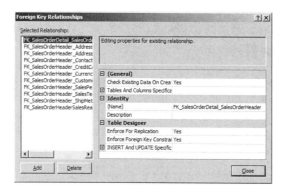

FIGURE 5.10
The Foreign Key Relationships dialog enables you to work with the relationships associated with a table.

3. Click a relationship to select it. The properties of that relationship appear.

Adding a Foreign Key Relationship

The Foreign Key Relationships dialog also allows you to add an index. Simply click the Add button. A new relationship appears with a default name and without a description. Before you take any further action you should supply the Tables and Columns Specification covered in the section "How to Designate Table and Column Specifications." You must designate the table and column specification before SQL Server Express will accept the new relationship.

Deleting a Foreign Key Relationship

Deleting a foreign key relationship is easy. Follow these steps:

1. While in the Foreign Key Relationships dialog, select the relationship you wish to remove.

2. Click the Delete button. SQL Server Express removes the relationship without warning.

> **Warning**
>
> When you remove a foreign key relationship, you are removing the data integrity protection that it affords you. This means, for example, that after you have removed the foreign key relationship between customers and orders, the user can add orders for customers that do not exist.

How to Designate Table and Column Specifications

By entering a Tables and Columns specification, you designate the foreign key table that will participate in the relationship, the field in the foreign key table that will participate in the relationship, and the field in the current table that will participate in the relationship. To work with the Tables and Columns Specification, follow these steps:

1. In the Foreign Key Relationships dialog, click to select Tables and Columns Specification.

2. Click the Build button (...) that appears to the right. The Tables and Columns dialog appears (see Figure 5.11).

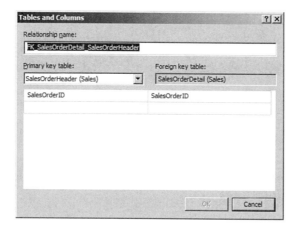

FIGURE 5.11
The Tables and
Columns dialog
enables you to
designate what
tables and
fields partici-
pate in the
relationship.

3. If you want to, modify the relationship name. You will generally want to rename the relationship to more accurately reflect the relationship that you are creating (for example, FK_Customers_Orders_CustomerID).

4. Click to select the primary key table that will participate in the relationship. For example, if you are creating foreign keys for the Orders table, you would designate the Customer table as the primary key table.

5. Use the drop-down on the left (under the primary key table) to select the field(s) that will participate in the relationship. For example, in the foreign key relationship between Orders and Customers, the CustomerID in the Customers table participates in the relationship.

6. Use the drop-down on the right (under the foreign key table) to select the field(s) in the current table that will participate in the relationship. The complete dialog appears in Figure 5.12. In the relationship between the Orders table and the Customers table, the foreign key field participating in the relationship would be the CustomerID field.

7. Click OK to complete the process. SQL Server Express returns you to the Foreign Key Relationships dialog.

FIGURE 5.12
The Completed
Tables and
Columns dialog,
showing the
relationship
between the
Customers
table and the
Orders table.

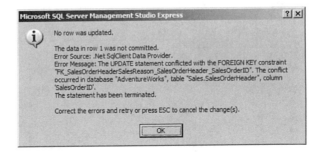

How to Add a Relationship Name and Description

It is helpful to provide a descriptive name for each relationship that you add, and for you to provide a brief description of each relationship. This way when you are viewing a relationship in the Foreign Key Relationships window you can easily see the nature of the relationship that you have selected.

To enter or change a name for the relationship simple click the (Name) property for the relationship. Enter or change the name as you desire.

To enter a description for the relationship, click the Description property for the index. Enter a short description of your choice.

How to Determine when Foreign Key Relationships Constrain the Data Entered in a Column

As you can see, establishing a relationship is quite easy. Establishing the right kind of relationship is a little more difficult. When you attempt to establish a relationship between two tables, SQL Server makes some decisions based on a few predefined factors:

▶ It establishes a one-to-many relationship if one of the related fields is a primary key or has a unique index.

▶ It establishes a one-to-one relationship if both the related fields are primary keys or have unique indexes.

▶ It cannot create a relationship if neither of the related fields is a primary key and neither has a unique index.

As covered earlier in this hour, *referential integrity* consists of a series of rules that SQL Server applies to ensure that the relationships between tables are maintained properly. At the most basic level, referential integrity rules prevent the creation of orphan records in the table on the many side of the one-to-many relationship. After establishing a relationship between a Customers table and an Orders table, for example, all orders in the Orders table must be related to a particular customer in the Customers table. Before you can establish referential integrity between two tables, the following conditions must be met:

▶ The matching field on the one side of the relationship must be a primary key field or must have a unique index.

▶ The matching fields must have the same data types. They also must have the same size. Number fields on both sides of the relationship must have the same size (int, for example).

▶ Both tables must be part of the same database.

▶ If you opt to set the Check Existing Data on Creation option to Yes, existing data within the two tables cannot violate any referential integrity rules. All orders in the Orders table must relate to existing customers in the Customers table, for example.

After you establish referential integrity between two tables, SQL Server applies the following rules:

▶ You cannot enter a value in the foreign key of the related table that does not exist in the primary key of the primary table. For example, you cannot enter a value in the CustomerID field of the Orders table that does not exist in the CustomerID field of the Customers table.

▶ You cannot delete a record from the primary table if corresponding records exist in the related table. For example, you cannot delete a customer from the Customers table if related records exist in the Orders table (records with the same value in the CustomerID field) unless you designate a Delete Rule (see the section that follows).

▶ You cannot change the value of a primary key on the one side of a relationship if corresponding records exist in the related table. For example, you cannot change the value in the CustomerID field of the Customers table if corresponding orders exist in the Orders table unless you designate an Update rule in the Foreign Key Relationships dialog for the relationship (see the section that follows).

If any of the previous three rules is violated and referential integrity is being enforced between the tables, an appropriate error message is displayed, as shown in Figure 5.13.

FIGURE 5.13
An appropriate error message appears if referential integrity is violated.

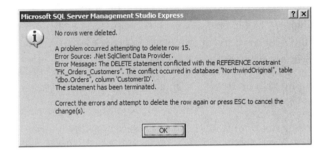

SQL Server's default behavior is to prohibit the deletion of parent records that have associated child records and to prohibit the change of a primary key value of a parent record when that parent has associated child records. You can override these restrictions by using the INSERT and UPDATE specification, covered in the next section.

For now, let's see how you can establish referential integrity between the tables in your database. The process is as follows:

1. From the Foreign Key Relationships dialog, select the relationship for which you want to establish referential integrity.

2. Set the Enforce Foreign Key Constraint property to Yes. This step alone is all you need to establish referential integrity.

3. If you want to check existing data when you save your changes to ensure that they do not violate the referential integrity rules, set the Check Existing Data on Creation or Re-enabling option to Yes.

4. If you are utilizing replication, and want to enforce referential integrity during the synchronization process, set the Enforce for Replication property to Yes.

Designating Insert and Update Specifications

SQL Server enables you to define rules that dictate what will happen when the user deletes or updates a record. You can find these rules under the INSERT and UPDATE

Specification node of the Foreign Key Relationships window. The text that follows explores this node, and why and how you should use it.

The Delete Rule

By setting the Delete rule, you determine what happens when the user deletes a record on the one side of a one-to-many relationship. For example, by setting the Delete rule to Cascade you establish the rule so that the user can delete a record on the one side of a one-to-many relationship, even if related records exist in the table on the many side of the relationship. The user can delete a customer even if the customer has existing orders, for example. Referential integrity is maintained between the tables because SQL Server automatically deletes all related records in the child table.

If you attempt to delete a record from the table on the one side of a one-to-many relationship and no related records exist in the table on the many side of the relationship, you are able to delete the record. On the other hand, if you attempt to delete a record from the table on the one side of a one-to-many relationship and related records exist in the child table, you will delete the record from the parent table as well as any related records in the child table.

Tip

Setting the Delete rule to Cascade is not always appropriate. It is an excellent feature, but you should use it prudently. Although it is usually appropriate to cascade delete from an Orders table to an Order Details table, for example, it generally is not appropriate to cascade delete from a Customers table to an Orders table. This is because you generally do not want all your order history deleted from the Orders table if for some reason you want to delete a customer. Deleting the order history causes important information, such as your profit and loss history, to change. It therefore is appropriate to prohibit this type of deletion and handle the customer in some other way, such as marking him as inactive or archiving his data. On the other hand, if you delete an order because it was canceled, you probably want the corresponding order detail information to be removed as well. In this case, the Cascade option is appropriate. You need to make the appropriate decision in each situation, based on business needs. The important thing is to carefully consider the implications of each option before making your decision.

Did you Know?

The Update Rule

With the Update rule set to Cascade, the user can change the primary key value of the record on the one side of the relationship. When the user makes an attempt to modify the field joining the two tables on the one side of the relationship, the change is cascaded down to the foreign key field on the many side of the relationship. This is useful if the primary key field is modifiable. For example, a purchase number on a purchase order master record may be updateable. If the user modifies the purchase order number of the parent record, you would want to cascade the change to the associated detail records in the purchase order detail table.

By the Way

> **Note**
>
> There is no need to select the Cascade option when the related field on the one side of the relationship is an identity field. An identity field can never be modified. The Cascade option has no effect on identity fields.

By the Way

> **Note**
>
> Other options for the Delete and Update rules include No Action, Set Null, and Set Default. No Action, the default value, does nothing, and therefore does not allow the deletion of parent records that have children or the modification of the key field(s) of parent records that have children. Set Null sets the value of the foreign key field to Null. Finally, Set Default sets the value of the foreign key field to its default value.

Summary

Even if your table design is sound, a database set up without proper relationships compromises both data integrity and application performance. It is therefore important that you establish the proper relationships between the tables in your database. This hour began with a discussion of the types of relationships available. You then learned about important topics such as how to establish relationships, how to designate table and column specifications, how to determine when foreign key relationships constrain the data entered in a column, and how to designate Insert and Update specifications.

Q&A

Q. *What is the Tables and Columns specification?*

A. The Tables and Columns specifications enable you to designate the foreign key table that will participate in the relationship, the field in the foreign key table that will participate in the relationship, and the field in the current table that will participate in the relationship.

Q. *Describe three uses of a one-to-one relationship.*

A. You use a one-to-one join when the number of fields required for a table exceeds the number of fields allowed in a SQL Server table, when certain fields that are included in a table need to be much more secure than other fields included in the same table, or when several fields in a table are required for only a subset of records in the table.

Q. *Describe a many-to-many relationship and how you create one.*

A. With a many-to-many relationship, records in both tables have matching records in the other table. You cannot create a many-to-many relationship directly. You must develop a junction table and relate the junction table to each of the two tables in one-to-many relationships.

Workshop

Quiz

1. Name the three types of relationships.

2. What is the most common type of relationship?

3. To create a relationship, matching fields must have the same data type (true/false).

4. By setting the Delete rule to Cascade, when a user deletes a row on the one side of the relationship, SQL Server Express deletes the corresponding rows on the many side of the relationship (true/false).

5. The Update rule is very useful when working with Identity columns (true/false).

6. List three advantages of establishing relationships between database tables.

Quiz Answers

1. One-to-one, one-to-many, and many-to-many.

2. One-to-many.

3. True.

4. True.

5. False. Because you cannot change the value of an identity column, the Update rule is not applicable to an identity column.

6. Data integrity, optimal performance, and ease of use in designing system objects.

Activities

Create a table that will store order information. Add a field called OrderID that will be the primary key field of the table. Make its data type Int and make it an identity field. Add a field called CustomerID. Give it the data type of Int. Add a Not Null constraint to the field. Add a field called OrderDate. Make it a DateTime field. Add another field called ShippedBy. Make it an Int field. Finally, add a field called FreightAmount. Make it a Money field. Now that you have created the table, establish a relationship between it and the Customers table created in Hour 4. Base the relationship on the CustomerID field from each table. Make sure that you set the Enforce Foreign Key Constraint property of the relationship to Yes. Add some customers to the Customers table. Make note of their CustomerIDs. Add orders to the Orders table for those customers. You should be able to add those orders without a problem. Try adding orders for customers that do not exist. You should not be able to do so because of the referential integrity that you applied. Try deleting customers who have orders. Once again, you should fail because of the referential integrity that you applied. If you are feeling really ambitious, set the Delete Rule of the relationship to Cascade. Then try deleting a Customer with orders. The process should delete the customer and its corresponding orders.

HOUR 6

Getting to Know the SELECT Statement

Knowledge of the T-SQL language is vital to your success as a SQL Express administrator or developer. You use the T-SQL language to manipulate the data in your database. Using T-SQL, you can select, insert, update, and delete data. In this hour you'll learn:

▶ What T-SQL Is

▶ How to Build a SELECT Statement

▶ How to Work with a WHERE Clause

▶ How to Order Your Output

▶ How to Work with the DISTINCT Clause

▶ How to Output Your Data as XML

▶ How to Create Top Values Queries

Introducing T-SQL

T-SQL, or Transact-SQL, is the dialect of the Structured Query Language (SQL) incorporated in SQL Server. To work effectively as a SQL Server developer, you must have a strong grasp of T-SQL. Fortunately, T-SQL is easy to learn. When retrieving data, you simply build a SELECT statement. SELECT statements are composed of clauses that determine the specifics of how the data is selected. When they're executed, SELECT statements select rows of data and return them as a recordset.

By the Way

> In the examples that follow, keywords appear in uppercase. Values that you supply appear italicized. Optional parts of the statement appear in square brackets. Curly braces, combined with vertical bars, indicate a choice. Finally, ellipses are used to indicate a repeating sequence.

By the Way

> The examples that follow are based on a database called Northwind which is included on the sample code CD. Instructions as to how to install the Northwind database are included in Appendix A.

Working with the SELECT Statement

The SELECT statement is at the heart of the SQL language. You use the SELECT statement to retrieve data from one or more tables. Its basic syntax is

```
SELECT column-list FROM table-list WHERE where-clause ORDER BY order-by-clause
```

The SELECT clause specifies what columns you want to retrieve from the table that SQL Server returns to the result set. The basic syntax for a SELECT clause is

```
SELECT column-list
```

The simplest SELECT clause looks like this:

```
SELECT * FROM Customers
```

This SELECT clause, combined with the FROM clause covered next, retrieves all columns from a table. Here's another example that retrieves only the CustomerID and CompanyName columns from a table:

```
SELECT CustomerID, CompanyName FROM Customers
```

Not only can you include columns that exist in your table, but you also can include expressions in a SELECT clause. Here's an example:

```
SELECT CustomerID, City + ', ' + Region + ' ' +
    PostalCode AS Address FROM Customers
```

This SELECT clause retrieves the CustomerID column as well as an alias called Address, which includes an expression that concatenates the City, Region, and PostalCode columns (see Figure 6.1).

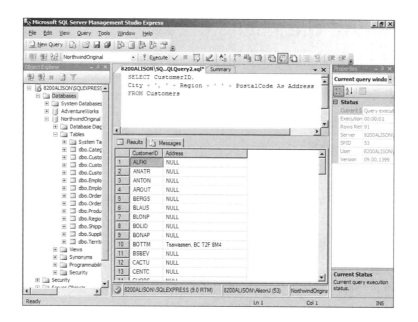

FIGURE 6.1
A *SELECT* clause
that retrieves
the CustomerID
column as well
as an alias
called Address,
which includes
an expression
that concate-
nates the City,
Region, and
PostalCode
columns.

Adding on the FROM **Clause**

The FROM clause specifies the tables or views from which the records should be selected. It can include an alias that you use to refer to the table. The FROM clause looks
like this:

FROM *table-list* [AS *alias*]

Here's an example of a basic FROM clause:

FROM *Customers*

In this case, the name of the table is Customers. If you combine the SELECT clause
with the FROM clause, the SQL statement looks like this:

SELECT *CustomerID, CompanyName* FROM *Customers*

This SELECT statement retrieves the CustomerID and CompanyName columns from
the Customers table.

Just as you can alias the fields included in a SELECT clause, you can also alias the
tables included in the FROM clause. The alias is used to shorten the name and to simplify a cryptic name, as well as for a variety of other reasons. Here's an example:

SELECT *CustomerID, CompanyName* FROM *Customers* AS *Clients*

Including the WHERE Clause

The WHERE clause limits the records retrieved by the SELECT statement. A WHERE clause can include columns combined by the keywords AND and OR. The syntax for a WHERE clause looks like this:

```
WHERE expression1 [{AND¦OR} expression2 […]]
```

A simple WHERE clause looks like this:

```
WHERE Country = 'USA'
```

Using an AND to further limit the criteria, the WHERE clause looks like this:

```
WHERE Country = 'USA' AND ContactTitle Like 'Sales%'
```

This WHERE clause limits the records returned to those in which the country is equal to USA and the ContactTitle begins with Sales. Notice that T-SQL uses the percent (%) sign as a wildcard. Using an OR, the SELECT statement looks like this:

```
WHERE Country = 'USA' OR Country = 'Canada'
```

This WHERE clause returns all records in which the country is equal to either USA or Canada. Compare that with the following example:

```
WHERE Country = 'USA' OR ContactTitle Like 'Sales%'
```

This WHERE clause returns all records in which the country is equal to USA or the ContactTitle begins with Sales. For example, the salespeople in China are returned from this WHERE clause because their ContactTitle begins with Sales. The WHERE clause combined with the SELECT and FROM clauses looks like this (see also Figure 6.2):

```
SELECT CustomerID, CompanyName FROM Customers
    WHERE Country = 'USA' OR Country = 'Canada'
```

You must follow several rules when building a WHERE clause. You must enclose the text strings for which you are searching in apostrophes. You must also surround dates with apostrophes. Finally, you must include the keyword LIKE when utilizing wildcard characters. Remember that T-SQL uses the percent symbol as the wildcard for zero or more characters. The underscore (_) is the wildcard for a single character.

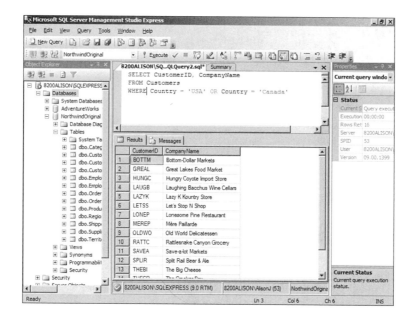

FIGURE 6.2
A *SELECT* clause that retrieves the CustomerID and CompanyName columns for all the customers in the U.S.A. and Canada.

Using the ORDER BY **Clause**

The ORDER BY clause determines the order in which SQL Server sorts the returned rows. It's an optional clause and looks like this:

```
ORDER BY column1 [{ASC¦DESC}], column2 [{ASC¦DESC}] [,…]]
```

Here's an example:

```
ORDER BY CustomerID
```

The ORDER BY clause can include more than one field:

```
ORDER BY Country, CustomerID
```

When you specify more than one field, SQL Server uses the leftmost field as the primary level of sort. Any additional fields are the lower sort levels. Combined with the rest of the SELECT statement, the ORDER BY clause looks like this:

```
SELECT CustomerID, CompanyName FROM Customers
    WHERE Country = 'USA' OR Country = 'Canada'
    ORDER BY CompanyName
```

The results appear in order by CompanyName (see Figure 6.3).

FIGURE 6.3
A *SELECT* clause that retrieves the CustomerID and CompanyName columns for all the customers in the U.S.A. and Canada. SQL Server orders the results by CompanyName.

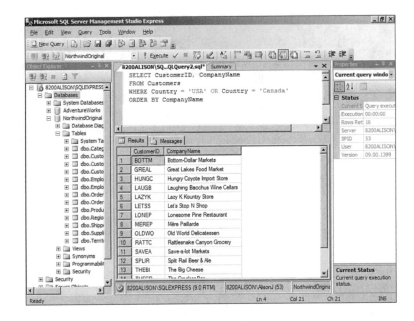

The ORDER BY clause enables you to determine whether the sorted output appears in ascending or descending order. By default, output appears in ascending order. To switch to descending order, use the optional keyword DESC. Here's an example:

```
SELECT CustomerID, CompanyName FROM Customers ORDER BY CustomerID DESC
```

This example selects the CustomerID and CompanyName fields from the Customers table, ordering the output in descending order by the CustomerID field (see Figure 6.4).

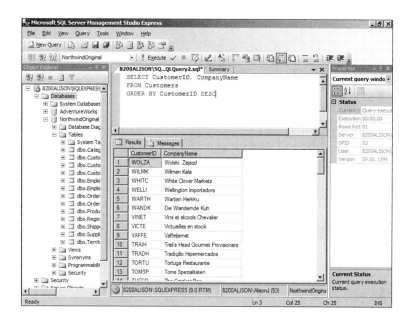

FIGURE 6.4
A *SELECT* clause that retrieves the CustomerID and CompanyName columns for all the customers in the U.S.A. and Canada. SQL Server orders the results in descending order by CustomerID.

Adding the DISTINCT Keyword

The DISTINCT keyword ensures uniqueness of values in the column or combination of columns included in the query result. Consider the following SQL statement:

```
SELECT Country FROM Customers
```

This statement returns one row for each customer (see Figure 6.5). The same country appears multiple times in the output.

Contrast the statement used in Figure 6.5 with this:

```
SELECT DISTINCT Country FROM Customers
```

This statement returns a list of unique countries from the list of customers (see Figure 6.6).

The statement that follows returns a unique list of country and city combinations (see Figure 6.7):

```
SELECT DISTINCT Country, City FROM Customers
```

FIGURE 6.5
A *SELECT* statement that returns one row for each customer. The same country appears multiple times in the output.

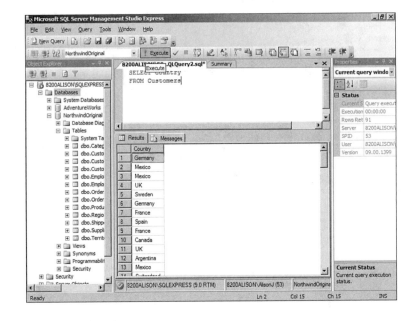

FIGURE 6.6
A *SELECT* statement that returns a list of unique countries from the list of customers.

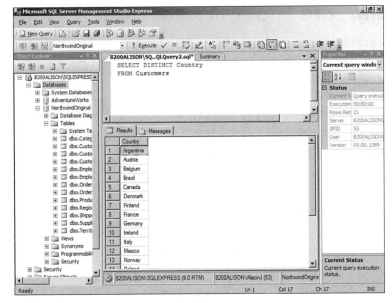

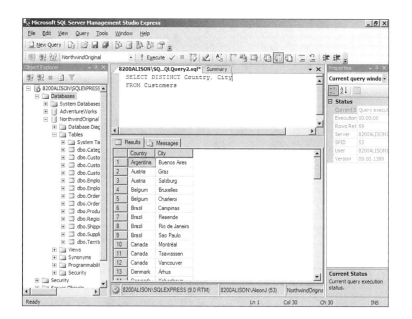

FIGURE 6.7
A *SELECT* statement that returns a list of unique country and city combinations from the list of customers.

Working with the FOR XML **Clause**

You use the FOR XML clause to return data as an XML document. When using the FOR XML clause, you must specify the mode as RAW, AUTO, or EXPLICIT. With the RAW option, SQL Server takes the result of the query and transforms each row in the result set into an XML element with a generic identifier. Here's an example:

```
SELECT CustomerID, CompanyName, ContactName, ContactTitle
FROM Customers
ORDER BY CustomerID
FOR XML RAW
```

The results appear as in Figure 6.8. With the AUTO option, SQL Server returns a simple nested XML tree. SQL Server represents each field in each table specified in the SELECT clause as an XML element. Here's an example:

```
SELECT CustomerID, CompanyName, ContactName, ContactTitle
FROM Customers
ORDER BY CustomerID
FOR XML AUTO
```

FIGURE 6.8
The result of
using the *FOR
XML RAW* clause
to return data.

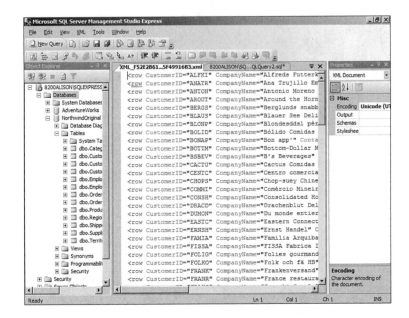

The results appear as in Figure 6.9. Finally, with the EXPLICIT option, you explicitly define the shape of the tree. You must write your queries so that the columns listed in the SELECT clause are mapped to the appropriate element attributes.

FIGURE 6.9
The result of
using the *FOR
XML AUTO*
clause to
return data.

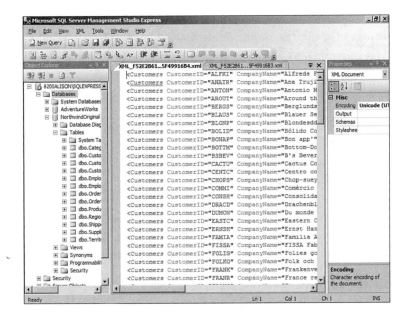

Creating Top Values Queries

You use the TOP clause to limit the number of rows that SQL Server includes in the output. Here's an example:

```
SELECT TOP 10 OrderDate, Freight FROM Orders
    ORDER BY Freight DESC
```

This example shows the 10 highest freight amounts along with their corresponding order dates (see Figure 6.10).

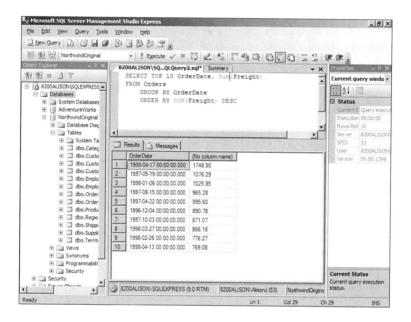

FIGURE 6.10
A *SELECT* statement that shows the 10 order dates associated with the highest 10 freight amounts.

In addition to enabling you to select the top number of rows, T-SQL also enables you to select the top percent of rows. Here's an example:

```
SELECT TOP 10 PERCENT OrderDate, Freight FROM Orders
    ORDER BY Freight DESC
```

Here the top 10% of freight amounts appear in the query result.

Summary

The T-SQL language is the foundation for most of what you do in SQL Server. It is therefore necessary that you have a strong understanding of the T-SQL language constructs. This chapter covered many of the basics of the T-SQL language. You learned about the SELECT statement, the FROM keyword, the WHERE clause, the ORDER

BY clause, and the DISTINCT keyword. You also learned about FOR XML and top value queries. We cover T-SQL in additional detail throughout the remainder of the book.

Q&A

Q *Why do you use a SELECT statement?*

A You use the SELECT statement to retrieve data from one or more tables.

Q *Name the wildcard characters that you can use when searching, and explain the differences between them.*

A The two wildcard characters are the percent (%) sign and the underscore (_). T-SQL uses the percent symbol as the wildcard for zero or more characters. The underscore (_) is the wildcard for a single character.

Q *Explain the DISTINCT keyword.*

A The DISTINCT keyword ensures uniqueness of values in the column or combination of columns included in the query result.

Q *Why would you use a Top Values query?*

A You use a Top Values query to limit the number of rows that appear in the output.

Workshop

Quiz

1. List the three modes of the FOR XML statement.

2. What keyword do you use to designate what tables you will include in the query?

3. PERCENT is a valid keyword when the TOP clause is used (true/false).

4. You use ALIAS to permanently rename a field in a table (true/false).

5. What is the keyword that you use if you want the data to appear in descending order?

Quiz Answers

1. The three modes of the FOR XML statement are RAW, AUTO, and EXPLICIT.

2. You use FROM to designate the tables you will include in the query.

3. True.

4. False. ALIAS provides only an alias for the field in the query output.

5. If you want the query output to appear in descending order, use the DESC keyword.

Activities

Build a simple SELECT statement based on the Orders table in the Northwind sample database. Add a WHERE clause to limit the date range of the orders that appear in the output. Order the data in descending order by Freight.

Building SQL Statements Based on Multiple Tables

Now that you've learned the basics of the T-SQL language, you're ready to move on to more advanced techniques. To really take advantage of what T-SQL has to offer, you must know how to return recordsets that contain data based on multiple tables. In this hour you'll learn:

▶ What Join Types Are Available and How to Use Them
▶ How to Output Data Based on Multiple Tables
▶ How to Group Your Query Output
▶ About the Aggregate Functions Available to You
▶ What the Having Clause Is and When to Use It
▶ How to Union Data from Multiple Tables
▶ How to Build Subqueries

The examples that follow are based on a database called Northwind which is included on the sample code CD. Instructions as to how to install the Northwind database are included in Appendix A.

By the Way

Working with Join Types

When you build a system based on normalized table structures, you must join the tables back together to see the data in a useable format. For example, if you have separated customers, orders, and order details, you need to join these tables in a query to see the name of the customer who placed an order for a particular item. Several types of joins are available. They include inner joins, outer joins, full joins, and self-joins. The sections that follow cover each of these join types.

Using Inner Joins

An inner join is the most common type of join. When you use an inner join, only rows on the one side of the relationship that have matching rows on the many side of the relationship are included in the output. Here's an example:

```
SELECT Customers.CustomerID,
    Customers.CompanyName, Orders.OrderID,
    Orders.OrderDate
    FROM Customers
    INNER JOIN Orders ON Customers.CustomerID = Orders.CustomerID
```

This example includes only those customers who have orders.

> The word OUTER is assumed in the LEFT JOIN clause used when building a left outer join.

At times you need to join more than two tables in a SQL statement. The most common syntax is

```
FROM table1 JOIN table2 ON condition1 JOIN table3 ON condition2
```

The following example joins the Customers, Orders, and OrderDetails tables:

```
SELECT Customers. CustomerID, Customers.CompanyName,
    Orders.OrderID, Orders.OrderDate
    FROM (Customers
    INNER JOIN Orders
    ON Customers.CustomerID = Orders.CustomerID)
    INNER JOIN [Order Details]
    ON Orders.OrderID = [Order Details].OrderID
```

In the example, the order of the joins is unimportant. The exception to this is when you combine inner and outer joins. When you combine inner and outer joins, the SQL Server engine applies two specific rules. First, the nonpreserved table in an outer join cannot participate in an inner join. The nonpreserved table is the one whose rows may not appear. In the case of a left outer join from Customers to Orders, the Orders table is considered the nonpreserved table. Therefore, it cannot participate in an inner join with OrderDetails. The second rule is that the nonpreserved table in an outer join cannot participate with another nonpreserved table in another outer join.

Creating Outer Joins

An outer join enables you to include rows from one side of the join in the output, regardless of whether matching rows exist on the other side of the join. Two types of outer joins exist: left outer joins and right outer joins. With a left outer join, SQL Server includes in the output all rows in the first table specified in the SELECT statement. Here's an example:

```
SELECT Customers.CustomerID,
    Customers.CompanyName, Orders.OrderID,
    Orders.OrderDate
    FROM Customers
    LEFT OUTER JOIN Orders ON Customers.CustomerID = Orders.CustomerID
```

In the previous example, customers are included regardless of whether they have orders. With the right outer join shown next, orders are included whether or not they have associated customers. If you have properly enforced referential integrity, this scenario should never exist.

```
SELECT Customers.CustomerID,
    Customers.CompanyName, Orders.OrderID,
    Orders.OrderDate
    FROM Customers
    RIGHT OUTER JOIN Orders ON Customers.CustomerID = Orders.CustomerID
```

Utilizing Full Joins

A full join combines the behavior of the left and right outer joins. It looks like this:

```
SELECT Customers.CustomerID,
    Customers.CompanyName, Orders.OrderID,
    Orders.OrderDate
    FROM Customers
    FULL JOIN Orders ON Customers.CustomerID = Orders.CustomerID
```

In this example, all customers appear in the output regardless of whether they have orders, and all orders appear in the output whether or not they are associated with customers.

Taking Advantage of Self-Joins

A self-join involves joining a table to itself. Although it is not the most common type of join, this join type is very valuable. Imagine the scenario in which an Employee table contains a field called EmployeeID and another field called ReportsTo. The ReportsTo field must contain a valid EmployeeID. It would not make sense to have separate Employee and Supervisor tables because supervisors are employees. This is where the self-join comes in. A self-join looks like this:

```
SELECT Employees.EmployeeID, Employees.LastName, Employees.FirstName,
    Supervisors.EmployeeID as SupervisorID,
    Supervisors.LastName as SupervisorLastName,
    Supervisors.FirstName as SupervisorFirstName
    FROM Employees INNER JOIN Employees as Supervisors
    ON Employees.ReportsTo = Supervisors.EmployeeID
```

In this example, the EmployeeID from the Employees table is joined to an alias of the ReportsTo field of an alias of the Employees table (called Supervisors). The resulting employee and supervisor information is output from the query (see Figure 7.1).

FIGURE 7.1
A *SELECT* statement that shows the result of joining the Employee table to itself.

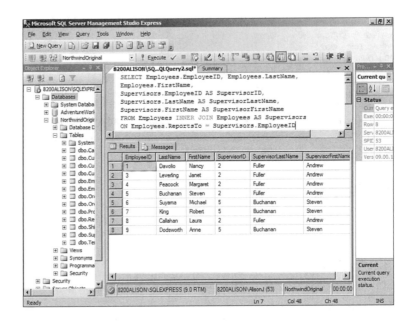

Working with the GROUP BY Clause

You can use the GROUP BY clause to calculate summary statistics. The syntax of the GROUP BY clause is

```
GROUP BY group-by-expression1 [,group-by-expression2 [,…]]
```

You use the GROUP BY clause to dictate the fields on which SQL Server groups the query result. When you include multiple fields in a GROUP BY clause, they are grouped from left to right. SQL Server automatically outputs the fields in the order designated in the GROUP BY clause. In the following example, the SELECT statement returns the country, city, and total freight for each country/city combination. The results are displayed in order by country and city (see Figure 7.2):

```
SELECT Customers.Country, Customers.City,
   Sum(Orders.Freight) AS SumOfFreight
   FROM Customers
   INNER JOIN Orders ON Customers.CustomerID = Orders.CustomerID
   GROUP BY Customers.Country, Customers.City
```

The GROUP BY clause indicates that SQL Server doesn't display the detail for the selected records. Instead, it displays the fields indicated in the GROUP BY uniquely. One of the fields in the SELECT statement must include an aggregate function. SQL Server displays this result of the aggregate function along with the fields specified in the GROUP BY clause.

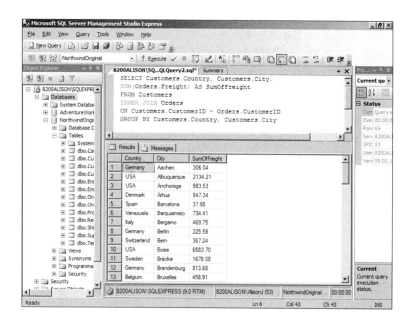

FIGURE 7.2
A *SELECT* statement that returns the country, city, and total freight for each country/city combination.

Including Aggregate Functions in Your SQL Statements

You use aggregate functions to summarize table data. The aggregate functions available include COUNT, COUNT_BIG, SUM, AVG, MIN, and MAX. The following sections discuss each of these aggregate functions. You can find additional aggregate functions in the Books Online.

Using the COUNT Function

You use the COUNT function to count the number of rows in a table. It looks like this:

```
SELECT COUNT(*) AS CountOfCustomers FROM Customers
```

The example counts the number of rows in the Customers table (see Figure 7.3).

As an alternative, you can count values in a particular column. The SQL statement looks like this:

```
SELECT COUNT(Region) AS CountOfCustomers FROM Customers
```

This example counts the number of regions found in the Customers table (see Figure 7.4).

FIGURE 7.3
A *SELECT* statement that counts the number of rows in the Customers table.

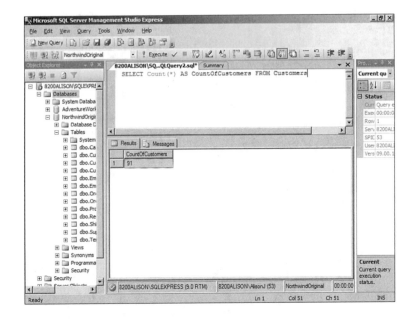

FIGURE 7.4
A *SELECT* statement that counts the number of regions found in the Customers table.

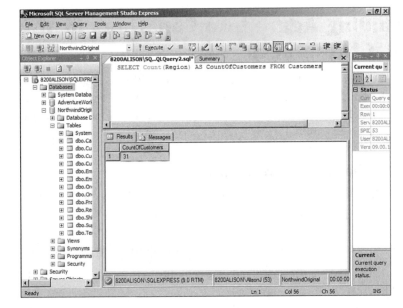

Working with the COUNT_BIG Function

The COUNT_BIG function is identical to the COUNT function, except that it returns a bigint data type. It looks like this:

```
SELECT COUNT_BIG(Region) AS CountOfCustomers FROM Customers
```

Exploring the SUM Function

The SUM function is available only for numeric columns. It adds the data in the columns. Here's an example:

```
SELECT SUM(Freight) FROM Orders
```

The example totals the Freight column for all rows in the Orders table. When used with the GROUP BY clause, the SUM function can easily total values for each grouping.

```
SELECT ShipVia, SUM(Freight) FROM Orders GROUP BY ShipVia
```

The example totals the freight for each shipper (see Figure 7.5).

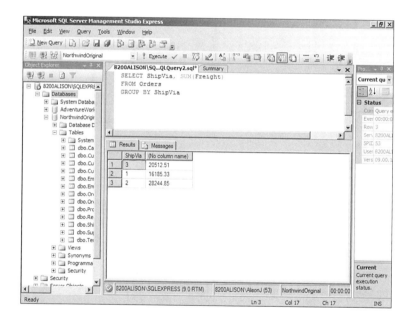

FIGURE 7.5
A *SELECT* statement that totals the freight for each shipper found in the Orders table.

Working with the AVG Function

Just as you can easily total data, you can average data. The following statement finds the average freight for all orders in the Orders table:

```
SELECT AVG(Freight) FROM Orders
```

When used with the GROUP BY clause, the AVG function can easily average values in each grouping.

```
SELECT ShipVia, AVG(Freight) FROM Orders GROUP BY ShipVia
```

The result provides the average freight for each shipper (see Figure 7.6).

FIGURE 7.6
A *SELECT* state-
ment that
provides the
average freight
for each shipper
found in the
Orders table.

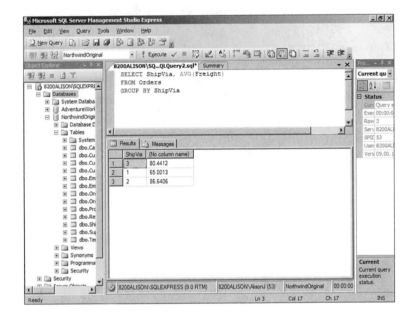

Using the MIN **Function**

Another important aggregate function is MIN. You use the MIN function to find the minimum value in a column. This statement finds the minimum freight in the Orders table:

```
SELECT MIN(Freight) FROM Orders
```

When used with the GROUP BY clause, the MIN function can easily find the minimum values in each grouping.

```
SELECT ShipVia, MIN(Freight) FROM Orders GROUP BY ShipVia
```

The result provides the minimum freight for each shipper (see Figure 7.7).

Using the MAX **Function**

A related aggregate function is MAX. You use the MAX function to find the maximum value in a column. This statement finds the maximum freight in the Orders table (see Figure 7.8):

```
SELECT MAX(Freight) FROM Orders
```

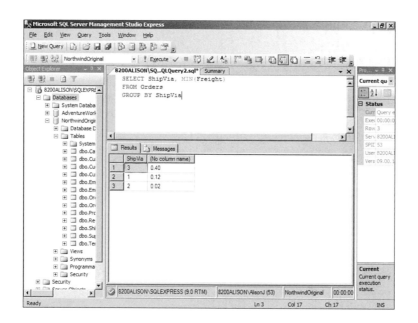

FIGURE 7.7
A *SELECT* statement that provides the minimum freight for each shipper found in the Orders table.

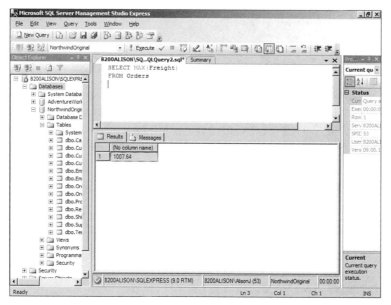

FIGURE 7.8
You use the *MAX* function to find the maximum value in a column.

When used with the GROUP BY clause, the MAX function can easily find the maximum values in each grouping.

```
SELECT ShipVia, MAX(Freight) FROM Orders GROUP BY ShipVia
```

The result provides the maximum freight for each shipper (see Figure 7.9).

FIGURE 7.9
When used with
the *GROUP BY*
clause, the *MAX*
function can
easily find the
maximum val-
ues in each
grouping.

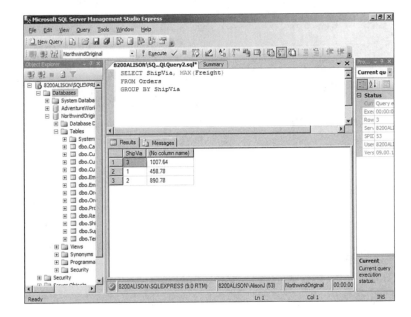

Taking Advantage of the HAVING Clause

A HAVING clause is similar to a WHERE clause, but it differs in one major respect: SQL Server applies it *after* it summarizes the data rather than beforehand. In other words, the WHERE clause is used to determine which rows are grouped. The HAVING clause determines which groups are included in the output. A HAVING clause looks like this:

```
HAVING expression1 [{AND¦OR} expression2[…]]
```

In the following example, SQL Server applies the criteria > 1000 after it applies the aggregate function SUM to the grouping. Therefore, SQL Server includes only country/city combinations with total freight greater than 1000 in the output (see Figure 7.10).

```
SELECT Customers.Country, Customers.City,
    Sum(Orders.Freight) AS SumOfFreight
    FROM Customers
    INNER JOIN Orders ON Customers.CustomerID = Orders.CustomerID
    GROUP BY Customers.Country, Customers.City
    HAVING (((Sum(Orders.Freight))>1000))
```

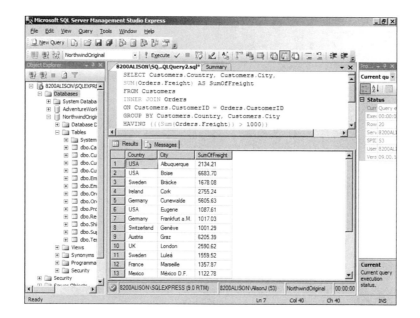

FIGURE 7.10
A *SELECT* statement that includes country/city combinations with total freight greater than 1000 in the output.

Exploring the Power of Union Queries

Union queries enable you to combine rather than join data from more than one table. A typical example of a union query is one that combines data from a Products table and a DiscontinuedProducts table. Another example is a query that combines data from a Customers table and a CustomerArchive table. Here's an example of a union query:

```
SELECT ProductID, ProductName, UnitPrice FROM Products
UNION ALL
SELECT ProductID, ProductName, UnitPrice FROM DiscontinuedProducts
```

This example outputs all rows from the Products table as well as from the DiscontinuedProducts table (see Figure 7.11).

The Northwind database does not contain a DiscontinuedProducts table. To follow along with this example, you need to create a table with the same structure as the Products table, except the primary key field should not be an IDENTITY column.

By the Way

FIGURE 7.11
A *SELECT* statement that outputs all rows from the Products table as well as from the Discontinued Products table.

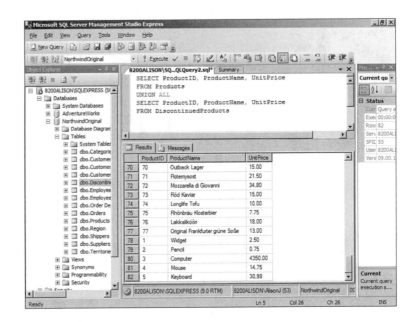

If you want to order the results, you must place the ORDER BY statement after the second SELECT statement:

```
SELECT ProductID, ProductName, UnitPrice FROM Products
UNION ALL
SELECT ProductID, ProductName, UnitPrice FROM DiscontinuedProducts
ORDER BY UnitPrice DESC
```

In this example, SQL Server combines the results of both SELECT statements in descending order by UnitPrice.

Working with Subqueries

A subquery is a query that SQL Server evaluates before it evaluates the main query. Here's an example:

```
SELECT CustomerID, CompanyName, City, Country FROM Customers WHERE
    CustomerID Not In(Select CustomerID FROM Orders)
```

In this example, SQL Server executes the statement that selects data from the Orders table *before* it evaluates the statement that selects data from the Customers table (see Figure 7.12).

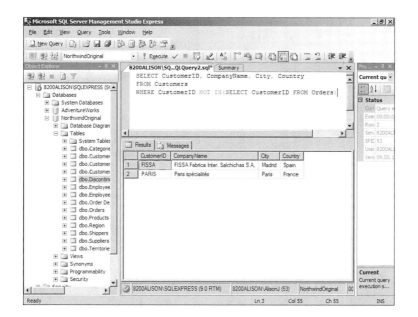

FIGURE 7.12
A *SELECT* statement that selects data from the Orders table before it evaluates the statement that selects data from the Customers table.

This is *not* a very efficient method of accomplishing the task of finding all the customers without orders. A better solution would be to use an outer join to solve this problem. You could modify the SQL statement to look like this:

```
SELECT Customers.CustomerID, CompanyName, City, Country
    FROM Customers LEFT JOIN Orders ON Customers.CustomerID = Orders.CustomerID
    WHERE Orders.CustomerID Is Null
```

This example uses a left outer join to select all customers who do not have orders. Because this uses a left outer join, customers are included whether or not they have orders. Because the criteria designate that only rows with a null CustomerID appear in the output, only Customers without orders are included (see Figure 7.13) .

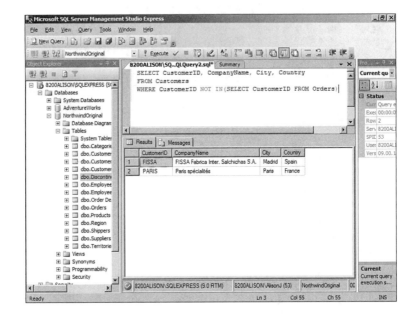

Summary

In a world of normalized data, it is important that you understand how to use
queries to join your tables back together. This chapter showed you how to join table
data. You learned about the various join types available to you. You also learned
how to group data, and how to work with aggregate functions. You learned about
the HAVING clause, a clause necessary for working with aggregated data. Finally, you
learned about two special types of queries: union queries and subqueries.

Q&A

Q *Why must you join tables together in a query?*

A When you build a system based on normalized table structures, you must join
the tables back together to see the data in a useable format.

Q *Explain what a full join is.*

A A full join combines the behavior of a left outer join and a right outer join. An
example is where you show all customers whether or not they have orders,
and all orders whether or not they are associated with a customer.

Q *Explain the difference between the* HAVING *clause and the* WHERE *clause.*

A SQL Server Express applies the HAVING clause *after* it summarizes the data,
whereas it applies the WHERE clause *before* it summarizes the data.

Q *Describe a subquery.*

A SQL Server Express evaluates a subquery before it evaluates the main query.

Workshop

Quiz

1. Name the five join types.

2. What is the purpose of aggregate functions?

3. Name four aggregate functions.

4. One of the aggregate functions is COUNT LARGE (true/false).

5. A union query joins two tables (true/false)?

Quiz Answers

1. Inner, left outer, right outer, full, and self.

2. They summarize table data.

3. Sum, Count, Min, Max, Avg.

4. False. It is called COUNT BIG.

5. False. Union queries allow you to combine two tables.

Activities

Practice joining the Customers and Orders tables in the Northwind sample database with an inner join, a left-outer join, a right-outer join, and a full join. Add a few customers without orders. Note that the number of rows in the output differs for the various join types. Perform a self-join by joining the EmployeeID in the Employees table to the ReportsTo field in the Employees table. Output the LastName and FirstName fields from each table instance used in the query. You should see a list of all employees and their supervisors. Finally, find the sum, average, minimum, and maximum freight amounts in the Orders table.

HOUR 8

Modifying Data with Action Queries

Not only can you use T-SQL to select data, you can also use it to update data. T-SQL enables you to update, insert into, and delete data from tables. In this hour you'll learn:

- ▶ How to use the UPDATE statement to update table data
- ▶ How to use the INSERT statement to insert data into an existing table
- ▶ How to use the SELECT INTO statement to insert data into a new table
- ▶ How to use the DELETE statement to selectively delete data from a table
- ▶ How to use the TRUNCATE statement to remove all data from a table

> The examples that follow are based on a database called Northwind which is included on the sample code CD. Instructions as to how to install the Northwind database are included in Appendix A.

Modifying Data with Action Queries

The queries that you have explored thus far are all SELECT queries. This means that they *select* data from one or more tables. The queries that we discuss now are action queries. They are queries that modify data. The five types of action queries discussed here are INSERT, UPDATE, SELECT INTO, DELETE, and TRUNCATE.

Adding Data with the INSERT Statement

You use the INSERT statement to insert data into an *existing* table. The INSERT statement has the following format:

```
INSERT [INTO] table_or_view [(col1, col2…)] VALUES (value1, value2)
```

Here's an example:

```
INSERT INTO Customers
(CustomerID, CompanyName, ContactName,
ContactTitle, City, Country)
VALUES
('INFO', 'InfoTechnology Partners, Inc.',
'Alison Balter', 'President',
'Camarillo', 'USA')
```

In this example, the designated values are inserted into the specified fields in the Customers table.

Using the SELECT INTO Statement

Whereas the INSERT statement inserts data into an existing table, the SELECT INTO statement creates a new table. Here's an example:

```
SELECT Customers.CustomerID,
Customers.CompanyName,
Customers.ContactName,
Customers.ContactTitle,
Customers.City,
Customers.Country
INTO USACustomers FROM Customers
WHERE Country = 'USA'
```

In this example, all customers with a country of USA are inserted into a new table called USACustomers.

Updating Data with the UPDATE Statement

As its name implies, an UPDATE statement updates table data. The format of the UPDATE statement is

```
UPDATE tablename SET column1=value1, [column2=value2….]
```

The following example updates the contents of the Customers table, changing the city to Oak Park for all rows in which the city is Camarillo.

```
UPDATE Customers
SET City = 'Oak Park'
WHERE City = 'Camarillo'
```

Deleting Data with the DELETE Statement

You use the DELETE statement to remove rows from a table. The format of the DELETE statement is

```
DELETE [FROM] table-name [WHERE search_conditions]
```

Here's an example:

```
DELETE FROM USACustomers WHERE ContactTitle = 'Owner'
```

This example removes all rows from the USACustomers table in which the contact title is Owner.

Using the TRUNCATE **Statement**

The TRUNCATE statement removes all rows from a table. It executes more quickly than a DELETE statement without a WHERE clause. Unlike the DROP statement, the TRUNCATE statement retains the structure of the table. It looks like this:

```
TRUNCATE TABLE USACustomers
```

Summary

An important use of T-SQL lies in its ability to modify table data. Using T-SQL, you can insert, update, and delete table data. In this chapter, you learned the syntax to perform these important tasks.

Q&A

Q *Explain the difference between* INSERT *and* SELECT INTO.

A INSERT adds data to an existing table, whereas SELECT INTO creates a new table containing the data that you are inserting.

Q *Explain the difference between a* DELETE *statement and a* TRUNCATE *statement.*

A A DELETE statement enables you to selectively remove data from a table, whereas the TRUNCATE statement unconditionally removes all rows from a table.

Q *Describe the difference between* TRUNCATE *and* DROP.

A TRUNCATE removes all data from the table while retaining the table structure, whereas DROP removes the table from the database.

Workshop

Quiz

1. Name the five action keywords available in T-SQL.

2. You can insert data into a view (true/false).

3. What keyword do you use when inserting data into a new table?

4. What statement do you use to *most efficiently* remove all data from the Customers table?

Quiz Answers

1. INSERT, SELECT INTO, UPDATE, DELETE, TRUNCATE.

2. True. You can insert data into a view just as you can insert data into a table. The INSERT statement affects all tables underlying the view.

3. INTO.

4. TRUNCATE TABLE Customers.

Activities

Write and execute T-SQL that inserts all orders where freight is between 500 and 1000 into a new table called tblCustomerMediumFreight. View the table data to validate that your T-SQL code ran successfully. Insert additional data into the tblCustomerMediumFreight table from the Orders table where the freight is between 0 and 200. View the table data to validate your T-SQL code. Update all freight amounts in the tblCustomerMediumFreight table, increasing them by one. Review the table data to make sure that your T-SQL code executed as expected. Delete all rows in the tblCustomerMediumFreight table where the freight amount is between 600 and 800. Review the table data to ensure that all the rows with the designated freight amount are removed. Truncate the tblCustomerMediumFreight table. Open it up and note that the data is unavailable. Finally DROP the tblCustomerMediumFreight table. Note that it is no longer listed in the list of available data.

HOUR 9

Getting to Know the T-SQL Functions

The T-SQL language contains numerous functions that you can incorporate into the T-SQL statements that you build. These functions perform a variety of important tasks. In this hour you'll cover some of the commonly used numeric, string, date/time, and null-related functions. For additional information on the plethora of T-SQL functions available, consult Books Online (online help for SQL Server). In this hour you'll learn:

- ▶ How to work with some of the numeric functions available in T-SQL
- ▶ How to work with some of the string functions available in T-SQL
- ▶ How to work with some of the date/time functions available in T-SQL
- ▶ How to use T-SQL to work with nulls

The examples that follow are based on a database called Northwind which is included on the sample code CD. Instructions as to how to install the Northwind database are included in Appendix A.

Working with Numeric Functions

Important numeric functions include `IsNumeric` and `ROUND`. The sections that follow examine these functions and provide examples of their uses.

Using The `IsNumeric` Function

The `IsNumeric` function returns information on whether a value is numeric. Here's an example:

```
SELECT CustomerID, PostalCode, IsNumeric(PostalCode) FROM Customers
```

The SELECT statement returns each customer's CustomerID, PostalCode, and information on whether the postal code is numeric (see Figure 9.1).

FIGURE 9.1
A *SELECT* statement that uses the *IsNumeric* function to determine whether the postal code is numeric.

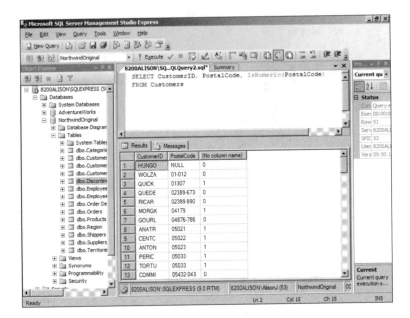

Exploring the ROUND **Function**

As its name implies, the ROUND function rounds an expression to a specified length. Here's an example:

```
SELECT OrderID, Freight, Round(Freight, 0) FROM Orders
```

This SQL statement returns the OrderID, Freight, and the Freight rounded to whole numbers from the Orders table (see Figure 9.2).

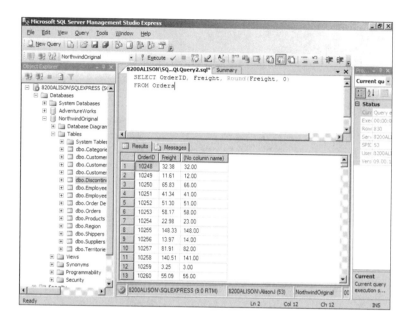

FIGURE 9.2
A *SELECT* statement that returns the OrderID, Freight, and the Freight rounded to whole numbers from the Orders table.

Taking Advantage of String Functions

Important string functions include LEFT, RIGHT, LEN, REPLACE, STUFF, SUBSTRING, LOWER, UPPER, LTRIM, and RTRIM.

Using the LEFT Function

The LEFT function extracts a designated number of characters from the left of a string:

```
SELECT CustomerID, LEFT(CompanyName, 5) FROM Customers
```

This example selects the CustomerID and the five leftmost characters from the Customers table (see Figure 9.3).

Working with the RIGHT Function

The RIGHT function works similarly but extracts the designated rightmost characters from a string. The same example using the RIGHT function looks like this:

```
SELECT CustomerID, RIGHT(CompanyName, 5) FROM Customers
```

This example returns the CustomerID and the five rightmost characters from the CompanyName (see Figure 9.4).

FIGURE 9.3
A *SELECT* statement that selects the CustomerID and the five leftmost characters from the Customers table.

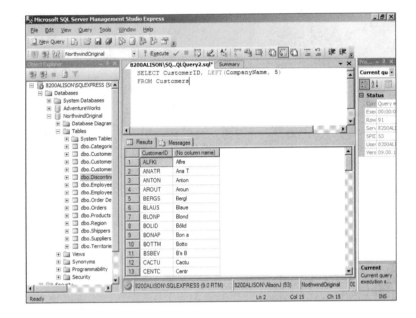

FIGURE 9.4
A *SELECT* statement that returns the CustomerID and the five rightmost characters from the CompanyName.

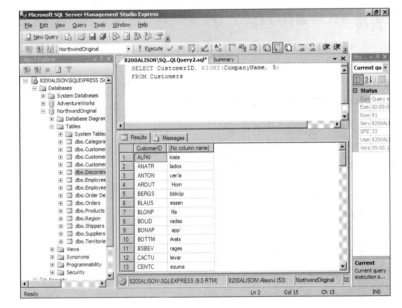

Using the SUBSTRING **Function**

The SUBSTRING function extracts specified characters from a string. Here's an example:

```
SELECT CustomerID, ContactTitle, SUBSTRING(ContactTitle, 5, 3) FROM Customers
```

This example returns the CustomerID, ContactTitle, and the fifth through seventh characters of the ContactTitle from the Customers table (see Figure 9.5).

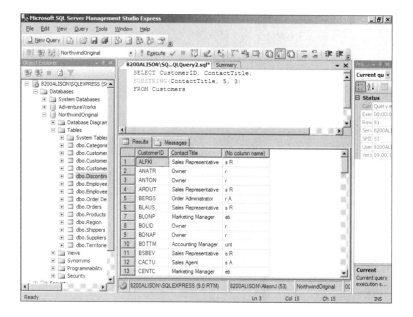

FIGURE 9.5
A *SELECT* statement that returns the CustomerID, ContactTitle, and the fifth through seventh characters of the ContactTitle from the Customers table.

Exploring the LEN **Function**

The LEN function returns the length of a string. It looks like this:

```
SELECT CustomerID, CompanyName, LEN(CompanyName) FROM Customers
```

This example returns the CustomerID, CompanyName, and the length of the company name for each row in the Customers table (see Figure 9.6).

Using the REPLACE **Function**

The REPLACE function replaces all occurrences of one string with another. Here's an example:

```
SELECT CustomerID, ContactTitle,
   REPLACE(ContactTitle, 'Sales', 'Marketing' )
   FROM Customers
```

FIGURE 9.6
A *SELECT* statement that returns the CustomerID, CompanyName, and the length of the company name for each row in the Customers table.

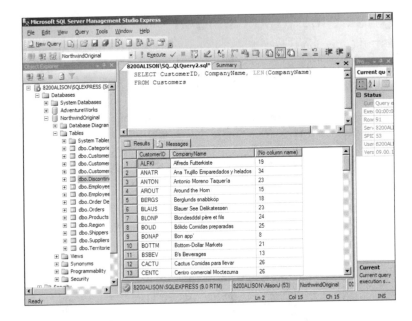

This example selects the CustomerID and ContactTitle from the Customers table. It includes an additional column that replaces all occurrences of the word Sales with the word Marketing (see Figure 9.7).

FIGURE 9.7
A *SELECT* statement that replaces all occurrences of the word *Sales* with the word *Marketing*.

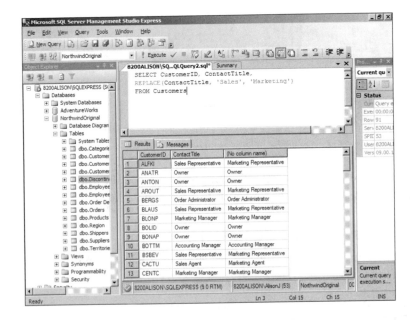

Taking Advantage of the STUFF Function

The STUFF function starts at a specific position and replaces a specified number of characters with other specified characters. Here's an example:

```
SELECT CustomerID, ContactTitle,
    STUFF(ContactTitle, 5, 3, '***' )
    FROM Customers
```

This example selects the CustomerID and ContactTitle from the Customers table. It includes an additional column that replaces the fifth through seventh characters with asterisks (see Figure 9.8).

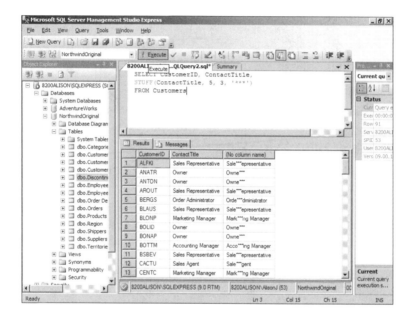

FIGURE 9.8
A *SELECT* statement that replaces the fifth through seventh characters with asterisks.

Using the LOWER Function

The LOWER function returns the lowercase version of a string. It looks like this:

```
SELECT CustomerID, LOWER(CompanyName) FROM Customers
```

The example returns the contents of the CustomerID field and then the lowercase version of the contents of the CompanyName field (see Figure 9.9).

FIGURE 9.9
A *SELECT* state-
ment that
returns the low-
ercase version
of the contents
of the
CompanyName
field.

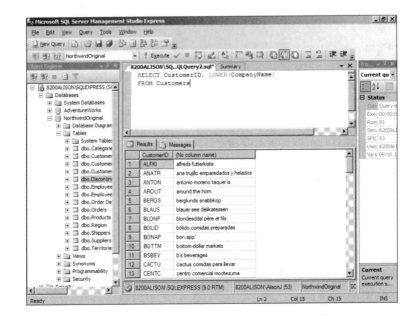

Using the UPPER Function

The UPPER function returns the uppercase version of a string. It looks like this:

```
SELECT CustomerID, UPPER(CompanyName) FROM Customers
```

The example returns the contents of the CustomerID field and then the uppercase
version of the contents of the CompanyName field (see Figure 9.10).

FIGURE 9.10
A *SELECT* state-
ment that
returns the
uppercase ver-
sion of the con-
tents of the
CompanyName
field.

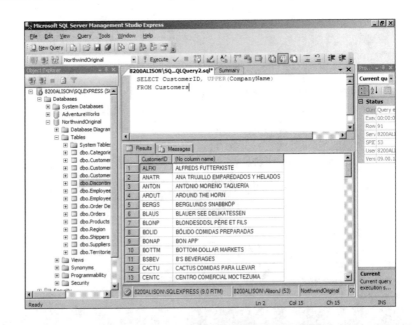

Working with the LTRIM Function

The LTRIM function returns the string without leading spaces. It looks like this:

```
SELECT CustomerID, LTRIM(CompanyName) FROM Customers
```

The example returns the contents of the CustomerID field and then the contents of the CompanyName field with any leading spaces removed.

Working with the RTRIM Function

The RTRIM function returns the string without trailing spaces. It looks like this:

```
SELECT CustomerID, RTRIM(CompanyName) FROM Customers
```

The example returns the contents of the CustomerID field and then the contents of the CompanyName field with any trailing spaces removed.

Exploring the Date/Time Functions

Important date/time functions include GETDATE, MONTH, DAY, YEAR, DATEPART, DATE-NAME, DATEADD, and DATEDIFF. The sections that follow cover these functions.

Using The GETDATE Function

The GETDATE function returns the system date and time. It looks like this:

```
SELECT GETDATE()
```

Learning About the MONTH Function

The MONTH function returns the month portion of a date. It looks like this:

```
SELECT OrderID, OrderDate, MONTH(OrderDate) FROM Orders
```

This SQL statement returns the OrderID, the OrderDate, and the month of the order date from the Orders table (see Figure 9.11).

Exploring the DAY Function

The DAY function returns the day portion of a date. It looks like this:

```
SELECT OrderID, OrderDate, DAY(OrderDate) FROM Orders
```

This SQL statement returns the OrderID, the OrderDate, and the day of the order date from the Orders table (see Figure 9.12).

FIGURE 9.11
A *SELECT* statement that returns the month of the order date from the Orders table.

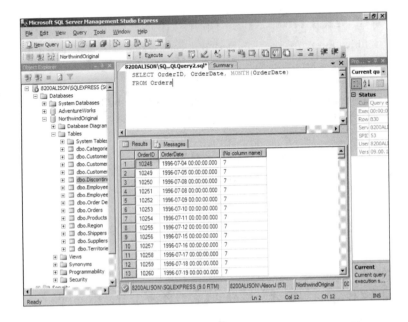

FIGURE 9.12
A *SELECT* statement that returns the day of the order date from the Orders table.

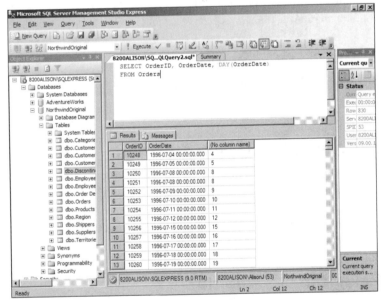

Working with the YEAR Function

The YEAR function returns the year portion of a date. It looks like this:

```
SELECT OrderID, OrderDate, YEAR(OrderDate) FROM Orders
```

This SQL statement returns the OrderID, the OrderDate, and the year of order date from the Orders table (see Figure 9.13).

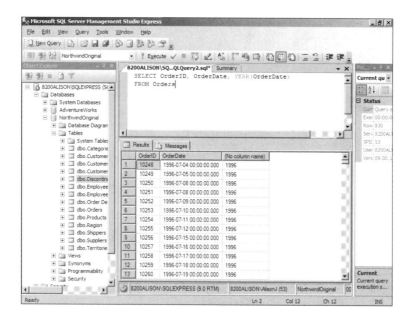

FIGURE 9.13
A *SELECT* statement that returns the year of order date from the Orders table.

Exploring the Powerful DATEPART Function

You use the DATEPART function to extract a part of a date. The first parameter to the DATEPART function is an abbreviation designating the part of the date that you want to extract. The second parameter is the date from which you want to extract it. Here's an example:

```
SELECT OrderID, OrderDate, DATEPART(qq, OrderDate) FROM Orders
```

This example selects the OrderID, the OrderDate, and the quarter of the OrderDate from the Orders table (see Figure 9.14).

Using the DATENAME Function

The DATENAME function returns a string representing a part of a date. It also receives two parameters. The first is the abbreviation indicating the part of the date that you want to extract. The second is the date from which you want to extract it. Here's an example:

```
SELECT OrderID, OrderDate, DATENAME(dw, OrderDate) FROM Orders
```

FIGURE 9.14
A *SELECT* statement that returns the quarter of the OrderDate from the Orders table.

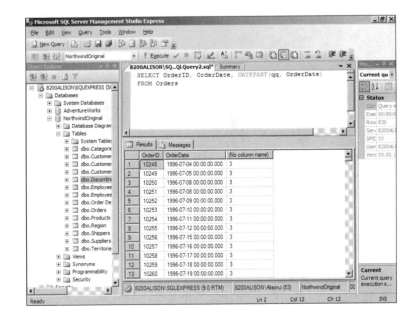

This example returns the OrderID, the OrderDate, and a text description of the day of the week of the OrderDate (see Figure 9.15).

FIGURE 9.15
A *SELECT* statement that returns a text description of the day of the week of the OrderDate.

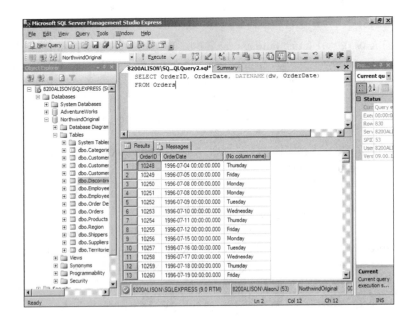

Working with the DATEADD Function

You use the DATEADD function to add or subtract time from a date. The first parameter is the time period that you want to add or subtract (for example day, month, year). The second parameter is the number of time periods that you want to add or subtract (for example 1 day, 3 months, or 5 years). The final parameter is the date to which you want to add it or from which you want to subtract it. Here's an example:

```
SELECT OrderID, OrderDate, DATEADD(mm, 1, OrderDate) FROM Orders
```

This returns the OrderID, the OrderDate, and the date one month greater than the order date (see Figure 9.16).

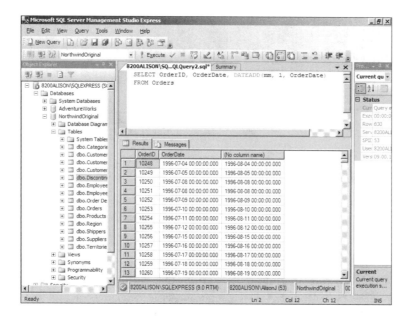

FIGURE 9.16
A *SELECT* statement that returns the OrderID, the OrderDate, and the date one month greater than the order date.

Using the DATEDIFF Function

The DATEDIFF function returns the difference between two dates. It receives three parameters. The first is the time period in which you want the difference to appear (days, months, and so on). The second and third parameters are the dates whose difference you want to evaluate. Here's an example:

```
SELECT OrderID, OrderDate, ShippedDate,
DATEDIFF(dd, OrderDate, ShippedDate) FROM Orders
```

This example returns the OrderID, OrderDate, ShippedDate, and number of days between the OrderDate and the ShippedDate (see Figure 9.17).

FIGURE 9.17
A *SELECT* statement that returns the OrderID, OrderDate, ShippedDate, and number of days between the OrderDate and the ShippedDate.

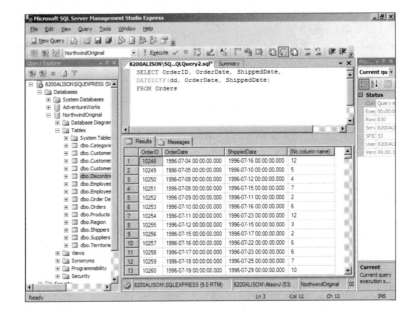

Working with Nulls

Several functions help you deal with nulls in your table data. They include ISNULL, NULLIF, and COALESCE. The sections that follow cover these functions.

Exploring the ISNULL Function

The ISNULL function returns information on whether the value in an expression is null. It receives two parameters. The first parameter is the expression that you want to evaluate. The second is the value that you want to return if the expression is null. The ISNULL function looks like this:

```
SELECT CustomerID, Region,
ISNULL(Region, 'No Region')
FROM Customers
```

This example returns the CustomerID and Region fields from the Customers table. If the region is null, the third column contains the words No Region. Otherwise, the third column contains the value for the region (see Figure 9.18).

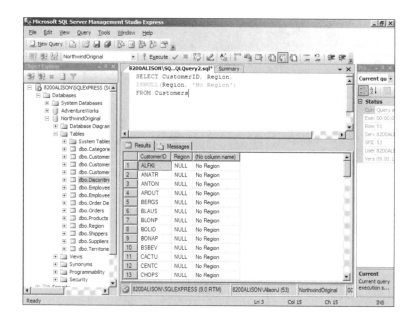

FIGURE 9.18
A *SELECT* statement that handles nulls in the Region field.

Taking Advantage of the NULLIF Function

The NULLIF function replaces specified values with nulls. It receives two parameters. The first is the name of the expression that you want to replace. The second is the value that you want to replace with nulls. Here's an example:

```
SELECT AVG(NULLIF(Freight, 0)) FROM Orders
```

This example calculates the average freight amount in the Orders table, eliminating 0 values from the calculation (see Figure 9.19).

Working with the COALESCE Function

The COALESCE function returns the first non-null expression in a series of expressions. SQL Server evaluates the first expression. If it is null, it evaluates the second expression. If the second expression is null, it evaluates the third expression. This continues until the function reaches the last expression. Here's an example:

```
SELECT CustomerID,
COALESCE(Region, PostalCode, Country)
FROM Customers
```

This example returns the CustomerID. It then returns the Region if it is not null. If the region is null, it evaluates the PostalCode. If it is non-null, the PostalCode is returned. Otherwise, it evaluates the country (see Figure 9.20).

FIGURE 9.19
A *SELECT* statement that calculates the average freight amount in the Orders table, eliminating 0 values from the calculation.

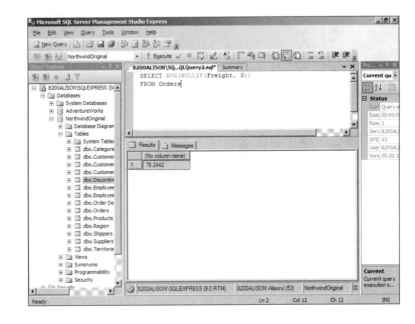

FIGURE 9.20
A *SELECT* statement that uses the *COALESCE* function to appropriately handle nulls in the Region and PostalCode fields.

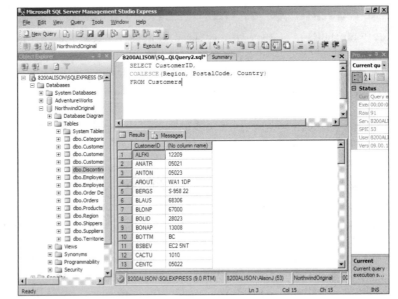

Summary

The T-SQL language provides you with a rich function library. Using this rich library of T-SQL functions, you can manipulate your data in ways that you probably haven't even dreamed of. In this chapter, you learned many of the commonly-used numeric, string, and date-time functions. You also learned how functions can help you with the process of handling null values in your data.

Q&A

Q *Explain what the* STUFF *function does.*

A The STUFF function starts at a certain position and replaces a specified number of characters with other specified characters.

Q *Explain what the* DATEPART *function does.*

A The DATEPART function extracts part of a date. You designate the part of the date you want to extract, and the date from which you want to extract it.

Q *Explain the* ISNULL *function.*

A The ISNULL function returns information about whether the value in an expression is null. It receives the expression that you want to evaluate, and the value that you want to return if the expression is null. It returns the specified value.

Workshop

Quiz

1. What function extracts specified characters from a string?

2. The NOW function returns the system date and time (true/false).

3. Name the two parameters to the DATEPART function.

4. What function finds the difference between two dates?

5. The NULLIF function determines whether a value is null (true/false).

Quiz Answers

1. The SUBSTRING function extracts specified characters from a string.

2. False. The GETDATE function returns the system date and time.

3. The first parameter is an abbreviation designating the part of the date you want to extract. The second parameter is the date from which you want to extract it.

4. The DATEDIFF function.

5. False. The ISNULL function determines whether a value is null.

Activities

Practice executing T-SQL statements that contain functions. First find the left four characters of each customer's CompanyName in the Customers table of the Northwind database. Next find the fourth through the eighth character of the Address. Find the right four characters of the ContractName. Next replace all occurrences of the ContactTitle of "Sales" with the word "Marketing." Find the month of each OrderDate in the Orders table. Then extract the quarter of each OrderDate in the Orders table. Find the difference in days between the OrderDate and the ShippedDate. Finally, use a SELECT statement to display "No Region" for all rows in the Customers table where the Region field is null.

HOUR 10

Working with SQL Server Views

A view is a saved `select` statement. A view can retrieve data from one or more tables. After it is created, you can select data from a view just as you can select it from a table. In this hour you'll learn:

▶ What views are and why you would want to use them

▶ How to use the SQL Server Management Studio Query Builder to create a view

▶ How to use T-SQL to create or modify a view

An Introduction to Views

Views can only select data. They cannot update it (although you can update the data in the result of a view). For example, a T-SQL UPDATE statement in a stored procedure updates data. Although you cannot use a T-SQL UPDATE statement in a view, you can update the results returned from a SELECT statement.

Views have several advantages. They enable you to

▶ Join data so that users can work with it easily

▶ Aggregate data so that users can work with it easily

▶ Customize data to users' needs

▶ Hide underlying column names from users

▶ Limit the columns and rows with which a user works

▶ Easily secure data

Although a normalized database is easy to work with and maintain from a programmer's viewpoint, it is not always easy for the user to work with. For example, if users look at the Sales.SalesOrderHeader table, they see only the CustomerID associated with the order. If they wish to see the customer's name, they must join the Sales.SalesOrderHeaderTable with the Sales.Customer table. This is not a particularly easy task for users to accomplish. Using a view, you can join the Sales.CustomerTable and Sales.SalesOrderHeaderTable and table. You provide the view to the user. The user can build forms, queries, and reports that are based on the view without having to understand how to join the underlying tables.

Just as a view can join data, it can also aggregate data. You can very easily create a view that contains the total order amounts for each customer. The user can use the view as the foundation for forms, queries, and reports that they build. Once again, it is not necessary for the user to understand the syntax required to aggregate the data.

Another advantage of views is their capability to customize data to the users' needs. For example, a column in a view can combine the first name and last name of a customer, or it can combine the customer's city, state, and zip code. Users do not need to understand how to combine this information. Instead, they use the view as the foundation for the forms, queries, and reports that they need.

Developers often use column names that are not particularly intuitive for users. This is another situation where views come to the rescue. You can easily build a view that aliases column names. Users will never see the underlying column names. You simply provide them with access to the view and they can easily build the forms, queries, and reports that they need.

The number of fields in a table can be overwhelming to users. Most of the time there are certain fields that users need for the majority of the work that they do. You can create views containing only the critical fields. This simplifies the process when users build forms, queries, and reports based on the table data.

A major advantage of views is the security that they provide. You can grant logins and roles the rights to views *without* granting them rights to the underlying tables. An example is an employee table. You can create a view that includes the EmployeeID, FirstName, LastName, Extension, and other non-sensitive fields. You can then grant rights to the view. Although the users have no rights to the Employee table, and therefore have no access to fields such as the employee salary, they gain rights to the rows and columns included in the view.

SQL Server Express views are very powerful. Using user-defined functions, you can parameterize views. Using the TOP syntax you can order view results. SQL Server 2005 Express enables you to create INSTEAD OF triggers. Finally, SQL Server 2000 introduced indexed views, also available in SQL Server 2005 Express. All these features make SQL Server 2005 Express views extremely powerful!

Creating a Simple View

A view is actually a SELECT statement with a CREATE VIEW statement that causes SQL Server to save it as a view. You can use a few different methods to create a SQL Server view. The following methods are discussed:

▶ You can use the Microsoft SQL Server Management Studio Express Query Builder to create a view.

▶ You can use T-SQL to create a view.

The sections that follow cover each of these options.

Using the Microsoft SQL Server Management Studio Query Builder to Create a View

The Management Studio Query Builder facilitates the process of creating a view. To create a view, follow these steps:

1. Right-click the Views node of the database in which you want the view to appear and select New View. The Add Table dialog appears (see Figure 10.1).

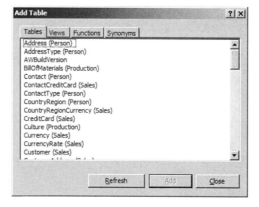

FIGURE 10.1
The Add Table dialog enables you to add tables, views, functions, and synonyms to your view.

2. Click each table, view, function, and synonym you want to add to the view and click Add. In the example shown in Figure 10.2, the Sales.Customer and Sales.SalesOrderHeader tables are included in the view.

3. Click Close when you have finished adding objects to the view. Your screen should appear as in Figure 10.3.

FIGURE 10.2
The
Sales.Customers
and Sales.
SalesOrderHeader
tables appear
joined in the view.

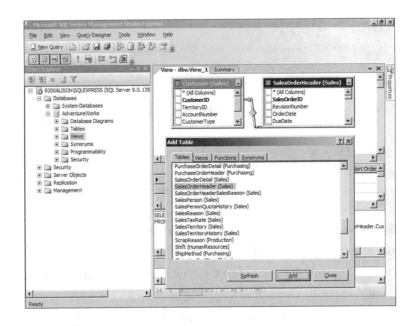

FIGURE 10.3
A new view that
includes the
Sales.Customers
and
Sales.SalesOrder
Header tables.

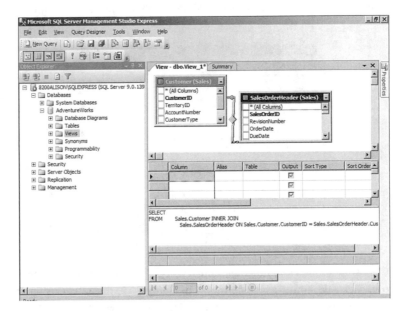

4. Click the check boxes to the left of the field names to select the fields that you
want to add to the view. If you prefer, you can drag and drop fields to the column list on the query grid. Figure 10.4 shows a view with the CustomerID,
AccountNumber, SalesOrderID, OrderDate, and Freight fields included.

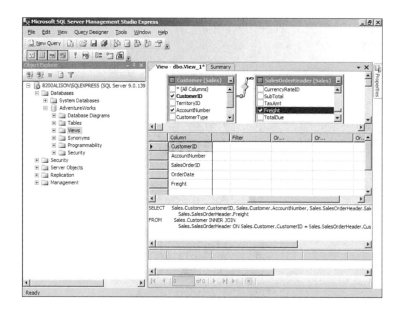

FIGURE 10.4
A view with selected fields.

5. Specify any criteria that you want to apply to the view. To add criteria, enter the desired criteria in the Criteria column of the appropriate field on the query grid. Adding criteria limits the records returned when you execute the view. Figure 10.5 shows criteria limiting the selected records to those with freight between 500 and 1000.

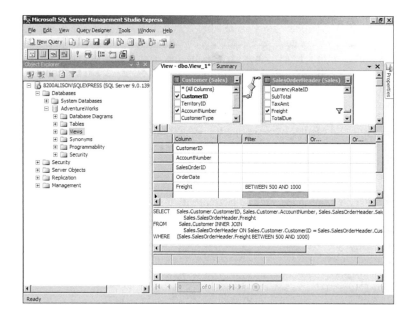

FIGURE 10.5
A view that limits the output to orders with freight between 500 and 1000.

7. Test the view using the Run button. The output should appear as in Figure 10.6.

FIGURE 10.6
The results of the view appear in the Output pane.

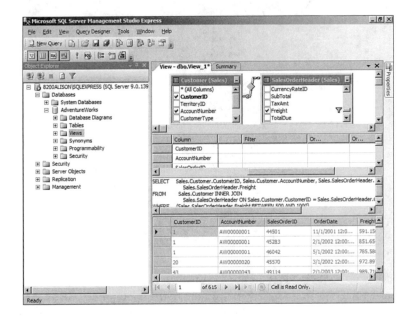

8. Attempt to close the view. SQL Server prompts you to save changes to the view.

9. The view appears in the list of views under the View node. You can treat it much like a table.

To use SQL Server Management Studio to modify a view:

1. Expand the Views node for the database until you can see the view you wish to modify.

2. Right-click the view you want to modify and select modify. The view appears as in Figure 10.7.

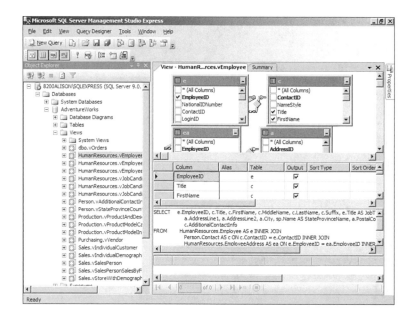

FIGURE 10.7
Modifying a view
is very similar
to building a
new view.

3. Make the desired changes and then close and save the view.

You can easily drag and drop tables to the diagram pane of the view. Simply resize the View and Console windows so that you can see both windows simultaneously and then drag and drop the tables from the Tables node of the appropriate database to the diagram pane of the view.

Did you Know?

Using T-SQL to Create or Modify a View

In addition to using the Management Studio View Builder to build a view, you can use T-SQL to create a view. Rather than building the view graphically, as outlined in the preceding section, you type the entire CREATE VIEW statement from scratch. The syntax for a CREATE VIEW statement is as follows:

```
CREATE VIEW [DatabaseName] [<owner>] ViewName
    [(column [,…n])]
    [WITH <ViewAttribute> [,…n]]
AS
SelectStatement
[WITH CHECK OPTION]

<ViewAttribute> :: = [ENTCRYPTION¦SCHEMASBINDING¦VIEW_METADATA]
```

An example of a CREATE VIEW statement is the following:

```
CREATE VIEW vwUSACustomers
AS
SELECT CustomerID, FirstName, City
FROM Sales.vIndividualCustomer
WHERE CountryRegionName = 'USA'
```

The statement creates a view named vwUSACustomers, which selects the contents of the CustomerID, FirstName, and City fields from the Sales.vIndividualCustomer view for all customers in the USA.

To type and execute the CREATE VIEW statement, follow these steps:

1. Click the New Query button on the toolbar. Your screen appears as in Figure 10.8.

FIGURE 10.8
The screen after clicking the New Query button on the toolbar.

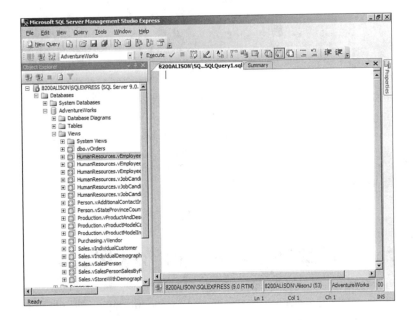

2. Type the SQL statement into the available pane.

3. Click the Execute button on the toolbar. The results should appear as in Figure 10.9.

If you wish use T-SQL to modify a view, you must use an ALTER VIEW statement rather than a CREATE VIEW statement. An example of an ALTER VIEW statement is

```
ALTER VIEW vwUSACustomers
AS
SELECT CustomerID, FirstName, LastName, City
FROM Sales.vIndividualCustomer
WHERE CountryRegionName = 'USA'
```

This example modifies the vwUSACustomers view, adding the LastName field to the view.

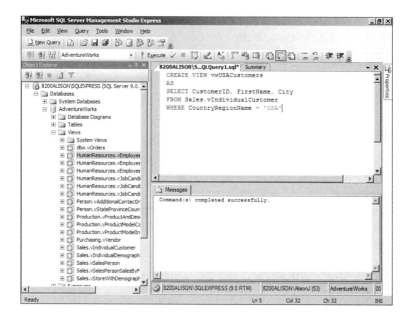

FIGURE 10.9
The results of using the Execute button to create a new view.

Summary

Views are a critical part of any application that you build. It is therefore important that you understand how to create and work with views. In this hour you learned how to create and modify simple views, using both the SQL Server Management Studio and T-SQL.

Q&A

Q. *Name some advantages of views.*

A. Views enable you to join data, aggregate data, customize data to the user's needs, hide underlying column names from users, limit the columns and rows that a user works with, and easily secure data.

Q. *Explain why you would want to join data so that users can easily work with it.*

A. A normalized database is not always easy for the user to work with. For example, only the CustomerID is stored in the Orders table. The Company Name is stored in the Customers table. To see both the Customer and Order information, the user must join the tables. Using a view, you can join the tables for the user, so that the user can work with the view as if it were a single table.

Q. *Explain what it means to customize data to a user's needs.*

A. Using a view, you can create a column that combines first, middle, and last name of an employee, or the city, state, and zip code from an address. This makes it much easier for the user to work with this data.

Q. *How do views help you to secure data?*

A. You can grant rights to logins and roles to the views that you create. It is not necessary to grant rights to the underlying tables. In this way you can give users access to just desired columns and rows. For example, you can give users rights to name and address data for the sales department in the employee table.

Workshop

Quiz

1. Name two ways that you can create a view.

2. What statement do you use to create a view?

3. The result of a view is updatable (true/false).

4. Name the four panes of the view builder.

5. You cannot drag and drop tables onto the diagram pane of the view (true/false).

6. What statement do you use to modify a view?

Quiz Answers

1. Using SQL Server Management Studio, and using T-SQL.

2. CREATE VIEW.

3. True.

4. Diagram, grid, SQL, and results.

5. False. You can drag and drop from the Tables node of the appropriate databases to the diagram pane of the view.

6. ALTER VIEW.

Activities

Create a view by using the Microsoft SQL Server Management Studio Query Builder. Include the EmployeeID, Title, BirthDate, Gender, HireDate, VacationHours, and SickLeaveHours from the HumanResources.Employee table. Sort the result in Ascending order, and return just the rows where the HireDate is between 1/1/1998 and 12/31/1998. Close and save the view as vw1998Hires. Modify the view and add the LoginID to the view. Create another view by using T-SQL. Include the SalesPersonID, SalesQuota, Bonus, SalesYTD, and SalesLastYear from the Sales.SalesPerson table. Sort in descending order by SalesYTD, and return just the rows where the SalesYTD is greater than 800,000. Close and save the view as vwBigHitters. Modify the view (using T-SQL), and add the CommissionPct field to the view. Change the criteria for the SalesYTD to 1,000,000.

HOUR 11

Creating Complex Views

Now that you've learned the basics of creating and working with views, you're ready to move on to more advanced techniques. These techniques enable you to fully harness the power of views and what they have to offer. In this hour you'll learn:

- ▶ How to create views based on data in multiple tables
- ▶ How to work with views and subqueries
- ▶ How to add outer joins to a view
- ▶ How to sort view results
- ▶ How to look at top values
- ▶ How to utilize functions in the views that you create
- ▶ How to use views to secure data
- ▶ How to modify data in a view
- ▶ How to modify, rename, and delete views
- ▶ How to work with indexed views
- ▶ How to optimize the views that you build

Creating Views Based on Data in Multiple Tables

Creating a view based on data from multiple tables is quite simple. While in the View Builder you use the Add Table tool on the toolbar to add tables to the view. SQL Server automatically joins the tables based on relationships established in the database. To create a new view, follow these steps:

1. Right-click the Views node within SQL Server Management Studio and select New View. The Add Table dialog appears (see Figure 11.1).

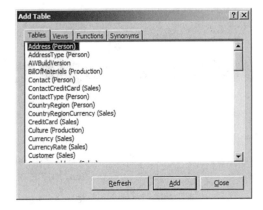

2. Select all the tables, views, functions, and synonyms that you want to include in the view and click Add.

3. Click Close to close the Add Table dialog. Your view should appear as in Figure 11.2.

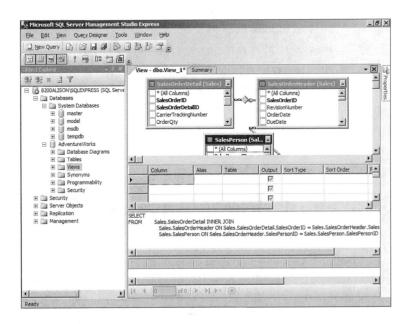

4. Add the desired fields to the output of the view. Your view should appear as in Figure 11.3.

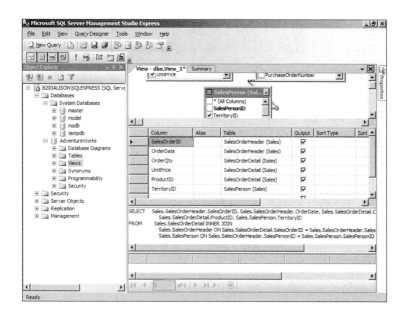

FIGURE 11.3
After you add the desired fields to the view, they appear on the query grid.

Views and Subqueries

Just as a T-SQL statement can contain a subquery (see Hour 7, "Building SQL Statements Based on Multiple Tables"), so can a view. The syntax looks like this:

```
CREATE VIEW vwCustomersWithoutOrders
AS
    SELECT CustomerID, AccountNumber
    FROM Sales.Customer
    WHERE NOT EXISTS
    (SELECT CustomerID FROM Sales.SalesOrderHeader WHERE
    Sales.Customer.CustomerID = Sales.SalesOrderHeader.CustomerID)
```

This example selects all customers who do not have orders. You call the view like this:

```
SELECT * FROM vwCustomersWithoutOrders
```

An alternative to the subquery would be a LEFT JOIN, which is type of outer join. A LEFT JOIN is almost always more efficient than a subquery. The section that follows covers views and outer joins.

Views and Outer Joins

As discussed in the section on views and subqueries, views, like T-SQL statements, can contain outer joins. Here's the subquery example, rewritten as follows:

```
ALTER VIEW vwCustomersWithoutOrders
AS
    SELECT Sales.Customer.CustomerID, Sales.Customer.AccountNumber
    FROM Sales.Customer LEFT JOIN Sales.SalesOrderHeader
    ON Sales.Customer.CustomerID = Sales.SalesOrderHeader.CustomerID
    WHERE Sales.SalesOrderHeader.CustomerID Is Null
```

This example uses a LEFT JOIN from the Sales.Customer table to the Sales.SalesOrderHeader table to accomplish its task. Because only Orders with a Null CustomerID appear in the result, the view returns only customers without orders.

Views and Top Values

The TOP syntax is available for both T-SQL statements and views. The TOP syntax for views works the same way as it does for tables. It looks like this:

```
SELECT TOP 100 Percent SalesOrderID, OrderDate, Freight
FROM Sales.SalesOrderHeader
```

This example shows only that the TOP clause is available for views. The following section, "Sorting View Results," provides practical examples of the TOP clause.

Sorting View Results

The syntax required to sort the results of a view is a little bit different than you might expect. It looks like this:

```
CREATE VIEW vwHighOrders
AS
SELECT TOP 100 Percent SalesOrderID, OrderDate, Freight
FROM Sales.SalesOrderHeader
ORDER BY Freight DESC
```

The combination of the TOP clause and the ORDER BY clause enables you to sort the view result. Of course, you can use similar syntax to return only the top values in the result:

```
ALTER VIEW vwHighOrders
AS
SELECT TOP 5 Percent SalesOrderID,
Sales OrderDate, Freight
FROM Sales.SalesOrderHeader
ORDER BY Freight DESC
```

Views and Functions

Prior to SQL Server 2000, a major limitation of views in SQL Server was that you could not parameterize them. SQL Server 2000 handled this limitation with the introduction of user-defined functions. User-defined functions enable you to pass parameters to functions as if they were stored procedures, but to work with the results as if they were views.

Two types of functions are available in SQL Server 2005 Express: system (built-in) functions and user-defined functions. The section that follows covers built-in functions. Hour 14, " Stored Procedure Special Topics," covers user-defined functions in detail.

Views and Built-in Functions

You can use built-in functions within the views that you build. Here's an example:

```
CREATE VIEW vwTodaysOrders
AS
SELECT SalesOrderID, OrderDate, Freight
FROM Sales.SalesOrderHeader
WHERE OrderDate = Convert(VarChar(10),GetDate(),101)
```

In this example, SQL Server returns only orders placed on the current day. The GetDate() function returns the current date and time. The Convert function converts the date to the mm/dd/yyyy format so that the current date and time can be compared to the order date.

Using Views to Secure Data

One major benefit of a view is the security that it provides. Consider the following view:

```
CREATE VIEW vwEmployeeList
AS
SELECT EmployeeID, FirstName, LastName, EmailAddress
FROM HumanResources.VEmployee
```

This view selects the EmployeeID, FirstName, LastName, and EmailAddress from the Employees table. In this scenario you would grant no rights to certain users for the Employees table. Instead, you would grant them rights to the view. Figure 11.4 shows the Permissions dialog for a view. Notice that the permissions available for a view are similar to those available for the table. As long as the owner of the table and the owner of the view are the same, the user can interact with the table based on the permissions granted to the view.

FIGURE 11.4
The permissions available for a view are similar to those available for the table.

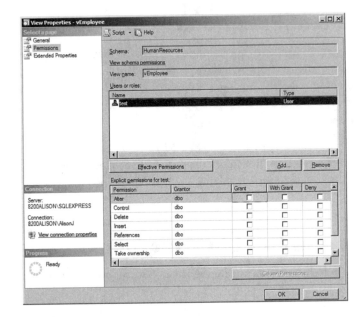

Modifying Data in a View

With a few exceptions, the results of views are updateable. Recognize that a view is not a table and does not contain any data. Therefore, when you are modifying the data in a view, you are modifying the underlying table. You cannot violate any rules, check constraints, referential integrity rules, or any other rules that govern the data that can be contained in the tables. The following are limitations to the updateability of a view:

▶ If a view joins multiple tables, you can insert and update data in only one table in the view.

▶ The results of a view that aggregates data are not updateable.

▶ The results of a view that contains a UNION clause are not updateable.

▶ The results of a view that contains a DISTINCT statement are not updateable.

▶ Text and image columns cannot be updated via a view.

▶ Data that you modify is not checked against the view criteria. For example, if the criteria for the view is to show only customers in the USA, and you change the country of a row in the result to Canada, no error occurs and the row remains in the result set until the view is run again.

Modifying Views

The process of modifying a view is similar to that of modifying a table. You simply go into the design of the view and then make the desired changes. Here are the steps involved:

1. Click to expand the Views node for the database.

2. Select the view whose attributes you want to modify.

3. Right-click and select Modify. The design of the existing view appears.

4. Modify the view's attributes.

5. Close the window and save your changes when you are finished.

Renaming Views

Renaming a view is a relatively simple process. The process is similar to that of a table. To rename a view, follow these steps:

1. Right-click the view that you want to rename and select Rename.

2. Enter a new name for the view.

No warning appears when you rename a view. Because other objects (such as stored procedures) may depend on the view that you are renaming, the results can be disastrous.

Deleting Views

Deleting a SQL Server view is very simple. In fact, it is *so* simple, that it is dangerous. To delete a view, taking the following steps:

1. Click to expand the Views node in the Objects list.

2. Right-click the view you want to delete.

3. Select Delete from the pop-up menu. The Delete Object dialog appears (see Figure 11.5).

4. If you want to look at the view's dependencies, click Show Dependencies. The Dependencies dialog appears (see Figure 11.6) .

5. Click OK when you are finished viewing dependencies.

6. If you want to drop the view, click OK. SQL Server deletes the view.

FIGURE 11.5
The Delete
Object dialog
enables you to
drop a view.

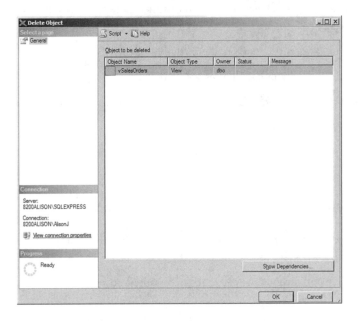

FIGURE 11.6
The Depend-
encies dialog
shows you on
what other
objects a view
depends.

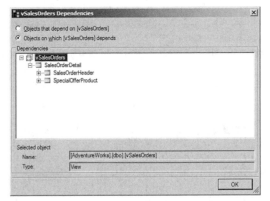

Indexed Views

SQL Server 2000 introduced indexed views. They provide you with greatly improved
performance by enabling you to create a unique clustered index for a view. Here's
the reason why: SQL Server does not store the result set of a standard view in the
database. Each time a query references the view, SQL Server creates the result set

dynamically. The overhead of building the result set can be substantial, particularly
for complex views. You can greatly improve performance by creating a unique clustered index for the view. When you create a unique clustered index, SQL server
stores the data that exists at the time you create the view. SQL Server then reflects
all modifications to table data within the stored view. This improves the efficiency of
data retrieval. After you create a unique clustered index for the view, you can then
create additional non-clustered indexes. The following is an example of the syntax
to create an indexed view:

```
CREATE UNIQUE CLUSTERED INDEX [vwCustomerInfoCustomerID]
ON [dbo].[vwCustomerInfo] ([CustomerID])
```

This example creates a clustered index for the view called vwCustomerInfo, based
on the CustomerID field. The index is called vwCustomerInfoCustomerID and is
based on the CustomerID field. Here's another example:

```
CREATE INDEX [vwCustomerInfoCountry] ON [dbo].[vwCustomerInfo] ([Country])
```

It is easy to use the SQL Server Management Studio to create an indexed view. To
create an indexed view, follow these steps:

1. Create the view.

2. Within the design of the view, click Properties.

3. Set the Bind to Schema property to Yes (see Figure 11.7).

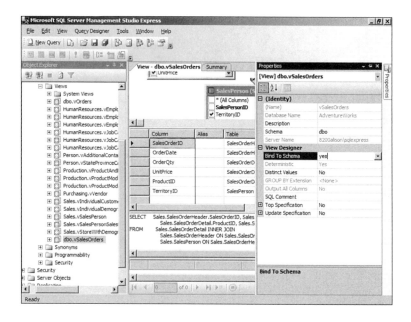

FIGURE 11.7
You must first
set the Bind to
Schema prop-
erty to Yes.

4. Close and save the view.

5. Right-click Indexes under the View node for the view and select New Index. The New Index dialog appears (see Figure 11.8).

6. Click Add to create a new index. The Select Columns dialog appears (see Figure 11.9).

FIGURE 11.8
The New Index dialog enables you to add an index to a view.

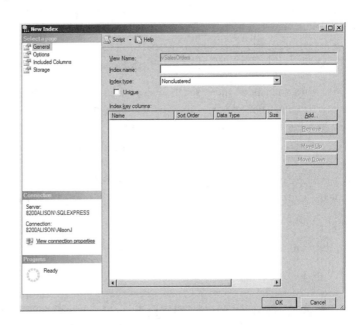

FIGURE 11.9
The Select Columns dialog lets you select the fields that will participate in the view.

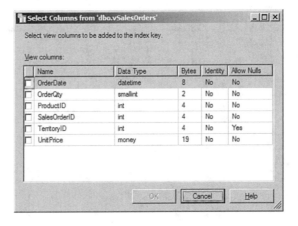

7. Click to select the columns that will participate in the index and click OK to close the dialog.

8. Enter a name for the index.

9. Specify index options such as whether the index is clustered and whether it is unique. Figure 11.10 shows an index called HumanResources.vEmployee.EmployeeID. It is based on the EmployeeID field and is clustered and unique.

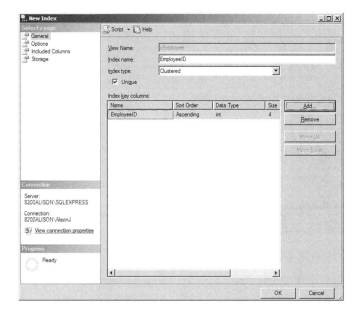

10. Click OK to create the index. You are returned to Management Studio, where you can create additional indexes, modify existing indexes, or delete unwanted indexes, as well as perform any other database administration tasks.

When to Use Indexed Views

Indexed views are not appropriate in all situations. Although indexed views speed up data retrieval, they slow data updates. You must therefore ascertain that the benefits of data retrieval performance outweigh the performance degradation experienced for data update operations.

Requirements for Indexed Views

Not all views can be indexed. A view must meet all the following requirements for you to index it:

▶ The view cannot reference other views.

▶ The tables underlying the view must be in the same database as the view and have the same owner as the view.

▶ You must set the ANSI_NULLS option to ON when you create the tables referenced by the view.

▶ You must set the ANSI_NULLS and QUOTED_IDENTIFIER options to ON before creating the view.

▶ You must create the view, and any functions underlying the view, with the SCHEMABINDING option. This means that you cannot modify or drop tables and other objects underlying the view without dropping the view first.

In addition to the limitations for the view, there are also limitations for the syntax within the view:

▶ You cannot use * to designate all columns.

▶ You cannot use the keyword UNION.

▶ You cannot use the keyword DISTINCT.

▶ You cannot include the keywords TOP or ORDER BY.

▶ You cannot use COUNT(*).

▶ You cannot include AVG, MAX, MIN, STDEV, STDEVP, VAR, or VARP.

▶ You cannot repeat a column in a view (for example, SELECT CustomerID, CompanyName, ContactName, CompanyName as Client).

▶ You cannot include derived tables or subqueries.

Optimizing the Views That You Build

The most important thing that you can do to improve the performance of your views is to design your indexes efficiently. The SQL Server query optimizer automatically selects the most efficient index for any query. It can select only from existing indexes. It is therefore necessary that you create all the indexes that your queries need to execute. Follow these guidelines:

▶ Create indexes for any fields used in the criteria of views.

▶ Create indexes for any fields that are included in the sorting or grouping of a view.

▶ Create indexes for all columns used in joins.

▶ *Do not* create indexes for columns that have very few unique values.

Displaying the Estimated Execution Plan

When in doubt about what indexes you need, the Express Manager can help you out. Using Express Manager, you can display the estimated execution plan for a view, perform index analysis, display the execution plan when the query executes, show a server trace, and show client statistics. Here's how:

1. Open Express Manager.

2. Click New Query on the toolbar.

3. Enter the SQL statement underlying the view (you can copy it from SQL View of the view).

2. Select Query, Display Estimated Execution Plan. The Query Analyzer appears as in Figure 11.11.

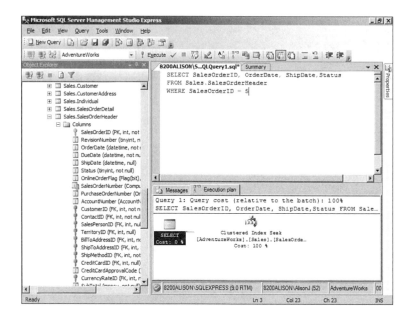

FIGURE 11.11
The Query Analyzer enables you to display the Estimated Execution Plan.

3. Hover your mouse pointer over each icon to show the statistics for that particular statement. In Figure 11.12 you can see that the search for the OrderDate

uses an index seek because an OrderDate index exists for the Orders table. Contrast this to Figure 11.13 where SQL Server must perform an index scan because no index exists for the ShipCountry field.

FIGURE 11.12
Because the necessary index is available, the search for the OrderDate uses an index seek.

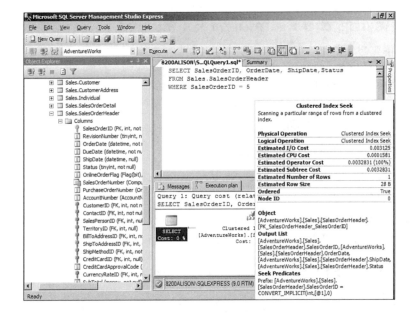

FIGURE 11.13
Because the necessary index is not available, the search for the ShipCountry uses an index scan.

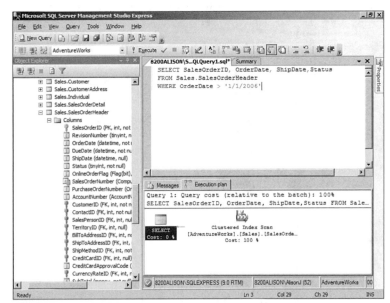

Summary

Views are a very powerful aspect of SQL Server. In this hour you learned advanced techniques that you can use to ensure that you are taking full advantage of what views have to offer. For example, you learned how you can use views to secure the data in your database.

Q&A

Q *Explain what an indexed view is and why it is beneficial.*

A With indexed views, you provide a unique, clustered index for a view. This means that SQL server stores the data in the designated order at the time that you save the view. It updates the index as you add, update, and delete data. Therefore, there is no need for SQL Server to create a result set dynamically each time the view is referenced.

Q *Describe the benefits of user-defined functions when working with views.*

A User-defined functions enable you to pass parameters to functions as if they were stored procedures, but to work with the results as if they were views.

Q *Explain how you can use a view to secure data.*

A You first create a view containing the appropriate columns. You then give the users rights to the view. Although they have no rights to the underlying tables, they are able to work with the data displayed in the view.

Workshop

Quiz

1. What type of join can you use to ensure that you display only customers who do not have orders?

2. What type of join can you use to ensure that you display only customers with orders?

3. What two clauses enable you to sort the results of a view?

4. What is the problem when renaming a view?

5. What dialog is beneficial when deleting a view?

6. Express Manager enables you to display the estimated execution plan for a query (true/false).

Quiz Answers

1. An outer join.

2. An inner join.

3. TOP and ORDER BY.

4. Other objects may be dependent on the view and will no longer run after you rename the view.

5. The Dependencies dialog shows you what objects are dependent on the view.

6. True.

Activities

Attach to the AdventureWorks database if you have not already done so (for more information, see Hour 3, "Getting to Know the SQL Server Object Explorer"). Create a new view in the AdventureWorks database. Add the Sales.Customer, Sales.SalesOrderheader, and Sales.SalesOrderDetail tables to the view. Add the CustomerID and AccountNumber fields from the Customer table to the view. Add the OrderDate, DueDate, and ShipDate from the SalesOrderHeader table. Finally, add the OrderQty, UnitPrice, and LineTotal to the view. Save the view as vOrders. Create a second view that finds all the customers who do not have orders. Note the number of rows returned. Modify the view to display all customers, whether they have orders or not. Note the number of rows returned. Finally, modify the view to display only the customers who have orders. Note the number of rows returned. The number of customers returned who have orders plus the number of customers returned without orders should equal the total number of rows returned (whether they have orders or not).

HOUR 12

Using T-SQL to Design SQL Server Stored Procedures

Stored procedures are at the heart of any client/server application. Using stored procedures, you can guarantee that processing is completed on the server. Stored procedures have many other benefits as well, including the following:

▶ Stored procedures help you to separate the client application from the database's structure.

▶ Stored procedures help you to simplify client coding.

▶ Stored procedures process at the server (reduces required bandwidth).

▶ Stored procedures enable you to create reusable code.

▶ Stored procedures enable you to perform error-handling at the server.

▶ Stored procedures facilitate the security of data.

▶ Because stored procedures are pre-compiled, they execute more quickly.

▶ Stored procedures improve the application's stability.

▶ Stored procedures reduce network locking.

▶ When you build a stored procedure, a query plan is created. This query plan contains the most efficient method of executing the stored procedure given available indexes and so on.

In this hour you'll learn:

▶ The basics of working with stored procedures

▶ How to declare and work with variables

▶ How to control the flow of the stored procedures that you write

The Basics of Working with Stored Procedures

Creating stored procedures in SQL Server 2005 Express is easy. You can create a stored procedure with the Query Editor or with T-SQL.

Designing a Stored Procedure in the Query Editor

Although you may not be able to design an entire stored procedure in the Query Editor, you will probably find it easiest to use the Query Editor to design the T-SQL statement that you include in your stored procedure. Take the steps that follow to build the SELECT statement that you want to include in your stored procedure:

1. Expand the Programmability node of the database that you are working with so that you can see the Stored Procedures node underneath it (see Figure 12.1).

FIGURE 12.1
The Stored Procedures node appears under the Programmability node.

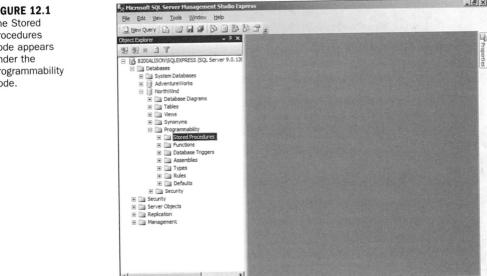

2. Right-click the Stored Procedure node and select New Stored Procedure. A template for a stored procedure appears in the Query Editor (see Figure 12.2).

3. Click and drag over the SELECT statement included in the template and press the Delete key to delete it.

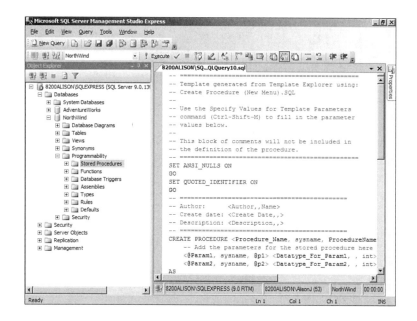

FIGURE 12.2
When you create a stored procedure, Management Studio provides you with a template for that stored procedure.

4. Right-click in that same location and select Design Query in Editor. The Add Table Dialog appears (see Figure 12.3).

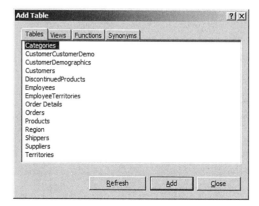

FIGURE 12.3
You replace the template SQL statement with the SQL state-ment generated by the Query Editor.

5. Add the desired tables to the query by selecting each table and clicking Add.

6. Click Close to complete the process. The Query Designer should look similar to Figure 12.4.

FIGURE 12.4
The Query
Designer
appears with
the selected
tables.

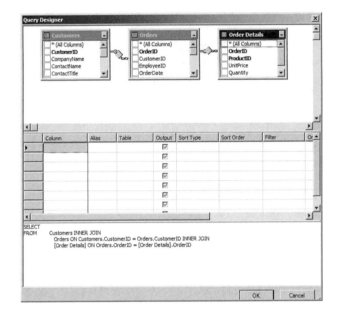

7. Click to add the desired fields to the SELECT statement. Click OK when finished. The stored procedure should appear as in Figure 12.5.

FIGURE 12.5
The generated
SQL statement
appears within
the stored
procedure
template.

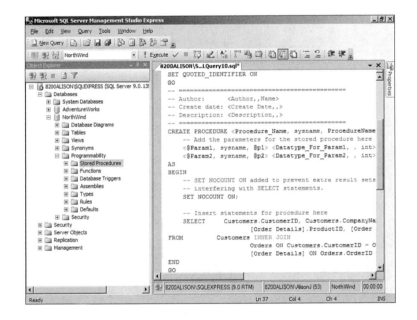

8. Modify the stored procedure, adding all the functionality you want it to have.

9. After completing the stored procedure, click Execute to execute the CREATE PROCEDURE statement.

10. You need to save only if you want to store the T-SQL behind the stored procedure in an *external* file.

> To make the generated stored procedure execute, you must provide the stored procedure with a name, and delete all the superfluous template code, such as the declaration of parameters.

By the Way

Using T-SQL to Create a Stored Procedure

Sometimes you may not find it useful to use the Query Editor to get started in creating a stored procedure. In that case you will simply create the stored procedure and begin modifying the template as desired. Here are the steps involved:

1. Expand the Programmability node of the database that you are working with so that you can see the Stored Procedures node underneath it.

2. Right-click the Stored Procedure node and select New Stored Procedure. A template for a stored procedure appears in the Query Editor.

3. Type the body of the stored procedure.

4. After completing the stored procedure, click Execute to execute the CREATE PROCEDURE statement.

5. You need to save only if you want to store the T-SQL behind the stored procedure in an *external* file.

Declaring and Working with Variables

Just as you can create variables within the subroutines and functions that you build, you can also declare variables in your stored procedures. You use the keyword DECLARE to create a variable. The syntax looks like this:

```
DECLARE @VariableName DataType [(length)], @VariableName DataType [(length)]
```

Here's an example:

```
DECLARE @FirstName VarChar(35)
```

Unintialized variables are assigned the value Null. You use a SELECT statement to assign a value to a variable. It looks like this:

```
SELECT @FirstName = 'Alexis'
```

The following is a stored procedure that illustrates the use of a variable:

```
DECLARE @strCompany varchar (50)
SELECT @strCompany = Upper(CompanyName)
FROM Customers
WHERE CustomerID = 'ALFKI'
SELECT @strCompany
```

The example declares a variable called @strCompany. The code stores the uppercase version of the CompanyName associated with the customer ALFKI into the variable. The procedure returns the variable in a SELECT. Figure 12.6 illustrates the result of executing the sample stored procedure.

FIGURE 12.6
An example of a variable used in a stored procedure.

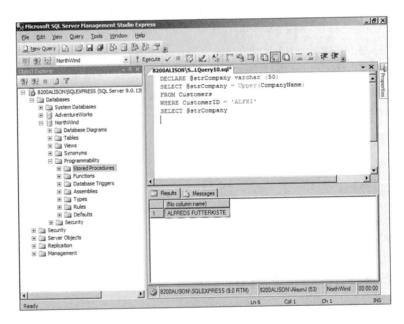

Controlling the Flow

Often you want specified statements in your stored procedure to execute only if certain conditions are true. T-SQL contains several constructs that enable you to control the flow of your stored procedures. These include BEGIN...END, IF...ELSE, GOTO, RETURN, CASE, and WHILE. The sections that follow cover each of these constructs.

Using IF...ELSE

You use the IF...ELSE construct to make a decision within the stored procedure. This decision is generally based on parameters supplied to the stored procedure. The IF...ELSE construct works like this:

```
IF (SomeCondition)
    BEGIN
        --Execute multiple statements
    END
```

With this version of the IF...ELSE construct, certain statements execute only if the condition is true. No special statements execute if the condition is false. The construct that follows accommodates the scenario when the condition is false:

```
IF (SomeCondition)
    BEGIN
        --Execute multiple statements
    END
ELSE
    BEGIN
        --Execute multiple statement
    END
```

Here's an example of an IF...THEN construct in action:

```
DECLARE @Locale VarChar(20), @Country VarChar(30)

SELECT @Country = Country
    FROM Customers
    WHERE CustomerID = 'ALFKI'

IF @Country   = 'USA'
    BEGIN
        SELECT @Locale = 'Domestic'
    END
ELSE
    BEGIN
        SELECT @Locale= 'Foreign'
    END

SELECT CustomerID, @Locale
    FROM Customers
    WHERE CustomerID = 'ALFKI'
```

The code begins by declaring two variables: @Locale and @Country. It stores the contents of the Country field for the customer ALFKI into the @Country variable. It then evaluates the contents of the @Country variable, storing the appropriate locale into the @Locale variable. Finally, it returns the CustomerID and the contents of the @Locale variable for the customer with the CustomerID ALFKI. Figure 12.7 provides an example of executing the stored procedure.

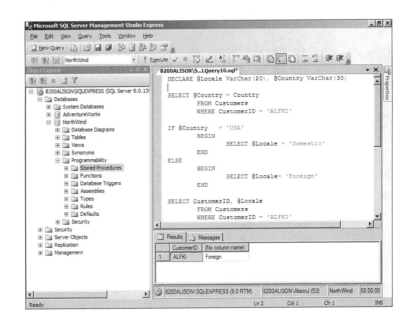

It is important to note that if you want to execute more than one statement under a specific condition, you must enclose the statements within the BEGIN...END construct (see the following section).

Working with BEGIN...END

The BEGIN...END construct enables you to group a series of statements together. Without the BEGIN...END construct, only the first statement after the IF or the ELSE executes. Consider the following example:

```
DECLARE @Locale VarChar(20), @Country VarChar(30)

SELECT @Country = Country
    FROM Customers
    WHERE CustomerID = 'ALFKI'

IF @Country   = 'USA'
    BEGIN
        SELECT @Locale = 'Domestic'
        PRINT 'This is domestic'
        PRINT ' '
        PRINT 'Hello there'
    END
ELSE
    BEGIN
        SELECT @Locale= 'Foreign'
        PRINT 'This is foreign'
```

```
        PRINT ' '
        PRINT 'Hello there'
    END

SELECT CustomerID, @Locale
    FROM Customers
    WHERE CustomerID = 'ALFKI'
```

In this example, multiple statements execute if the condition is true, and multiple statements execute if the condition is false. Without the BEGIN...END construct after the IF, the code renders an error. Figure 12.8 shows this stored procedure in action.

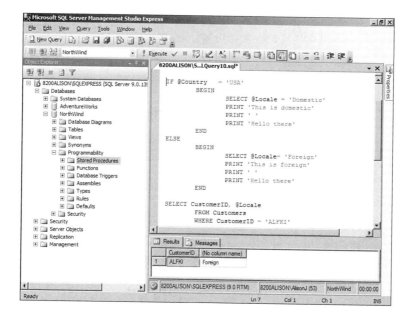

FIGURE 12.8
An example of executing a stored procedure that includes a BEGIN...END construct.

Exploring GOTO, RETURN, **and Labels**

You use the GOTO statement to jump to a label in your stored procedure. Programmers seem to use this statement most commonly in error handling. The RETURN statement unconditionally exits the stored procedure without executing any other statements. These three keywords are covered together because they generally work as a group. Consider the following examples:

```
IF Month(GetDate()) > 6
    BEGIN
        PRINT 'In IF Statement'
        GOTO MyLabel
    END
```

```
SELECT CustomerID, CompanyName FROM Customers

MyLabel:
    SELECT  OrderID, OrderDate FROM Orders
```

This example evaluates to see whether the month associated with the current date is greater than the value six. If it is, the statement In IF Statement appears and code execution jumps to the label MyLabel. The procedure then selects data from the Orders table. If the month associated with the current date is less than or equal to the value six, the procedure first selects data from the Customers table. Code execution then continues at the label, where the procedure selects data from the orders table. Figure 12.9 shows an example of executing the code when the month associated with the current date is greater than six. Figure 12.10 shows the sample procedure where the month associated with the current date is less than or equal to six.

As mentioned, a RETURN statement unequivocally exits from the procedure. Take a look at the procedure that follows:

```
IF Month(GetDate()) > 6
    BEGIN
        PRINT 'In IF Statement'
        GOTO MyLabel
    END
SELECT CustomerID, CompanyName FROM Customers
RETURN

MyLabel:
    SELECT  OrderID, OrderDate FROM Orders
```

FIGURE 12.9
An example of executing a stored procedure that includes GOTO and a label.

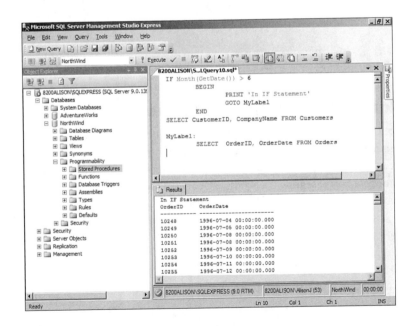

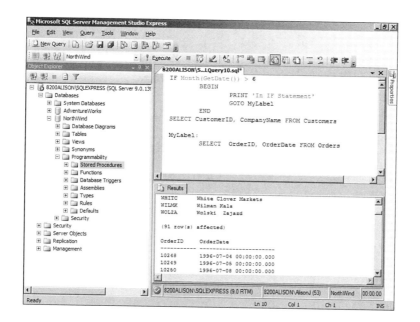

FIGURE 12.10
An example of executing the same stored procedure with a different value for the month of the current date.

In this example, if the month associated with the current date is greater than the value six, the In IF Statement message appears and then the procedure returns data from the Orders table. If the month associated with the current date is less than or equal to the value six, the code selects data from the Customers table and then exits the procedure. Because of the RETURN statement, the procedure does not select data from the Orders table. Figure 12.11 shows an example of executing the code when the month associated with the current date is less than or equal to six. Figure 12.12 shows the sample procedure where the month associated with the current date is greater than six.

Working with the CASE Statement

Most developers use the CASE statement to compare a result from a SQL statement against a set of simple responses. The CASE statement replaces a table value with an alternate value. The CASE statement looks like this:

```
CASE InputExpression
    WHEN WhenExpression THEN ResultExpression
        [...n]
    [ELSE ElseResultExpression]
END
```

FIGURE 12.11
An example of executing a stored procedure that includes the RETURN statement.

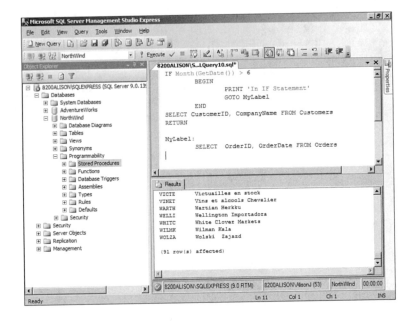

FIGURE 12.12
An example of executing the same stored procedure with a different value for the month of the current date.

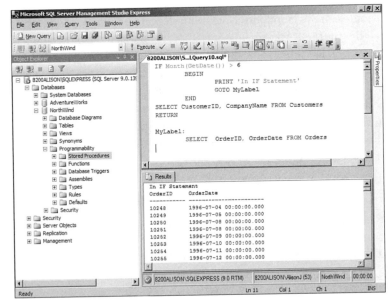

Here's an example of this use of a case statement:

```
SELECT OrderID, OrderDate,
    CASE ShipVIA
        WHEN 1 THEN 'UPS'
```

```
      WHEN 2 THEN 'FedEx'
      WHEN 3 THEN 'U.S. Mail'
   END AS Shipper,
   Freight FROM Orders
```

The expression selects the OrderID, OrderDate, and Freight fields from the Orders table. The CASE statement evaluates the contents of the ShipVia field. It returns an appropriate string depending on the value in the ShipVia field. Figure 12.13 illustrates this example.

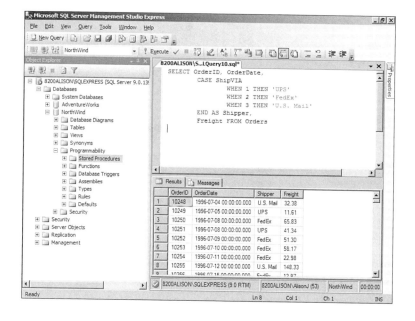

FIGURE 12.13
An example of executing a CASE statement replaces a table value with an alternate value.

The second use of the CASE construct looks like this:

```
CASE
   WHEN Expression THEN TruePart
   ELSE FalsePart
END
```

Here's an example:

```
DECLARE @AverageFreight Money
SELECT @AverageFreight = AVG(Freight) FROM Orders

SELECT OrderID, OrderDate, Freight,
   CASE
      WHEN FREIGHT <= @AverageFreight
      THEN 'Low Freight'
      ELSE 'High Freight'
   END AS Shipper,
   Freight FROM Orders
```

The example first declares the @AverageFreight variable. It sets the variable equal to the average freight amount from the Orders table. The CASE statement evaluates whether the freight of the current row is less or equal to the average freight amount. If so, the statement returns Low Freight. Otherwise, it returns High Freight. This value is combined with the OrderID, OrderDate, and Freight amounts which are also selected from the table. Figure 12.14 shows this use of the CASE statement in action.

FIGURE 12.14
An alternative
use of the CASE
statement.

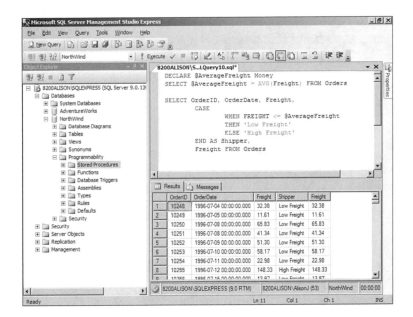

Exploring the WHILE Statement

You use the WHILE statement when you want to set up a loop. The loop continues to execute until the specified condition is met. The WHILE construct looks like this:

```
WHILE BooleanExpression
    (SQLStatement ¦ SQLBlock)
```

Here's an example:

```
CREATE TABLE MyTable
(
LoopID INT,
LoopText VarChar(25)
)
```

```
DECLARE @LoopValue INT
DECLARE @LoopText CHAR(25)

SELECT @LoopValue = 1

WHILE (@LoopValue < 100)
BEGIN
    SELECT @LoopText = 'Iteration #' + Convert(VarChar(25), @LoopValue)
    INSERT INTO MyTable(LoopID, LoopText)
        VALUES (@LoopValue, @LoopText)
    SELECT @LoopValue = @LoopValue + 1
END

SELECT * FROM MyTable
```

The routine first creates a table called MyTable. The table contains two fields: an INT
field and a CHAR field. The routine then declares two variables, an INT variable and
a CHAR variable. It sets the value of the @LoopValue variable to one. The code then
loops from one to one hundred. As it loops, it sets the CHAR variable equal to the
text Iteration # combined with the contents of the @LoopValue variable converted
to a VarChar. Next it inserts the contents of the @LoopValue and @LoopText variables into the table. Finally it increments the value of the @LoopValue variable.
Figure 12.15 shows the results of executing the WHILE statement.

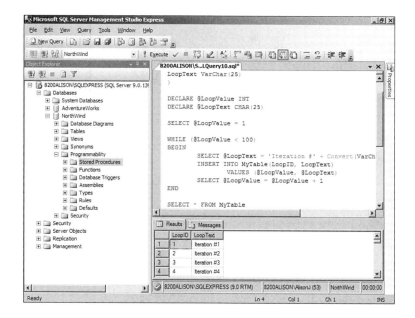

FIGURE 12.15
With a WHILE
statement the
loop continues
to execute until
the specified
condition
is met.

Summary

Stored procedures have many benefits. In this hour you learned the ins and outs of working with stored procedures. You learned the basics of stored procedures, and how to declare and work with variables. Finally, you learned numerous ways that you can control the flow of the stored procedures that you write.

Q&A

Q. *What happens if you forget to use* BEGIN *and* END *with the* IF...ELSE...ENDIF *construct?*

A. If you forget to place a BEGIN...END construct on the line immediately following the IF statement or the ELSE statement, only the first statement after the IF or the ELSE executes.

Q. *What does the* RETURN *statement do?*

A. The RETURN statement unconditionally exits a stored procedure without executing any other statements.

Q. *Why would you use the* CASE *statement?*

A. You use the CASE statement to compare a result from a SQL statement against a set of simple responses. For example, a CASE statement might evaluate the contents of the ContactTitle field and return an appropriate string based on those contents.

Workshop

Quiz

1. What is the *main* benefit of stored procedures?

2. What keyword do you use to assign a value to a variable?

3. What construct do you use to group a series of SQL statements together?

4. When is the GOTO statement most commonly used?

5. What does a GOTO statement do?

Quiz Answers

1. You guarantee that the code will execute on the server.

2. The SELECT keyword.

3. BEGIN...END.

4. In error handling.

5. Jump to a label in your stored procedure.

Activities

Use the SQL Express Manager to practice creating a stored procedure. Build a procedure that determines whether the ContactTitle in the Customer table in the Northwind database is Owner. If the ContactTitle is Owner, store Head Honcho into a variable called @TitleName. If the ContactTitle is not Owner, store Peon into the @TitleName variable. Finally, return the contents of the CustomerID field and the @TitleName variable for the customer with the CustomerID of ALFKI.

HOUR 13

Important Stored Procedure Techniques

In the previous hour you learned the basics of working with stored procedures. To really be effective in working with stored procedures, you must learn additional techniques. In this hour you'll learn about:

- ▶ The SET NOCOUNT statement
- ▶ How to use the @@ functions in the stored procedures that you build
- ▶ How to work with input and output parameters
- ▶ How to add error handling to your stored procedures
- ▶ How to use stored procedures to modify data
- ▶ How to add transaction processing to your stored procedures

The SET NOCOUNT Statement

The SET NOCOUNT statement, when set to ON, eliminates the *xx* row(s) affected message in the SQL Express Manager window. It also eliminates the DONE_IN_PROC communicated from SQL Server to the client application. For this reason the SET NOCOUNT ON statement, when included, improves the performance of the stored procedure. Here's an example:

```
CREATE PROCEDURE procEmployeesGetNoCount AS
SET NOCOUNT ON
SELECT EmployeeID, Title, HireDate, VacationHours
FROM HumanResources.Employee
ORDER BY Title, HireDate
```

If you execute this stored procedure from the SQL Express Manager, you'll notice that the *xx* row(s) affected message does not appear (see Figure 13.1). You might wonder how with SET NOCOUNT ON in effect you can return the number of rows affected to the client application. Fortunately this is easily accomplished with the @@RowCount system variable. The following section covers the @@RowCount system variable as well as other system variables.

FIGURE 13.1
With a NOCOUNT statement, the xx row(s) affected message does not appear.

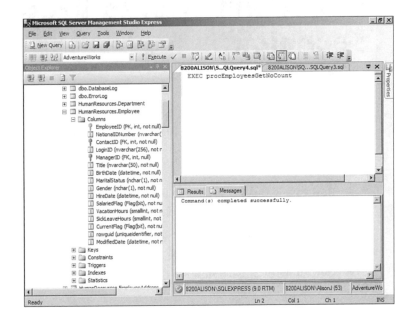

Using the @@ Functions

Developers often refer to the @@ functions as global variables. In fact, they don't really behave like variables. You cannot assign values to them or work with them as you would work with normal variables. Instead they behave as functions that return various types of information about what is going on in SQL Server.

Using the @@RowCount System Variable

The @@RowCount variable returns the number of rows returned by a selected statement or affected by a statement that modifies data. It returns zero if no values are returned by the select statement or modified by the action query. Here's an example:

```
SELECT EmployeeID, Title
FROM HumanResources.Employee
WHERE Title = 'Sales Representative'
SELECT @@RowCount as NumSalesReps
```

The example selects all employees who are sales representatives from the Employee table. It returns the number of rows selected (see Figure 13.2).

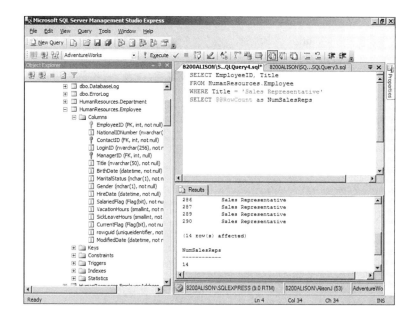

FIGURE 13.2
The @@RowCount
variable returns
the number of
rows returned
by a selected
statement or
affected by a
statement that
modifies data.

You can also see the results of the SELECT @@RowCount statement if you change the query results to display as text rather than as grid. To do this select Query, Results To, Results to Text.

By the Way

Using the @@TranCount System Variable

The @@TranCount function is applicable when you are using explicit transactions. Transactions are covered later in this chapter. The BEGIN TRAN statement sets the @@TranCount to one. Each ROLLBACK TRAN statement decrements @@TranCount by one. The COMMIT TRAN statement also decrements @@TranCount by one. When you use nested transactions @@TranCount helps you to keep track of how many transactions are still pending.

Using the @@Identity System Variable

The @@Identity function retrieves the new value inserted into a table that has an identity column. Here's an example:

```
INSERT INTO Purchasing.ShipMethod
    (Name, ShipBase, ShipRate)
    VALUES ('Great Shipper', 120, 150)
    SELECT @@Identity
```

The example inserts a row into the ShipMethod table. It returns the identity value of the inserted row (see Figure 13.3).

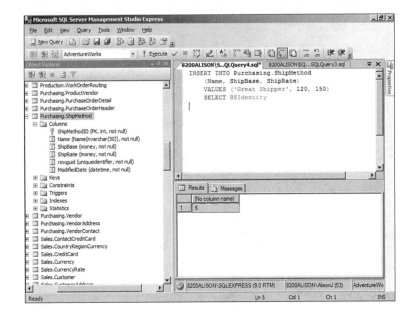

Using the @@Error **System Variable**

The @@Error function returns the number of any error that occurred in the statement immediately preceding it. Here's an example:

```
INSERT INTO Sales.SalesOrderDetail
    (CarrierTrackingNumber, OrderQty, ProductID, SpecialOfferID,
    UnitPrice, UnitPriceDiscount)
    VALUES (1, 1, 1, 1, 100.00, .05)
    SELECT @@Error
```

This example attempts to insert a row into the SalesOrderDetail table. If it is successful, @@Error returns zero. If you attempt to insert an sales order detail record for a sales order that doesn't exist, it returns 547, a referential integrity error (see Figure 13.4).

It is important to note that @@Error returns the error number associated with the line of code *immediately* preceding it. Consider this example:

```
INSERT INTO Sales.SalesOrderDetail
    (CarrierTrackingNumber, OrderQty, ProductID, SpecialOfferID,
    UnitPrice, UnitPriceDiscount)
    VALUES (1, 1, 1, 1, 100.00, .05)
    SELECT @@Identity
    SELECT @@Error
```

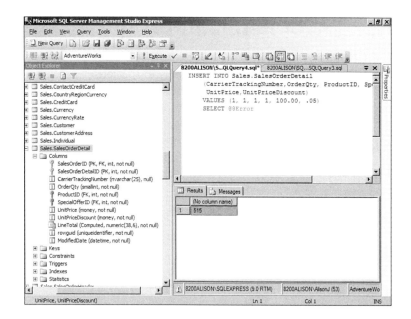

FIGURE 13.4
The @@Error function returns the number of any error that occurred in the statement immediately preceding it.

Although the INSERT statement renders an error, the @@Error function returns zero (see Figure 13.5) because the SELECT @@Identity statement executes without error.

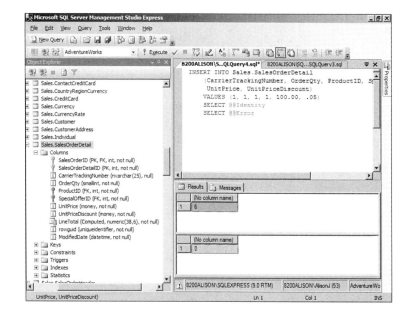

FIGURE 13.5
An example where the error number is not properly reported.

Working with Parameters

Some stored procedures have no interface. They are called, but they do not receive or return anything. Other procedures are input only. These stored procedures have input parameters but no output parameters. A third type of stored procedure has both input parameters and output parameters.

Input Parameters

An example of a stored procedure that has neither input nor output parameters is this one:

```
CREATE PROCEDURE procEmployeesGetYoungSalesReps
AS
SELECT EmployeeID, Title, BirthDate, HireDate,
    VacationHours
FROM HumanResources.Employee
WHERE Title = 'Sales Representative' AND
    BirthDate > '1/1/1981'
ORDER BY BirthDate
```

Contrast this stored procedure with the following:

```
CREATE PROCEDURE procEmployeesGetByTitleAndBirthDate
    @Title nVarChar(50),
    @BirthDate DateTime
AS
SELECT EmployeeID, Title, BirthDate, HireDate,
    VacationHours
FROM HumanResources.Employee
WHERE Title = @Title AND
    BirthDate >= @BirthDate
ORDER BY BirthDate
```

The procedure receives two input parameters, @Title and @BirthDate. The procedure uses these input parameters as variables for the WHERE clause for title and birth date. Here's how you execute the procedure:

```
procEmployeesGetByTitleAndBirthDate 'Sales Representative', '1/1/1960'
```

The parameters in this stored procedure are required. If you do not supply them when you call the procedure, an error results (see Figure 13.6). The following is the same procedure with the title set up as an optional parameter.

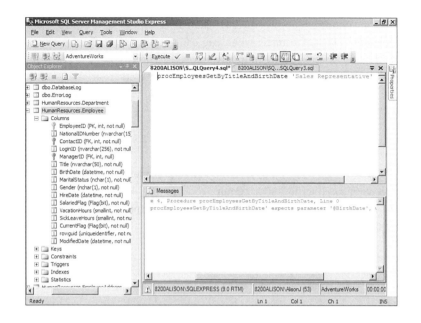

FIGURE 13.6
An error occurs
if you omit a
required
parameter.

```
CREATE PROCEDURE procEmployeesGetByTitleAndBirthDateOpt
    @Title nVarChar(50) = NULL,
    @BirthDate DateTime
AS
IF @Title IS NULL
    BEGIN
    SELECT EmployeeID, Title, BirthDate,
        HireDate, VacationHours
    FROM HumanResources.Employee
    WHERE BirthDate >= @BirthDate
    ORDER BY BirthDate
    END
ELSE
    BEGIN
    SELECT EmployeeID, Title, BirthDate,
        HireDate, VacationHours
    FROM HumanResources.Employee
    WHERE Title = @Title AND
        BirthDate >= @BirthDate
    ORDER BY BirthDate
    END
```

You establish an optional parameter by supplying SQL Server with a default value
for the parameter. In this example, @Title is an optional parameter, but
@BirthDate is required. If you opt to omit the @Title parameter, you would call the
stored procedure like this:

```
procEmployeesGetByTitleAndBirthDateOpt @BirthDate = '1/1/1960'
```

Notice that the example supplies the @BirthDate parameter as a named parameter. If you omit the @Title parameter when you call the procedure, the procedure sets its value to Null. The stored procedure evaluates the value of the @Title variable. If it is Null (it wasn't supplied), the WHERE clause omits the title from the selection criteria. If the user of the stored procedures supplies the @Title parameter, the procedure uses the @Title parameter in the criteria for the WHERE clause.

Output Parameters

So far we have looked only at input parameters—parameters that the user of the stored procedure supplies to the procedure. You can also declare output parameters in the stored procedures that you build. SQL Server returns output parameters to the caller (as their name implies). Here's an example:

```
CREATE PROCEDURE procEmployeesGetByTitleAndBirthDateOutput
    @Title nVarChar(50) = NULL,
    @BirthDate DateTime,
    @MyMessage VarChar(50) = NULL OUTPUT
AS
IF @Title IS NULL
    BEGIN
    SELECT EmployeeID, Title, BirthDate,
        HireDate, VacationHours
    FROM HumanResources.Employee
    WHERE BirthDate >= @BirthDate
    ORDER BY BirthDate
    SELECT @MyMessage = 'No Title'
    END
ELSE
    BEGIN
    SELECT EmployeeID, Title, BirthDate,
        HireDate, VacationHours
    FROM HumanResources.Employee
    WHERE Title = @Title AND
        BirthDate >= @BirthDate
    ORDER BY BirthDate
    SELECT @MyMessage = 'Country Supplied'

    END
SELECT @MyMessage
```

In addition to receiving two parameters, this procedure also has an output parameter called @MyMessage. The IF statement within the procedure sets the value of @MyMessage to the appropriate string (see Figure 13.7). You will see additional examples of OUPUT parameters and their uses as you move through the material. In particular, you will see examples of ADO code that utilize the output parameters within the client/server applications that you build.

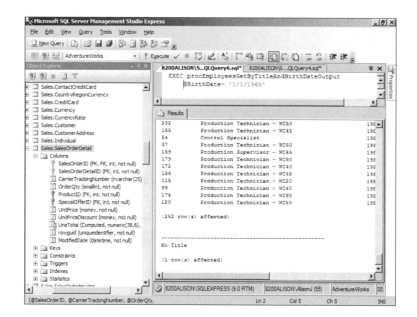

FIGURE 13.7
The IF statement within the procedure sets the value of @MyMessage to the appropriate string.

To see the output parameter you can also change the query results to display as text. To do this select Query, Results To, Results to Text.

By the Way

Modifying Data with Stored Procedures

Probably the most common use of a stored procedure is to modify the data in your database. You can easily design stored procedures to insert, update, and delete data. The sections that follow cover stored procedures that perform each of these tasks.

Inserting Data

Stored procedures are very effective at inserting data into your databases. Stored procedures that insert data generally contain several input parameters, one corresponding with each field in the underlying table. They often contain output parameters containing status or error information. Take a look at the following stored procedure:

```
CREATE PROCEDURE procOrderDetailAdd
@SalesOrderID int,
@CarrierTrackingNumber nvarchar(25),
@OrderQty smallint,
@ProductID int,
```

```
@SpecialOfferID int,
@UnitPrice money,
@UnitPriceDiscount money
AS
INSERT INTO Sales.SalesOrderDetail
(SalesOrderID, CarrierTrackingNumber, OrderQty,
ProductID, SpecialOfferID, UnitPrice, UnitPriceDiscount)
VALUES
(@SalesOrderID, @CarrierTrackingNumber, @OrderQty,
@ProductID, @SpecialOfferID, @UnitPrice, @UnitPriceDiscount)
```

The procedure receives seven input parameters, one for each field in the
Sales.SalesOrderDetail table into which the procedure inserts data. The INSERT INTO
statement uses the input parameters as values to insert into the table. As you can
see, the previous example contains no output parameters. The following procedure,
which inserts data into the Sales.SalesOrderDetail table, contains an output parameter called @SalesOrderDetailID:

```
CREATE PROCEDURE procOrderDetailAddOutput
@SalesOrderID int,
@CarrierTrackingNumber nvarchar(25),
@OrderQty smallint,
@ProductID int,
@SpecialOfferID int,
@UnitPrice money,
@UnitPriceDiscount money,
@SalesOrderDetailID int = 0 OUTPUT
AS
INSERT INTO Sales.SalesOrderDetail
(SalesOrderID, CarrierTrackingNumber, OrderQty,
ProductID, SpecialOfferID, UnitPrice, UnitPriceDiscount)
VALUES
(@SalesOrderID, @CarrierTrackingNumber, @OrderQty,
@ProductID, @SpecialOfferID, @UnitPrice, @UnitPriceDiscount)
SET @SalesOrderDetailID = @@IDENTITY
```

In addition to receiving six input parameters, this procedure uses the output parameter to house the identity value of the inserted row. Notice that the code populates
the @SalesOrderDetailID output parameter with the value of the system function
@@IDENTITY. The client application can use the output parameter via ADO code
that you write.

Updating Data

Stored procedures are also excellent in their capability to update data. Here's an
example:

```
CREATE PROCEDURE procSalesOrderHeaderUpdate
@SalesOrderID int,
@NewFreight money
AS
```

```
UPDATE Sales.SalesOrderHeader
SET Freight = @NewFreight
WHERE SalesOrderID = @SalesOrderID
```

The procedure receives two input parameters. One is for the SalesOrderID of the order whose freight you want to modify. The other parameter contains the new value for the freight. Notice that the UPDATE statement sets the freight to the @NewFreight value where the SalesOrderID matches the customer passed in as the @SalesOrderID parameter. Consider this more complex example:

```
CREATE PROCEDURE procSalesOrderDetailUpdate
@SalesOrderDetailID int,
@SalesOrderID int,
@CarrierTrackingNumber nvarchar(25),
@OrderQty smallint,
@ProductID int,
@SpecialOfferID int,
@UnitPrice money,
@UnitPriceDiscount money,
@ResultCode int = NULL Output,
@ResultMessage varchar(20) = NULL Output
AS
UPDATE Sales.SalesOrderDetail
SET SalesOrderID = @SalesOrderID,
    CarrierTrackingNumber = @CarrierTrackingNumber,
    OrderQty = @OrderQty,
    ProductID = @ProductID,
    SpecialOfferID = @SpecialOfferID,
    UnitPrice = @UnitPrice,
    UnitPriceDiscount = @UnitPriceDiscount
WHERE SalesOrderID = @SalesOrderID AND
    SalesOrderDetailID = @SalesOrderDetailID

SET @ResultMessage =
    Convert(varchar(20),  @@RowCount) +
    ' Records Affected'
SET @ResultCode = 0


SET @ResultMessage =
    Convert(varchar(20),  @@RowCount) +
    ' Records Affected'
SET @ResultCode = 0
```

This example is more similar to the INSERT example. It receives one input parameter for each field in the SalesOrderDetails table that you want to modify. It updates the fields in the SalesOrderDetails table with the values of the input parameters for the customer with the SalesOrderDetailID designated in the @SalesOrderDetailID parameter. It then sets the @ResultMessage output parameter to a string containing the @@RowCount value. Finally, it sets the @ResultCode output parameter to zero.

Deleting Data

Stored procedures are also very effective at deleting data. Here's an example:

```
CREATE PROCEDURE procSalesOrderDetailsDelete
@SalesOrderDetailID int
AS
DELETE FROM Sales.SalesOrderDetails
WHERE SalesOrderDetailID = @SalesOrderDetailID
```

This example receives one parameter: the SalesOrderDetailID of the customer you wish to delete. Notice that the DELETE statement contains a WHERE clause that references the @SalesOrderDetailID input parameter.

Errors and Error Handling

So far the examples in this chapter have contained no error handling. This means that they leave what happens when an error occurs up to chance. Although T-SQL provides a means of handling errors, the error handling model in T-SQL is not as powerful as that in VBA. Because there's no ON ERROR GOTO statement, you must handle errors as they occur.

Handling Runtime Errors

One alternative to handling errors as they occur is to prevent errors from occurring in the first place. The SalesOrderDetail table in the AdventureWorks database requires that data be entered for the several of the fields. The SalesOrderDetailID field is an IDENTITY column, so this is not of concern. Here's the error that occurs if a value is not supplied for the SalesOrderID field:

```
Msg 515, Level 16, State 2, Line 1
Cannot insert the value NULL into column 'SalesOrderID',
table 'AdventureWorks.Sales.SalesOrderDetail';
column does not allow nulls. INSERT fails.
The statement has been terminated.
```

Here's an example of how you can prevent this error message from ever occurring:

```
CREATE PROCEDURE procOrderDetailAddHandleErrors
@SalesOrderID int = Null,
@CarrierTrackingNumber nvarchar(25) = Null,
@OrderQty smallint = 0,
@ProductID int = Null,
@SpecialOfferID int = Null,
@UnitPrice money = 0,
@UnitPriceDiscount money = 0
AS

IF @SalesOrderID Is Null
    BEGIN
```

```
        PRINT 'SalesOrderID Cannot be Null'
        RETURN
    END

IF @CarrierTrackingNumber Is Null
    BEGIN
        PRINT 'CarrierTrackingNumber Cannot be Null'
        RETURN
    END

IF @ProductID Is Null
    BEGIN
        PRINT 'ProductID Cannot be Null'
        RETURN
    END

IF @SpecialOfferID Is Null
    BEGIN
        PRINT 'SpecialOfferID Cannot be Null'
        RETURN
    END

INSERT INTO Sales.SalesOrderDetail
(SalesOrderID, CarrierTrackingNumber, OrderQty,
ProductID, UnitPrice, UnitPriceDiscount)
VALUES
(@SalesOrderID, @CarrierTrackingNumber, @OrderQty,
@ProductID, @UnitPrice, @UnitPriceDiscount)
```

In the example the several of the parameters are optional. The procedure begins
by testing to see whether the value of the @SalesOrderID is Null. If it is, a message
is printed and the RETURN statement exits the procedure. This prevents the error message from ever occurring. The code repeats the process of testing the value and
printing a message for both the CarrierTrackingNumber and ProductID parameters.
Of course you could add an output parameter that would report the problem back
to the client application. The section that follows discusses this technique. Hour 20,
"ADO.NET V2 and SQL Server," covers it in detail.

Returning Success and Failure Information from a Stored Procedure

As discussed in the previous section, it is important for the server to communicate to
the client application the success or failure information about what happened
within the stored procedure. You can select between two techniques to accomplish
this task. The first method involves returning a recordset with status information.
Here's an example:

```
CREATE PROCEDURE procOrderDetailAddHandleErrors2
@SalesOrderID int,
@CarrierTrackingNumber nvarchar(25),
```

```
@OrderQty smallint,
@ProductID int,
@UnitPrice money,
@UnitPriceDiscount money
AS
DECLARE @SalesOrderDetailID int,
    @LocalError int, @LocalRows int
INSERT INTO Sales.SalesOrderDetail
(SalesOrderID, CarrierTrackingNumber, OrderQty,
ProductID, UnitPrice, UnitPriceDiscount)
VALUES
(@SalesOrderID, @CarrierTrackingNumber, @OrderQty,
@ProductID, @UnitPrice, @UnitPriceDiscount)
SELECT @SalesOrderDetailID = @@Identity,
    @LocalError = @@Error, @LocalRows = @@RowCount
SELECT @SalesOrderDetailID, @LocalError, @LocalRows
```

The procedure first declares three variables: @SalesOrderID, @LocalError, and @LocalRows. It then inserts an order into the SalesOrderDetail table. The statement immediately following the INSERT statement populates the three variables with the identity value, error number (if any), and number of rows affected. The alternative to this technique is to use output parameters. Here's an example:

```
CREATE PROCEDURE procOrderDetailAddHandleErrors3
@SalesOrderID int,
@CarrierTrackingNumber nvarchar(25),
@OrderQty smallint,
@ProductID int,
@UnitPrice money,
@UnitPriceDiscount money,
@SalesOrderDetailID int = 0 OUTPUT,
@LocalError int = 0 OUTPUT,
@LocalRows int = 0 OUTPUT
AS
INSERT INTO Sales.SalesOrderDetail
(SalesOrderID, CarrierTrackingNumber, OrderQty,
ProductID, UnitPrice, UnitPriceDiscount)
VALUES
(@SalesOrderID, @CarrierTrackingNumber, @OrderQty,
@ProductID, @UnitPrice, @UnitPriceDiscount)
SELECT @SalesOrderDetailID = @@Identity,
    @LocalError = @@Error, @LocalRows = @@RowCount
SELECT @SalesOrderDetailID, @LocalError, @LocalRows
```

Notice that the procedure does not declare any variables. Instead it contains three output parameters: one for the SalesOrderDetailID, another for the error information, and the last for the number of rows affected. The procedure populates the output parameters just as it populated the variables, with a SELECT statement immediately following the INSERT statement.

Stored Procedures and Transactions

It is a good idea to place transactions in all the stored procedures that you build. Transactions ensure that a piece of work is completed in entirety, or not at all. One of the classic examples is a banking transaction. You want all the debits and credits to complete properly or not at all. This is where transactions come in. When using a SQL Server backend, you should place all transaction processing inside the stored procedures that you build.

Types of Transactions

Two types of transactions exist: implicit transactions and explicit transactions. Implicit transactions happen regardless of what you do in your programming code. Each time that you issue an INSERT, UPDATE, or DELETE statement, SQL Server invokes an implicit transaction. If any piece of an INSERT, UPDATE, or DELETE statement fails, the entire statement is rolled back. For example, if your DELETE statement attempts to delete all the inactive customers, and somewhere in the process a record fails to delete (for example for referential integrity reasons), SQL Server does not delete any of the records. Explicit transactions, on the other hand, are transactions that you define and control. Using explicit transactions you package multiple statements within BEGIN TRANSACTION and COMMIT TRANSACTION statements. In your error handling you include a ROLLBACK TRANSACTION statement. This ensures that all the statements complete successfully or not at all.

Implementing Transactions

As mentioned, you use the BEGIN TRANSACTION, COMMIT TRANSACTION, and ROLL-BACK TRANSACTION statements to implement transactions. The following is a stored procedure that utilizes a transaction.

```
CREATE PROCEDURE procOrderDetailAddTransactions
@SalesOrderID int,
@CarrierTrackingNumber nvarchar(25),
@OrderQty smallint,
@ProductID int,
@UnitPrice money,
@UnitPriceDiscount money
AS
SET NOCOUNT ON
DECLARE @SalesOrderDetailID int, @LocalError int, @LocalRows int
BEGIN TRANSACTION
INSERT INTO Sales.SalesOrderDetail
(SalesOrderID, CarrierTrackingNumber, OrderQty,
ProductID, UnitPrice, UnitPriceDiscount)
VALUES
(@SalesOrderID, @CarrierTrackingNumber, @OrderQty,
@ProductID, @UnitPrice, @UnitPriceDiscount)
```

```
SELECT @LocalError = @@Error, @LocalRows = @@RowCount
IF NOT @LocalError = 0 or @LocalRows = 0
    BEGIN
    ROLLBACK TRANSACTION
    SELECT SalesOrderDetailID = Null, Error = @LocalError,
        NumRows = @LocalRows
    END
ELSE
    BEGIN
    COMMIT TRAN
    SELECT @SalesOrderDetailID = @@Identity
    SELECT OrderOrderDetailID = @SalesOrderDetailID, Error = 0, NumRows =
@LocalRows
    END
```

In the example, the BEGIN TRANSACTION starts the transaction. The procedure attempts to insert a row into the Sales.SalesOrderDetail table. It populates the @LocalError variable with the value returned from the @@Error function ,and the @LocalRows variable with the value returned from the @@RowCount function. An IF statement evaluates whether either @LocalError or @LocalRows is zero. If either variable contains zero, the procedure was unsuccessful at inserting the row. The ROLLBACK TRANSACTION statement is used to terminate the transaction, and the procedure returns error information to the caller. If neither variable equals zero, you can assume that the process completed successfully. The COMMIT TRANSACTION statement commits the changes and the procedure returns the status and identity information to the caller.

Summary

You can use many techniques to make your stored procedures more powerful. In this hour you learned many of them. You learned about the SET NOCOUNT statement, and how to use the built-in @@ functions. You also learned how to pass parameters to the stored procedures that you build as well as how to return values from your stored procedures. You learned how you can use stored procedures to modify data, and how to add error handling to your stored procedures. Finally, you learned how you can add transaction processing to the stored procedures that you build.

Q&A

Q. Why would you use the SET NOCOUNT statement?

A. When it is set to ON, SET NOCOUNT eliminates the *xx* row(s) affected message in the SQL Express Manager window and the DONE_IN_PROC communicated from SQL Server to the client application. This improves the performance of the stored procedure.

Q. *The @@ functions are actually variables (true/false).*

A. False. You cannot assign values to them or work with them like normal variables. They are instead functions that return information about SQL Server.

Q. *Describe the parameters used when a stored procedure is used to insert data.*

A. You generally have one input parameter for each field in the underlying table. It is also common to have output parameters that return error and status information, as well as the identity value of the row that the stored procedure inserted.

Workshop

Quiz

1. What does @@Identity do?

2. What keyword do you use to return a value from a stored procedure?

3. You use the ON ERROR GOTO statement to write error handling into the stored procedures that you build (true/false).

4. What is the TSQL function that you use to determine whether the caller has passed a parameter value to a stored procedure?

5. What keywords do you use to start a transaction?

Quiz Answers

1. Retrieves the new value inserted into an identity column.

2. The OUTPUT keyword.

3. False. The ON ERROR GOTO statement is not available in T-SQL stored procedures. You must therefore handle errors as they occur.

4. The ISNULL keyword.

5. The BEGIN TRANSACTION keywords.

Activities

Build a stored procedure that inserts an order into the AdventureWorks Sales.SalesOrderDetail table. Before you attempt to insert the row, write to ensure that the OrderID associated with the order detail record is included in the Sales.SalesOrderHeader table. If the order associated with the sales order detail is not included in the Sales.SalesOrderHeader table, return an error message to the caller and exit the stored procedure. If the order does exist in the Sales.SalesOrderHeader table, add the order. Return the Identity value of the new row to the caller, using an output parameter.

HOUR 14

Stored Procedure Special Topics

You should be aware of some special topics when writing your stored procedures. In some cases understanding these topics can help you to provide a more efficient solution to a problem. In other cases, these topics address functionality available only with the techniques covered during this hour. In this hour you'll learn about:

▶ How to work with stored procedures and temporary tables
▶ How stored procedures interact with the security of your database
▶ How to build and work with user-defined functions
▶ How to create and work with triggers

Stored Procedures and Temporary Tables

SQL Server creates temporary tables in a special system database called TempDB. SQL Server creates TempDB each time it starts, and destroys it each time it shuts down. SQL Server uses TempDB to house many temporary objects that it needs to run. You can use TempDB to share data between procedures or to help you to accomplish complex tasks. You often will need to incorporate temporary tables into the stored procedures that you write. Here's an example of how you create and use a temporary table:

```
CREATE PROCEDURE procCustomersGetTemp AS
BEGIN
CREATE TABLE #TempEmployees
(EmployeeID int NOT NULL PRIMARY KEY,
Title varchar(50),
HireDate varchar (50),
Rate varchar (50))
INSERT INTO #TempCustomers
(EmployeeID, Title, HireDate, Rate)
EXEC procEmployeesGetByHireDateAndRate '>#', ''
```

```
SELECT Employ, ContactName, ContactTitle, City
FROM #TempCustomers
ORDER BY City, CompanyName
END
```

This procedure uses a second procedure called
procCustomersGetByCountryAndTitle. It looks like this:

```
CREATE PROCEDURE procCustomersGetByCountryAndTitle
    @CountryName VarChar(50),
    @ContactTitle VarChar(50)
AS
SELECT CompanyName, ContactName, ContactTitle, City
FROM Customers
WHERE Country = @CountryName AND
ContactTitle = @ContactTitle
ORDER BY City, CompanyName
```

The procCustomersGetByCountryAndTitle procedure receives two parameters. It
uses those parameters for the WHERE clause for Country and ContactTitle. The
procCustomersGetTemp procedure creates a temporary table that holds customer
information. It inserts into the temporary table the results of executing the
procCustomersGetByCountryAndTitle procedure, passing it USA and Owner as the
country and title values. Finally, the procedures select data from the temporary
table, ordering the result by City and CompanyName.

Stored Procedures and Security

Like views, stored procedures provide an excellent tool for securing your application's data. You can grant rights to a stored procedure without providing any rights
to the underlying table(s). Consider the following scenario: Imagine that you create
an unbound Access form where users can select various customers. You then execute
stored procedures to insert, update, and delete data. In this scenario you can grant
users view rights to the Customers table. You do not need to grant them insert,
update, or delete rights to the table. Instead you grant them execute rights to the
appropriate stored procedures. In this way you can allow your users to easily create
queries and reports that use the Customer data (you granted them view rights to the
table). They can only insert, update, and delete data via the stored procedures that
you call from your application code.

Building and Working with User-Defined Functions

SQL 2000 introduced user-defined functions. User-defined functions add power and flexibility previously unavailable with views and stored procedures. Three types of user-defined functions exist: scalar, inline table-valued, and multi-statement table-valued. The sections that follow cover each of these types of user-defined functions in detail.

Scalar Functions

Scalar functions return a single value of the type defined in the RETURNS clause. The body of the function is between a BEGIN and END block. Scalar functions can return any data type *except* text, ntext, image, cursor, or timestamp. Here's an example of a scalar function:

```
CREATE FUNCTION dbo.FullName
    (@FirstName nVarChar(10),
    @LastName nVarChar(20))
RETURNS nVarChar(35)
BEGIN
    RETURN (@LastName + ', ' + @FirstName)
END
```

This function receives two parameters: @FirstName and @LastName. It returns an nVarChar(35) value. The return value is the combination of the @LastName and @FirstName input parameters combined with a comma and a space. You could call the function like this:

```
SELECT FirstName, LastName, dbo.FullName(FirstName, LastName) FROM Employees
```

The example displays the FirstName, LastName and result of the FullName function (see Figure 14.1).

FIGURE 14.1
Scalar functions
return a single
value of the
type defined in
the RETURNS
clause.

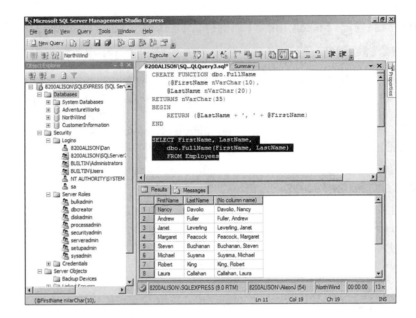

Inline Table-Valued Functions

As their name implies, inline table-valued functions return a table. Inline table-valued functions have no body. They simply return the result of a simple SELECT statement. Here's an example:

```
CREATE FUNCTION dbo.CustGetByTitle
    (@Title nVarChar(30))
RETURNS Table
AS
RETURN SELECT CustomerID, CompanyName, ContactName, City, Region
FROM Customers WHERE ContactTitle = @Title
```

This example receives a parameter called @Title. It returns a table containing selected fields from the Customers table where the ContactTitle equals the @Title parameter value. You would call the function like this:

```
SELECT * FROM dbo.CustGetByTitle('Owner')
```

The example selects all fields from the table returned from the CustGetByTitle function. Because the example passes Owner as a parameter, only the owners are included in the result set (see Figure 14.2).

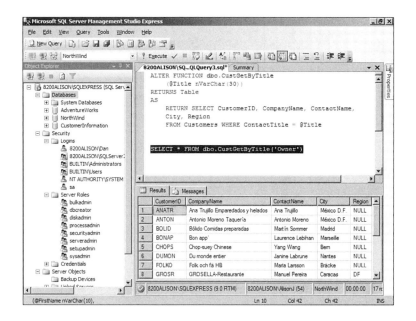

FIGURE 14.2
Inline table-
valued functions
return a table.

Multi-Statement Table-Valued Functions

Multi-statement table-valued functions are similar to inline table-valued functions. The main difference is that like scalar functions, they have a body defined by a BEGIN...END block. Like inline table-valued functions, they return a table.

Creating and Working with Triggers

A trigger is like an event procedure that runs when data changes. You can create triggers that execute in response to inserts, updates, and deletes. Developers use triggers to enforce business rules and even to perform tasks such as inserting data into an audit log.

Creating Triggers

To create or modify a trigger:

1. Click to expand the node for the table to which you want to add the trigger. The Triggers node appears (see Figure 14.3).

2. Right-click the Triggers node and select New Trigger. A new query window appears, enabling you to type the text for the trigger (see Figure 14.4).

FIGURE 14.3
The Triggers
node shows you
the existing trig-
gers associated
with a table.

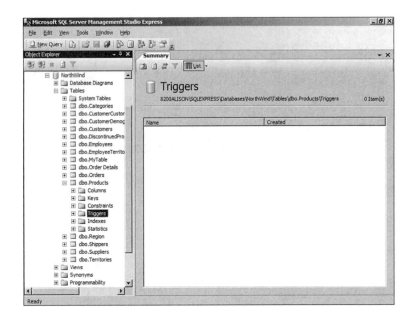

FIGURE 14.4
The new query
window enables
you to type the
T-SQL that
comprises the
trigger.

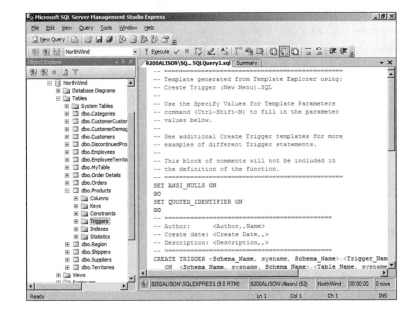

3. Type the T-SQL that comprises the Trigger.

4. Execute the CREATE TRIGGER statement (see Figure 14.5). After refreshing the list of triggers, it appears under the list of triggers associated with that table (see Figure 14.6).

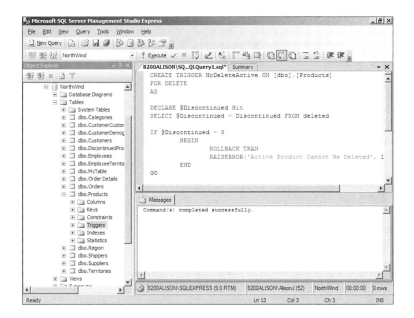

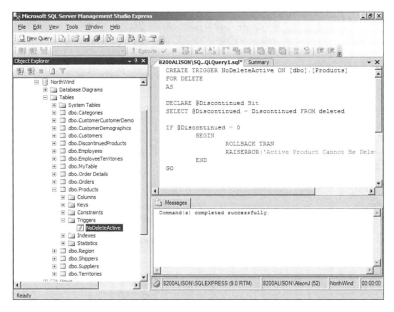

The syntax for a trigger is

```
CREATE TRIGGER TriggerName
    On TableName
    FOR [INSERT], [UPDATE], [DELETE]
    AS
    --Trigger Code
```

Here's an example:

```
CREATE TRIGGER NoDeleteActive ON [dbo].[Products]
FOR DELETE
AS

DECLARE @Discontinued Bit
SELECT @Discontinued = Discontinued FROM deleted

IF @Discontinued = 0
    BEGIN
        ROLLBACK TRAN
        RAISERROR('Active Product Cannot Be Deleted', 16,1)
    END
```

This trigger evaluates to see whether the product the user is attempting to delete is discontinued. If it is, SQL Server aborts the delete process and displays an error message.

The following is an example of a trigger that inserts data into an audit log whenever the user updates a row:

```
CREATE TRIGGER InsertProductAudit ON dbo.Products
FOR UPDATE
AS
DECLARE  @ProductID int, @ProductName NVarChar(40),
        @UnitPrice Money, @UnitsInStock SmallInt
SELECT @ProductID = ProductID, @ProductName = ProductName,
        @UnitPrice = UnitPrice, @UnitsInStock = UnitsInStock FROM inserted
INSERT ProductsAudit VALUES (@ProductID, @ProductName, @UnitPrice,@UnitsInStock)
```

This example inserts data into an audit log whenever the user modifies data in the Products table.

INSTEAD OF **Triggers**

An INSTEAD OF trigger fires in place of the triggering action. It executes after SQL Server creates the inserted and deleted tables, but before SQL Server takes any other actions. SQL Server executes INSTEAD OF triggers *before* constraints are applied. This enables you to perform pre-processing that supplements existing constraints.

Downsides of Triggers

Many developers avoid triggers entirely. Probably the biggest disadvantage of triggers is that they get buried in your database and are difficult to debug and troubleshoot. This has been ameliorated slightly in SQL Server 2005 Express because triggers appear as a node under the table that they are associated with. Triggers also slow down database operations. Furthermore, they often lock data for relatively long periods of time, increasing the chance of concurrency problems. For these reasons, most developers opt to utilize stored procedures functions, or even middle-tier components to replace the role of triggers in the applications that they build.

Summary

There are some special topics that you should be aware of when working with stored procedures. These topics not only include options available when you work with stored procedures, but they also provide you with some alternatives to stored procedures. In this hour we began by talking about how you can use temporary tables to enhance the stored procedures that you build. We then discussed the implications of stored procedures on the security of your database and the data contained within it. You learned about an alternative to stored procedures called user-defined functions. User-defined functions are a close relative to stored procedures. Finally, you learned about another cousin of stored procedures called triggers. Armed with this arsenal of techniques, you are ready to create any database application.

Q&A

Q. *Why would you create temporary tables?*

A. You create temporary tables to share data between procedures or to help you to accomplish complex tasks.

Q. *Explain what a trigger is.*

A. A trigger is like an event procedure that runs when data changes. You create triggers that respond to inserts, updates, and deletes.

Q. *Explain why you use triggers.*

A. Developers use triggers to enforce business rules and even to perform tasks such as inserting data into any audit log.

Workshop

Quiz

1. What database does SQL Server use for temporary tables?

2. With stored procedures, the user must have rights to the tables that are affected by the stored procedure (true/false).

3. Name the three types of user-defined functions.

4. Scalar functions return a single value (true/false).

5. The statements in an inline table-valued function are between a BEGIN clause and an END clause (true/false).

Quiz Answers

1. TempDB.

2. False. They need rights to only the stored procedure.

3. Scalar, inline table-valued, and multi-statement table-valued.

4. True.

5. False. The statements between scalar functions and multi-statement table-valued functions are between a BEGIN clause and an END clause.

Activities

Build a stored procedure that creates a temporary table containing OrderID, CustomerID, OrderDate, and Freight. Execute a second stored procedure that selects those fields from the Orders table, ordering by CustomerID and OrderDate. The first stored procedure should pass the second stored procedure a parameter for the freight amount. The second stored procedure receives the parameter for the freight amount. It selects all fields from the Orders table WHERE Freight is greater than the parameter value, ordering by CustomerID and Freight. It returns the result into the temporary table in the first stored procedure. Finally, have the first stored procedure display the contents of the temporary table. For help, consult the example in the "Stored Procedures and Temporary Tables" section of this chapter.

HOUR 15

ADO.NET and SQL Server

Hour 16 shows you how to use VB.NET to design SQL Server stored procedures. Before you can understand the content of Hour 16, "Using VB to Design SQL Server Stored Procedures"you must first learn a little bit about ADO.NET. In this hour you'll learn:

▶ The history of data access

▶ The basics of ADO.NET

▶ How to use ADO.NET to modify data

The History of Data Access

To get a sense of the benefits of ADO.NET, let's begin with a little history. Microsoft's first data access methodology was Data Access Objects (DAO). Microsoft introduced DAO in the early '90s. Microsoft developed DAO to access JET data. As more and more companies began accessing SQL Server, Oracle, and other client/server databases, the shortcomings of DAO became apparent. The need for a database access methodology optimized for relational ODBC databases became obvious. In response to this need, Microsoft released Remote Data Objects (RDO). Microsoft designed RDO specifically to access ODBC databases. Although it did a fairly good job interfacing with ODBC databases, RDO was not capable of accessing nonrelational data. Furthermore, you could use RDO only with ODBC-compliant databases. It became apparent that a more universal data access model was required.

In 1995 Microsoft released OleDb. Microsoft designed OleDb to access all types of data from a single programming model. To achieve this goal, each provider supplies a standard set of interfaces. The client requires no knowledge of the underlying implementation of the provider.

OleDb was difficult to program against, particularly from a Visual Basic application. Microsoft released ActiveX Data Objects (ADO) in response to this problem. ADO is a thin layer over OleDb, which is much easier to program against from a client application.

Although the solution to many problems, ADO did not facilitate the process of dealing with disparate data and was sometimes difficult to scale well over the Internet.

In today's world many people access data remotely. Furthermore, data is stored in many disparate formats. For example, one company might have Microsoft SQL Server databases, Oracle databases, and Excel spreadsheets, all of whose data must interface. The situation becomes even more complex when a company shares its data with other companies. The more data formats, and the more disparate these formats, the more difficult it becomes to write client applications that interface with the data. Furthermore, it is necessary to ensure that the methodology used does not tie up server resources for a long period of time. ADO.NET addresses dealing with disparate data formats and scalability quite well.

ADO.NET provides one programming model for accessing all types of data, regardless of the format in which it is stored in and where it is stored. It utilizes XML to accomplish its task. XML is widely supported and free of implementation dependencies. Furthermore, whereas ADO supported a limited number of disconnected operations, ADO.NET is focused on disconnected operations (although not all ADO.NET objects support disconnected operations).

The Basics of ADO.NET

You will spend the most time working with five objects. They are the `Connection` object, the `Command` object, the `DataReader` object, the `DataSet` object, and the `DataAdapter` object. Like its predecessor, ADO, ADO.NET provides you with predefined objects and methods. These objects and methods insulate you from the disparate data providers with which your application must interact. ADO.NET implements four main data provider objects. They are `Connection`, `Command`, `DataReader`, and `DataAdapter`. Microsoft provides an implementation of these objects for SQL Server. They are called the `SqlConnection`, `SqlCommand`, `SqlDataReader`, and `SqlDataAdapter` objects. They ship as part of the .NET Common Language Runtime (CLR). The `Connection` object represents a single persistent connection to a data source. The `Command` object represents a string that ADO.NET can execute via a connection. The `DataReader` object provides you with a very efficient set of results that are based on a `Command` object. Finally, the `DataAdapter` object provides a link between the data provider objects and the `DataSet` object.

Working with a SQL Connection Object

The ADO.NET `Connection` object provides you with a persistent connection to data. After you have that connection, you can return rowsets and update data. When

working with the Connection object, you can pass all or some of the following information to the provider:

▶ Server name

▶ Provider name

▶ UserID and password

▶ Default database

▶ Other provider-specific information

Listing 15.1 provides an example of the use of the Connection object. Notice that it
declares a SqlConnection object. The code instantiates the Connection object, passing it the connection string. The connection string includes the data source, default
database, and type of security you want to use (in this case NT Integrated security).
The code uses the Open method of the Connection object to open the connection. It
displays the value of the ConnectionString property in a text box and then closes
the connection.

LISTING 15.1   An Example That Uses Windows NT Integrated Security
to Establish a Connection to SQL Server

```
Private Sub btnSQLConnectionIntegrated_Click _
    (ByVal sender As System.Object, ByVal e As System.EventArgs) _
    Handles btnSQLConnectionIntegrated.Click
    'Declare necessary variables
    Dim conn As SqlClient.SqlConnection
    Dim strConn As String
     'Build a connection string
    strConn = "Data Source=.\SQLEXPRESS;AttachDBFilename=" & _
        "'C:\Program Files\Microsoft SQL Server\MSSQL.1\" & _
        "MSSQL\Data\AdventureWorks_Data.mdf';" & _
        "Integrated Security=True;Connect Timeout=30;User Instance=True"

    'Instantiate the SqlConnection object, passing it the
    'connection string
    conn = New SqlClient.SqlConnection(strConn)
     'Open the connection
    conn.Open()
     'Display the connection string
    txtOutput.Text = conn.ConnectionString & " - " & "State = " & conn.State

    'Close the connection
    conn.Close()

End Sub
```

The data source may not be local if you are accessing a remote server. You then need to supply the actual server name in Listing 15.1.

Notice that the example references `SqlClient.SqlConnection`. You will notice that the references to `System.Data` in all the code examples have been omitted. Alternatively, I could have used `System.Data.SqlClient.SqlConnection`, or I could have imported the `System.Data.SqlClient` namespace to further shorten the reference to `SqlConnection`. I have refrained from using the complete shorthand in the examples so that the code is extremely clear as to what objects it is using.

ADO.NET takes advantage of connection pooling. This means that with ADO.NET, your code is able to reuse a connection when appropriate. It is important that you call the `Close` method of the `Connection` object when you are finished using a connection. This releases the connection back to the connection pool. If you don't explicitly call the `Close` method yourself, you are leaving it up to the .NET garbage collector to determine when it closes the connection. This has potential negative performance implications. Therefore, it is important that you explicitly close connections when you are finished working with them.

To keep the sample code simple, the examples in this chapter are devoid of error handling. This means that should an error occur, the code will not handle the error gracefully. For your production code, you should include all the necessary error handling.

Listing 15.2 provides an example that utilizes SQL Server security, rather than Windows NT Integrated security, to connect to the server. Notice that rather than using `integrated security=SSPI`, the code designates the user ID and password. Apart from that, the code in Listing 15.2 is identical to that in Listing 15.1.

LISTING 15.2   An Example That Uses SQL Server Security to Establish a Connection to SQL Server

```
Private Sub btnSQLConnectionPassword_Click _
(ByVal sender As System.Object, ByVal e As System.EventArgs) _
Handles btnSQLConnectionPassword.Click

    'Declare necessary variables
    Dim conn As SqlClient.SqlConnection
    Dim strConn As String
    'Build a connection string
    strConn = "Data Source=.\SQLEXPRESS;AttachDbFilename=" & _
```

LISTING 15.2 Continued

```
"'C:\Program Files\Microsoft SQL Server\MSSQL.1\MSSQL\Data\" & _
"AdventureWorks_Data.mdf';;" & _
"Integrated Security=False;user id=sa;password=;" & _
"Connect Timeout=30;User Instance=True"

'Instantiate the SqlConnection object, passing it the
'connection string
conn = New SqlClient.SqlConnection(strConn)

'Open the connection
conn.Open()

'Display the connection string
txtOutput.Text = conn.ConnectionString & " - " & "State = " & conn.State

'Close the connection
conn.Close()

End Sub
```

> **By the Way**
>
> For the example code to work, you must have Integrated Security turned on in SQL Server, and you must supply a valid user ID and password in the login string.

> **By the Way**
>
> Note that you may need to modify the data source, the user ID, and the password in Listing 15.2. The data source may not be local if you are accessing a remote server. You then need to supply the actual server name. If the user ID that you use is other than "sa", and the password is other than blank, you also need to modify those accordingly. If your server does not support Mixed security, you will not be able to execute Listing 15.2 successfully. Hour 21, ""SQL Server Authentication,"" explains Mixed security.

In the examples thus far, we have passed the connection string to the Open method of the Connection object. An alternative is to set the ConnectionString property of the Connection object before calling the Open method. Listing 15.3 provides an example.

LISTING 15.3 An Example That Sets the ConnectionString **Property Before Opening the Connection**

```
Private Sub btnSQLConnectionAlt_Click _
(ByVal sender As System.Object, ByVal e As System.EventArgs) _
Handles btnSQLConnectionAlt.Click
    'Declare necessary variables
    Dim conn As SqlClient.SqlConnection
    Dim strConn As String
    'Build a connection string
```

LISTING 15.3   Continued

```
strConn = "Data Source=.\SQLEXPRESS;AttachDbFilename=" & _
"'C:\Program Files\Microsoft SQL Server\MSSQL.1\MSSQL\Data\" & _
"AdventureWorks_Data.mdf';;" & _
"Integrated Security=True;Connect Timeout=30;User Instance=True"
 'Instantiate the SqlConnection object, passing it the
 'connection string
conn = New SqlClient.SqlConnection()
  'Set ConnectionString property
conn.ConnectionString = strConn

'Open the connection
conn.Open()

'Display the connection string
txtOutput.Text = conn.ConnectionString & " - " & "State = " & conn.State

'Close the connection
conn.Close()

End Sub
```

By the Way

Note that you may need to modify the data source, the user ID, and the password in Listing 15.3. The data source may not be local if you are accessing a remote server. You will then need to supply the actual server name.

Working with a SQL Command Object

The Command object is one of the most important and useful ADO.NET objects. It enables you to execute commands that retrieve or update data. The Command object holds information about the command that you want to execute. The CommandText property of the Command object contains the SQL statement or the name of the stored procedure that you want to execute. Alternatively, it can contain the name of a table whose data you want to retrieve. The CommandType property contains a value indicating the type of statement contained in the CommandText property. It can contain one of the three following values:

▶ Text—Indicates that the CommandText is a SQL statement.

▶ StoredProcedure—Indicates that the CommandText is a stored procedure.

▶ TableDirect—Indicates that the CommandText is the name of a table.

The SQL statement or stored procedure might contain parameters. If so, you use the Parameters collection of the Command object to designate the parameters.

The `Command` object can return streams of data to the `DataReader` object, or it can cache results in a `DataSet` object. If you designate the name of a table in the `CommandText` property, ADO.NET instructs the database to return the contents of the entire table. If you specify a SQL statement or stored procedure that selects data in the `CommandText` property, the database returns a set of rows from one or more tables. If you specify a SQL statement or stored procedure that modifies data, the database updates the data, but does not return any rows.

The `Command` object has four methods that you can use to execute the contents of the `CommandText`:

▶ `ExecuteReader`—Returns a forward-only `DataReader` object.

▶ `ExecuteScalar`—Returns a result of one column and one row.

▶ `ExecuteNonQuery`—Returns no results.

▶ `ExecuteXMLReader`—Returns an XML version of a `DataReader` object.

Besides the `CommandText` and `CommandType` properties, the `Command` object has several other important properties and collections. You use the `Connection` property to designate a connection string or a Connection object associated with the `Command` object. You use the `Parameters` collection to designate parameter values for the SQL statement or stored procedure named in the `CommandText` property. You use the `Transaction` property to indicate the transaction in which the command executes. These are just a few of the properties and methods available for the `Command` object.

Listing 15.4 provides an example of the use of a `Command` object to retrieve data from a database. Notice that it declares `SqlConnection` and `SqlCommand` objects. After instantiating and opening a connection, the code instantiates the `Command` object. It sets the `CommandText` property of the `Command` object to a `SELECT` statement that selects specific fields from the Sales.SalesOrderHeader table. It designates the `CommandType` property as text, indicating that `CommandText` contains a SQL statement. Then it sets the `Connection` property of the `Command` object to the `SqlConnection` object instantiated and opened earlier in the code. Finally, the code creates a new `BindingSource` object and sets its `DataSource` property to the `DataReader` object. It then sets the `DataSource` property of the `DataGrid` control to the `BindingSource` object.

LISTING 15.4   An Example of Using the `Command` Object to Execute a SQL Statement That Retrieves Data from a Database

```
Private Sub btnSqlCommandSELECT_Click(ByVal sender As System.Object, _
ByVal e As System.EventArgs) Handles btnSqlCommandSELECT.Click
        'Declare necessary variables
        Dim cmd As SqlClient.SqlCommand
```

LISTING 15.4   Continued

```
Dim conn As SqlClient.SqlConnection
Dim strConn As String

'Build a connection string
 strConn = "Data Source=.\SQLEXPRESS;AttachDbFilename=" & _
    "'C:\Program Files\Microsoft SQL    Server\" & _
    "MSSQL.1\MSSQL\Data\AdventureWorks_Data.mdf';" & _
    "Integrated Security=True;Connect Timeout=30;User Instance=True"

'Instantiate the SQLConnection object, passing it the
'connection string
conn = New SqlClient.SqlConnection(strConn)

'Open the connection
conn.Open()

'Instantiate the SqlCommand object
cmd = New SqlClient.SqlCommand()

'Set the CommandText property
cmd.CommandText = "SELECT  SalesOrderID, OrderDate, DueDate, " & _
    "ShipDate, CustomerID, SubTotal, TaxAmt, Freight, TotalDue " & _
    "FROM Sales.SalesOrderHeader " & _
    "ORDER BY OrderDate"

'Designate the CommandType
cmd.CommandType = Data.CommandType.Text

'Set the Connection property of the SqlCommand
cmd.Connection = conn

'Output contents of DataReader to a grid
Dim source As New BindingSource
source.DataSource = source
grdOutput.DataSource = source

'Close the connection
conn.Close()
End Sub
```

The example in Listing 15.4 retrieved multiple rows and columns from a table in the database. The code in Listing 15.5 retrieves only a single row and column from the database. It uses the ExecuteScalar method of the Command object, rather than the ExecuteReader method, to accomplish its task. Notice that the SQL statement retrieves the number of orders that have freight greater than 500. This SQL statement returns only one row and column. Therefore, it is most efficient to use the ExecuteScalar method to handle the result. The code displays the result in a text box and then closes the connection.

LISTING 15.5   An Example of Using the Command Object to Execute a
SQL Statement That Retrieves a Single Row and Column from a Table in
a Database

```
Private Sub btnCommandSelectSingle_Click _
(ByVal sender As System.Object, ByVal e As System.EventArgs) _
Handles btnCommandSelectSingle.Click
    'Declare necessary variables
    Dim cmd As SqlClient.SqlCommand
    Dim conn As SqlClient.SqlConnection
    Dim strConn As String

    'Build a connection string
    strConn = "Data Source=.\SQLEXPRESS;AttachDbFilename=" & _
        "'C:\Program Files\Microsoft SQL Server\MSSQL.1\MSSQL\Data\" & _
        "AdventureWorks_Data.mdf';;" & _
        "Integrated Security=True;Connect Timeout=30;User Instance=True"

    'Instantiate the SQLConnection object, passing it the
    'connection string
    conn = New SqlClient.SqlConnection(strConn)

    'Open the connection
    conn.Open()

    'Instantiate the SqlCommand object
    cmd = New SqlClient.SqlCommand()

    'Set the CommandText property
    cmd.CommandText = "SELECT COUNT(SalesOrderID) AS NumHighFreight " & _
        "FROM Sales.SalesOrderHeader " & _
        "WHERE Freight > 500"

    'Designate the CommandType
    cmd.CommandType = Data.CommandType.Text

    'Set the Connection property of the SqlCommand
    cmd.Connection = conn

    'Populate the text box with the output
    txtOutput.Text = CStr(cmd.ExecuteScalar)

    'Close the connection
    conn.Close()

End Sub
```

One of the most important and common uses of the Command object is to execute
action queries, which are queries that update data. Listing 15.6 provides an example. Notice that after establishing a connection and instantiating a Command object,
the code sets the CommandText property equal to a SQL statement that updates data.
It uses the ExecuteNonQuery method of the Command object to execute the SQL statement. The ExecuteNonQuery method returns the number of rows affected by the
update. The code places this value in a text box on the form.

LISTING 15.6   An Example of Using the Command Object to Execute a
SQL Statement That Updates in a Database

```
Private Sub btnCommandUpdate_Click _
(ByVal sender As System.Object, ByVal e As System.EventArgs) _
Handles btnCommandUpdate.Click
    'Declare necessary variables
    Dim cmd As SqlClient.SqlCommand
    Dim conn As SqlClient.SqlConnection
    Dim strConn As String
     'Build a connection string
    strConn = "Data Source=.\SQLEXPRESS;AttachDbFilename=" & _
        "'C:\Program Files\Microsoft SQL Server\" _
        "MSSQL.1\MSSQL\Data\AdventureWorks_Data.mdf';;" & _
        "Integrated Security=True;Connect Timeout=30;User Instance=True"

    'Instantiate the SQLConnection object, passing it the
    'connection string
    conn = New SqlClient.SqlConnection(strConn)

    'Open the connection
    conn.Open()

    'Instantiate the SqlCommand object
    cmd = New SqlClient.SqlCommand()

    'Set the CommandText property
    cmd.CommandText = "UPDATE Sales.SalesOrderHeader " & _
        "SET Freight = Freight + 1 " & _
        "WHERE SalesOrderID = 43659"

    'Designate the CommandType
    cmd.CommandType = Data.CommandType.Text

    'Set the Connection property of the SqlCommand
    cmd.Connection = conn

    'Populate the text box with the output
    txtOutput.Text = cmd.ExecuteNonQuery.ToString

    'Close the connection
    conn.Close()

End Sub
```

Working with a SQL DataReader Object

The DataReader object provides the fastest means for retrieving read-only sets of
data. The DataReader object is much more efficient than the DataSet object. The
DataSet object generally loads much more into memory than you actually need.
You can think of the DataReader object as supplying a forward-only, read-only,
server-side cursor. Its biggest danger is that it has the potential for tying up a
Connection object. Therefore, it is very important to close the connection as soon as

you are finished working with it. Listing 15.7 provides an example. Notice that the code instantiates a Connection object. After opening the connection, the code uses the connection to instantiate a Command object. It uses the ExecuteReader method of the Command object to return a result into the DataReader object. Finally, it uses the DataReader object as the DataSource for a DropDownList control and closes the connection.

LISTING 15.7   An Example That Uses the DataReader Object as the Source for a DropDownList Control

```
Private Sub btnDataReader_Click _
(ByVal sender As System.Object, ByVal e As System.EventArgs) _
Handles btnDataReader.Click
    Dim conn As SqlClient.SqlConnection
    Dim dr As SqlClient.SqlDataReader
    Dim cmd As SqlClient.SqlCommand
    Dim strConn As String
    Dim strSQL As String

    'Build a connection string
    strConn = "Data Source=.\SQLEXPRESS;AttachDbFilename=" & _
        "'C:\Program Files\Microsoft SQL Server\MSSQL.1\MSSQL\Data\' & _
        "AdventureWorks_Data.mdf';;" & _
        "Integrated Security=True;Connect Timeout=30;User Instance=True"

    'Build the SELECT statement
    strSQL = "SELECT ContactID, LastName " & _
            "FROM Person.Contact " & _
            "ORDER BY LastName"

    'Instantiate and open the connection
    conn = New SqlClient.SqlConnection(strConn)
    conn.Open()

    'Instantiate the SqlCommand object
    cmd = New SqlClient.SqlCommand(strSQL, conn)

    'Use the ExecuteReader method of the SqlCommand object
    'to execute the SQL statement and return the results
    'into the DataReader object
    dr = cmd.ExecuteReader

    'Display results in a DropDownList
    If Not dr Is Nothing Then
        While (dr.Read())
            ddlContacts.Items.Add(dr("LastName"))
        End While
    End If

    dr.Close()
    conn.Close()

End Sub
```

Listing 15.8 is similar to Listing 15.7. It uses the Read method of the DataReader object to loop through the rows in the DataReader. As it loops, it uses the GetString method of the DataReader object to retrieve the data from that row in the DataReader.

LISTING 15.8 An Example That Uses the Read Method of the DataReader Object to Loop Through Each Row in the DataReader

```
Private Sub btnDataReaderLoop_Click(ByVal sender As System.Object, _
ByVal e As System.EventArgs) Handles btnDataReaderLoop.Click
    Dim conn As SqlClient.SqlConnection
    Dim dr As SqlClient.SqlDataReader
    Dim cmd As SqlClient.SqlCommand
    Dim strConn As String
    Dim strSQL As String
    Dim strOutput As New System.Text.StringBuilder()

    'Build a connection string
    strConn = "Data Source=.\SQLEXPRESS;AttachDbFilename=" & _
        "'C:\Program Files\Microsoft SQL Server\MSSQL.1\MSSQL\Data\" & _
        "AdventureWorks_Data.mdf';;" & _
        "Integrated Security=True;Connect Timeout=30;User Instance=True"

    'Build the SELECT statement
    strSQL = "SELECT DepartmentID, Name " & _
        "FROM HumanResources.Department " & _
        "ORDER BY Name"

    'Instantiate and open the connection
    conn = New SqlClient.SqlConnection(strConn)
    conn.Open()

    'Instantiate the SqlCommand object
    cmd = New SqlClient.SqlCommand(strSQL, conn)

    'Use the ExecuteReader method of the SqlCommand object
    'to execute the SQL statement and return the results
    'into the DataReader object
    dr = cmd.ExecuteReader

    'Loop through the DataReader appending to the DataReader object
    While dr.Read
        strOutput.Append(dr.GetString(1) & ", ")
    End While

    'Display the contents of the StringBuilder object in a text box
    txtOutput.Text = strOutput.ToString

    dr.Close()
    conn.Close()

End Sub
```

Introducing the ADO.NET `DataAdapter` **Object**

The `DataAdapter` object acts as a liaison between the permanent data store and the in-memory data store. It provides a means of marshalling data from the data store into the `DataSet` and back again. This object enables you to *fully* separate the `DataSet` from its underlying data store. The `DataAdapter` object is capable of sending `DataSet` changes back to the data source.

The `DataAdapter` object works very well with the `Connection` object. When you create a `Connection` object implicitly through the `DataAdapter` object, the `DataAdapter` object checks the status of the connection. If it finds an existing open connection, it uses it. Otherwise, it opens the connection. Then the `DataAdapter` closes the connection when it is finished with it.

Listing 15.9 provides an example of the `DataAdapter` object and its close ties to the `DataSet` object (discussed in the next section). The code creates a connection string and a SQL statement. It instantiates the `DataAdapter` object, passing it both the connection string and the SQL statement. It then uses the `Fill` method of the `DataAdapter` object to fill the `DataSet` with data based on the connection string and the SQL statement. It uses the resulting `DataSet` as the `DataSource` property of the grid. Finally, it uses the `Dispose` method of the `DataSet` and `DataAdapter` objects to clean up after itself.

LISTING 15.9   An Example That Uses the `DataAdapter` Object to Populate a `DataSet` with Data

```
Private Sub btnDataAdapter_Click _
(ByVal sender As System.Object, ByVal e As System.EventArgs) _
Handles btnDataAdapter.Click
    Dim da As SqlClient.SqlDataAdapter
    Dim ds As New DataSet()
    Dim strConn As String
    Dim strSQL As String

    'Build a connection string
    strConn = "Data Source=.\SQLEXPRESS;AttachDbFilename=" & _
        "'C:\Program Files\Microsoft SQL Server\MSSQL.1\MSSQL\Data\" & _
        "AdventureWorks_Data.mdf';" & _
        "Integrated Security=True;Connect Timeout=30;User Instance=True"

    'Build the SELECT statement
    strSQL = "SELECT  SalesOrderID, OrderDate, DueDate, " & _
        "ShipDate, CustomerID, SubTotal, TaxAmt, Freight, TotalDue " & _
        "FROM Sales.SalesOrderHeader " & _
        "ORDER BY OrderDate"

    'Instantiate the SqlDataAdapter
    da = New SqlClient.SqlDataAdapter(strSQL, strConn)

    'Use the Fill method of the DataAdapter to
```

LISTING 15.9   Continued

```
'fill a DataSet with data
da.Fill(ds, "SalesOrderHeader")

'Display the contents of the stringbuilder object in a grid
grdOutput.DataSource = ds.Tables("SalesOrderHeader")

ds.Dispose()
da.Dispose()

End Sub
```

Introducing the ADO.NET DataSet Object

Because the discussion of the DataAdapter object required the introduction of the DataSet object, you received a brief introduction to this powerful object in the previous section. The DataSet object is a powerful in-memory database that enables you to store and update relational or hierarchical data. There is only one DataSet object, regardless of the data provider that you use. In fact, the DataSet object is completely database agnostic. It works the same, regardless of where the data contained in it came from. Because the DataSet is divorced from its data source, it needs something to fill it with data. This is where the DataAdapter object comes in. It is the marriage between the DataSet and DataAdapter objects that enables you to have powerful interaction with data through your .NET applications. The following are the benefits of DataSets:

- ▶ DataSets separate connected and disconnected operations.

- ▶ DataSets can be cached easily on a web server.

- ▶ Because DataSets maintain their own state, they don't tie up server resources.

- ▶ You can safely store DataSets in an ASP .NET Session object.

- ▶ Because of their strong tie to XML, .NET and non-.NET applications can both utilize DataSets.

- ▶ DataSets interact well with bound controls.

Listing 15.10 provides an example of how you can loop through each column and row in a DataSet, retrieving values from the DataSet. The example uses the Fill method of the DataAdapter object to fill the dataset with data. It then sets the DataSource property of the grid to the SalesOrderHeader table contained in the DataSet.

LISTING 15.10   An Example That Utilizes a `DataSet` as the RowSource
for a Grid.

```vb
Private Sub btnDataSet_Click(ByVal sender As System.Object, _
ByVal e As System.EventArgs) _
Handles btnDataSet.Click
    Dim da As SqlClient.SqlDataAdapter
    Dim ds As New DataSet()
    Dim strConn As String
    Dim strSQL As String
    Dim strOutput As New System.Text.StringBuilder()

    'Build a connection string
    strConn = "Data Source=.\SQLEXPRESS;AttachDbFilename=" & _
        "'C:\Program Files\Microsoft SQL Server\MSSQL.1\MSSQL\Data\" & _
        "AdventureWorks_Data.mdf';;" & _
        "Integrated Security=True;Connect Timeout=30;User Instance=True"

    'Build the SELECT statement
    strSQL = "SELECT  SalesOrderID, OrderDate, DueDate, " & _
        "ShipDate, CustomerID, SubTotal, TaxAmt, Freight, TotalDue " & _
        "FROM Sales.SalesOrderHeader " & _
        "ORDER BY OrderDate"

    'Instantiate the SqlDataAdapter
    da = New SqlClient.SqlDataAdapter(strSQL, strConn)

    'Use the Fill method of the DataAdapter to
    'fill a DataSet with data
    da.Fill(ds, "SalesOrderHeader")

    'Populate a grid with the DataSet
    grdOutput.DataSource = ds.Tables("SalesOrderHeader")

    ds.Dispose()
    da.Dispose()

End Sub
```

A `DataSet` object can contain multiple tables. Listing 15.11 provides an example.
Notice that the code declares two `SqlDataAdapter` objects. It instantiates each
`SqlDataAdapter` object, sending each a different SQL statement: one that retrieves
data from the `SalesOrderHeader` table and another that retrieves data from the
`SalesOrderDetail` table. The code uses the `Fill` method of the first `DataAdapter`
object to fill the `DataSet` with data from the `SalesOrderHeader` table. Then it uses
the `Fill` method of the second `DataAdapter` object to fill the *same* `DataSet` with
data from the `SalesOrderDetail` table. The `DataSet` contains data from two tables.
The code uses the `GetXML` method of the `DataSet` object to retrieve the data from the
XML stream and display it in a text box. Because the code does not relate the tables,
the contents of the `SalesOrderHeader` table print, followed by the contents of the
`SalesOrderDetail` table.

LISTING 15.11   A `DataSet` Object with Multiple Tables

```
Private Sub btnMultipleTables_Click _
(ByVal sender As System.Object, ByVal e As System.EventArgs) _
Handles btnMultipleTables.Click

    Dim daOrders As SqlClient.SqlDataAdapter
    Dim daOrderDetails As SqlClient.SqlDataAdapter
    Dim rel As DataRelation
    Dim ds As New DataSet()
    Dim strConn As String
    Dim strSQL1 As String
    Dim strSQL2 As String

    'Build a connection string
    strConn = "Data Source=.\SQLEXPRESS;AttachDbFilename=" & _
        "'C:\Program Files\Microsoft SQL Server\MSSQL.1\MSSQL\Data\ " & _
        "AdventureWorks_Data.mdf';;" & _
        "Integrated Security=True;Connect Timeout=30;User Instance=True"

    'Build the SELECT statements
    strSQL1 = "SELECT SalesOrderID, OrderDate, DueDate, " & _
    "ShipDate, CustomerID, SubTotal, TaxAmt, Freight, TotalDue " & _
    "FROM Sales.SalesOrderHeader WHERE SalesOrderID >= 75061 " & _
    "ORDER BY OrderDate"

    strSQL2 = "SELECT SalesOrderDetailID, SalesOrderID, " & _
    "ProductID, OrderQty, UnitPrice " & _
    "FROM Sales.SalesOrderDetail WHERE SalesOrderID >= 75061"

    'Instantiate the SqlDataAdapters
    daOrders = New SqlClient.SqlDataAdapter(strSQL1, strConn)
    daOrderDetails = New SqlClient.SqlDataAdapter(strSQL2, strConn)

    'Use the Fill method of the DataAdapters to
    'fill a DataSet with data from both tables
    daOrders.Fill(ds, "SalesOrderHeader")
    daOrderDetails.Fill(ds, "SalesOrderDetail")

    'Create the DataRelation object and set its
    'Nested property to True
    rel = New DataRelation("OrdersOrderDetail", _
        ds.Tables("SalesOrderHeader").Columns("SalesOrderID"), _
        ds.Tables("SalesOrderDetail").Columns("SalesOrderID"))
    rel.Nested = True

    'Add the DataRelation object
    'to the Relations collection of the DataSet
    ds.Relations.Add(rel)

    'Display the XML stream in a textbox
    txtOutput.Text = ds.GetXml

    ds.Dispose()
    daOrders.Dispose()
    daOrderDetails.Dispose()

End Sub
```

It is easy to relate the tables in a DataSet. Listing 15.15 provides an example. Like the previous example, the code uses two DataAdapter objects to fill a DataSet with data. The difference between the code in Listing 15.11 and that in Listing 15.12 is that the code uses a DataRelation object to relate the data in the two tables. It instantiates the DataRelation object indicating that the SalesOrderID field from the SalesOrderHeader table relates to the SalesOrderID field from the SalesOrderDetail table. It sets the Nested property to True. This causes the generated XML to reflect the one-to-many relationship between the two tables in the DataSet. If you do not set the Nested property to True, the XML will contain all the data from the SalesOrderHeader table followed by all the data from the SalesOrderDetail table. The code uses the Add method of the Relations collection to add the DataRelation object to the Relations collection of the DataSet. Finally, it uses the GetXML method of the DataSet to retrieve the XML and display it in a text box.

LISTING 15.12   Relating the Tables in a DataSet

```
Private Sub btnRelations_Click( _
ByVal sender As System.Object, ByVal e As System.EventArgs) _
Handles btnRelations.Click
    Dim daSalesOrderHeader As SqlClient.SqlDataAdapter
    Dim daSalesOrderDetail As SqlClient.SqlDataAdapter
    Dim ds As New DataSet()
    Dim strConn As String
    Dim strSQL1 As String
    Dim strSQL2 As String
    Dim rel As DataRelation

    'Build a connection string
    strConn = "Data Source=.\SQLEXPRESS;AttachDbFilename=" & _
        "'C:\Program Files\Microsoft SQL Server\MSSQL.1\MSSQL\Data\" & _
        "AdventureWorks_Data.mdf';;" & _
        "Integrated Security=True;Connect Timeout=30;User Instance=True"

        'Build the SELECT statements
        strSQL1 = "SELECT SalesOrderID, OrderDate, DueDate, " & _
        "ShipDate, CustomerID, SubTotal, TaxAmt, Freight, TotalDue " & _
        "FROM Sales.SalesOrderHeader WHERE SalesOrderID >= 75061 " & _
        "ORDER BY OrderDate"
        strSQL2 = "SELECT SalesOrderDetailID, SalesOrderID, " & _
        "ProductID, OrderQty, UnitPrice " & _
        "FROM Sales.SalesOrderDetail WHERE SalesOrderID >= 75061"

    'Instantiate the SqlDataAdapters
    daSalesOrderHeader = New SqlClient.SqlDataAdapter(strSQL1, strConn)
    daSalesOrderDetail = New SqlClient.SqlDataAdapter(strSQL2, strConn)

    'Use the Fill method of the DataAdapters to
    'fill a DataSet with data from both tables
    daSalesOrderHeader.Fill(ds, "SalesOrderHeader")
    daSalesOrderDetail.Fill(ds, "SalesOrderDetail")
```

LISTING 15.12   Continued

```
'Create the DataRelation object and set its
'Nested property to True
rel = New DataRelation("HeaderDetail", _
    ds.Tables("SalesOrderHeader").Columns("SalesOrderID"), _
    ds.Tables("SalesOrderDetail").Columns("SalesOrderID"))
rel.Nested = True

'Add the DataRelation object
'to the Relations collection of the DataSet
ds.Relations.Add(rel)

'Display the XML stream in a text box
txtOutput.Text = ds.GetXml

ds.Dispose()
daSalesOrderHeader.Dispose()
daSalesOrderDetail.Dispose()

End Sub
```

Building Queries That Modify Data

It's important that you understand how to use ADO.NET code to insert, update, and delete data. This section provides examples of how to accomplish each task, using both the Command object as well as the DataSet object.

Using ADO.NET to Update Data

Listing 15.13 shows you how to use a SqlCommand object to insert data. The code opens a connection, then instantiates a SqlCommand object. It sets the CommandText property of the SqlCommand object to an INSERT INTO statement that inserts data into the HumanResources.Department table. It sets the Connection property of the SqlCommand object to the connection established earlier in the routine. The code then adds Parameter objects to the Parameters collection of the SqlCommand object. These parameters supply the values that the INSERT INTO statement inserts into the table. The code uses the ExecuteNonQuery method of the SqlCommand object to execute the INSERT INTO statement. Finally, the code uses the Fill method of the SqlDataAdapter object to fill a DataSet with data, and then populates a DataGrid control with data for the inserted department.

LISTING 15.13   An Example That Uses the SqlCommand **Object to Insert Data into a Table**

```
Private Sub btnInsert_Click(ByVal sender As System.Object, _
ByVal e As System.EventArgs) _
Handles btnInsert.Click
    'Declare necessary variables
```

LISTING 15.13   Continued

```
Dim cmd As New SqlClient.SqlCommand()
Dim conn As SqlClient.SqlConnection
Dim da As New SqlClient.SqlDataAdapter()
Dim ds As New DataSet()
Dim strConn As String
Dim strSQL As String

'Build a connection string
strConn = "Data Source=.\SQLEXPRESS;AttachDbFilename=" & _
   "'C:\Program Files\Microsoft SQL Server\" & _
   "MSSQL.1\MSSQL\Data\" & _
   "AdventureWorks_Data.mdf';" & _
   "Integrated Security=True;Connect Timeout=30;User Instance=True"

'Instantiate the SqlConnection object, passing it the
'connection string
conn = New SqlClient.SqlConnection(strConn)

'Open the connection
conn.Open()

'Instantiate the SqlCommand object
cmd = New SqlClient.SqlCommand()

    'Set the CommandText property
    cmd.CommandText = "INSERT INTO HumanResources.Department " & _
        "(Name, GroupName) " & _
        "VALUES (@Name, @GroupName) "

    'Designate the CommandType
    cmd.CommandType = CommandType.Text

    'Set the Connection property of the SqlCommand
    cmd.Connection = conn

    'Add parameters and set their values
    'NOTE THAT THE ORDER DOESN'T MATTER!
    Dim nameParameter As New SqlClient.SqlParameter("@Name",
SqlDbType.NVarChar)
    nameParameter.Value = txtName.Text
    cmd.Parameters.Add(nameParameter)

    Dim groupNameParameter As New SqlClient.SqlParameter("@GroupName",
SqlDbType.NVarChar)
    groupNameParameter.Value = txtGroupName.Text
    cmd.Parameters.Add(groupNameParameter)

    'Execute the Insert statement
    cmd.ExecuteNonQuery()

    'Fill the DataSet with data from the inserted row
    strSQL = "SELECT DepartmentID, Name, GroupName " & _
        "FROM HumanResources.Department " & _
        "WHERE Name = '" & _
        txtName.Text & "' And " & _
        "GroupName = '" & txtGroupName.Text & "'"
```

LISTING 15.13   Continued

```
        da = New SqlClient.SqlDataAdapter(strSQL, conn)
        da.Fill(ds, "DepartmentInfo")

        'Display the contents of the stringbuilder object in a textbox
        txtOutput.Text = ds.ToString

    'Close the connection
    conn.Close()
End Sub
```

By the Way

You must enter the name and group name *before* you click the Insert button. This ensures that the code inserts the correct data into the database.

The code required to update data is similar to that necessary to insert data. Listing 15.13 provides an example. The CommandText property contains an UPDATE statement. The code adds all the necessary parameters to the Parameters collection of the SqlCommand object, and then uses the ExecuteNonQuery method of the SqlCommand object to execute the action query. Finally, it displays the modified row in a DataGrid control.

LISTING 15.13   An Example That Uses the SqlCommand Object to Update Data in a Table

```
Private Sub btnUpdate_Click(ByVal sender As System.Object, _
ByVal e As System.EventArgs) Handles btnUpdate.Click
    'Declare necessary variables
    Dim cmd As New SqlClient.SqlCommand()
    Dim conn As SqlClient.SqlConnection
    Dim da As New SqlClient.SqlDataAdapter()
    Dim ds As New DataSet()
    Dim strConn As String
    Dim strSQL As String

    'Build a connection string
    strConn = "Data Source=.\SQLEXPRESS;AttachDbFilename=" & _
        "'C:\Program Files\Microsoft SQL Server\" & _
        "MSSQL.1\MSSQL\Data\AdventureWorks_Data.mdf';" & _
        "Integrated Security=True;Connect Timeout=30;User Instance=True"

    'Instantiate the SqlConnection object, passing it the
    'connection string
    conn = New SqlClient.SqlConnection(strConn)

    'Open the connection
    conn.Open()

    'Instantiate the SqlCommand object
    cmd = New SqlClient.SqlCommand()
```

LISTING 15.13   Continued

```
'Set the CommandText property
cmd.CommandText = "UPDATE HumanResources.Department " & _
    "SET Name = @Name, " & _
    "GroupName = @GroupName " & _
    "WHERE DepartmentID = @DepartmentIDCriteria"

'Designate the CommandType
cmd.CommandType = CommandType.Text

'Set the Connection property of the SqlCommand
cmd.Connection = conn

'Add parameters and set their values
'NOTE THAT THE ORDER DOESN'T MATTER!
cmd.Parameters.Add _
    (New SqlClient.SqlParameter("@DepartmentIDCriteria", _
    SqlDbType.SmallInt)).Value = Convert.ToInt32(txtDepartmentID.Text)
cmd.Parameters.Add _
    (New SqlClient.SqlParameter("@Name", _
    SqlDbType.NVarChar)).Value = txtName.Text
cmd.Parameters.Add _
    (New SqlClient.SqlParameter("@GroupName", _
    SqlDbType.NVarChar)).Value = txtGroupName.Text

'Execute the Insert statement
cmd.ExecuteNonQuery()

'Fill the DataSet with data from the updated row
strSQL = "SELECT DepartmentID, Name, GroupName " & _
    "FROM HumanResources.Department " & _
    "WHERE DepartmentID = '" & _
    txtDepartmentID.Text & "'"
da = New SqlClient.SqlDataAdapter(strSQL, conn)
da.Fill(ds, "DepartmentInformation")

'Display the contents of the stringbuilder object in a textbox
txtOutput.Text = ds.ToString

'Close the connection
conn.Close()

End Sub
```

> To run the code in Listing 15.13, you must enter the Department ID into the Department ID text box. You enter the new name and group name into the Name and Group Name text boxes, respectively.

By the Way

Listing 15.14 contains the code necessary when using the SqlCommand object to delete data. It sets the CommandText property to a DELETE statement. The code adds a parameter to the Parameters collection of the SqlCommand object. It uses this parameter to designate which department you want to delete. It is important to understand that the code contains no error handling. In a real-life application it is important to handle the occurrence of a user attempting to delete a department that may have associated child records, as well as any other potential problems that could occur.

LISTING 15.14   An Example That Uses the `SqlCommand` **Object to Delete Data from a Table**

```
Private Sub btnDelete_Click(ByVal sender As System.Object, _
ByVal e As System.EventArgs) Handles btnDelete.Click
    'Declare necessary variables
    Dim cmd As New SqlClient.SqlCommand()
    Dim conn As SqlClient.SqlConnection
    Dim da As New SqlClient.SqlDataAdapter()
    Dim ds As New DataSet()
    Dim strConn As String
    Dim strSQL As String

    'Build a connection string
    strConn = "Data Source=.\SQLEXPRESS;AttachDbFilename=" & _
        "'C:\Program Files\Microsoft SQL Server\" & _
        "MSSQL.1\MSSQL\Data\AdventureWorks_Data.mdf';" & _
        "Integrated Security=True;Connect Timeout=30;User Instance=True"

    'Instantiate the SqlConnection object, passing it the
    'connection string
    conn = New SqlClient.SqlConnection(strConn)

    'Open the connection
    conn.Open()

    'Instantiate the SqlCommand object
    cmd = New SqlClient.SqlCommand()

        'Set the CommandText property
        cmd.CommandText = "DELETE FROM HumanResources.Department " & _
            "WHERE DepartmentID = @DepartmentIDCriteria"

        'Designate the CommandType
        cmd.CommandType = CommandType.Text

        'Set the Connection property of the SqlCommand
        cmd.Connection = conn

        'Add parameters and set their values
        'NOTE THAT THE ORDER DOESN'T MATTER!
        cmd.Parameters.Add _
            (New SqlClient.SqlParameter("@DepartmentIDCriteria", _
            SqlDbType.NChar, 5)).Value = txtDepartmentID.Text

        'Execute the Delete statement
        cmd.ExecuteNonQuery()

        'Fill the DataSet with data from the deleted row
        strSQL = "SELECT DepartmentID, Name, GroupName " & _
            "FROM HumanResources.Department " & _
```

LISTING 15.14   Continued

```
            "WHERE DepartmentID = '" & _
            txtDepartmentID.Text & "'"
    da = New SqlClient.SqlDataAdapter(strSQL, conn)
    da.Fill(ds, "Departments")

    'Display the contents of the stringbuilder object in a textbox
    txtOutput.Text = ds.ToString

  'Close the connection
  conn.Close()

End Sub
```

Watch Out!

You cannot delete a department that has associated child records. If you attempt to do so, you will receive a referential integrity error.

By the Way

For the code in Listing 15.14 to run successfully, you must enter the DepartmentID of the department you want to delete into the DepartmentID text box.

Summary

ADO.NET revolutionizes the handling of data in Windows and Web applications. This chapter introduced you to ADO.NET. It began by discussing the history and benefits of ADO.NET. Next, it introduced you to the basics of ADO.NET as it delved into the important ADO.NET objects, exploring examples of each. Finally, you learned important techniques in modifying data with ADO.NET.

Q&A

Q. *Explain why ADO.NET is superior to its predecessors.*

A. ADO.NET is superb at dealing with disparate data formats and scalability in enterprise situations. It provides one programming model for accessing all types of data, no matter in what format it is stored and where it is stored. It utilizes XML to accomplish this task. Finally, ADO.NET is focused on disconnected operations, contributing to its scalability.

Q. *Name four methods of the* SqlCommand *object and explain what they do.*

A. The ExecuteReader method returns a forward-only DataReader object. The ExecuteScalar method returns a result of one column and one row. The ExecuteNonQuery method returns no results (you use it, for example, to update data). The ExecuteXLMReader method returns an XML version of a DataReader object.

Q. *Explain the benefits of the* SqlDataReader *object.*

A. It provides the fastest means for retrieving read-only sets of data. It supplies a forward-only, read-only, server-side cursor, loading only what it needs into memory.

Workshop

Quiz

1. Name five Microsoft data access methodologies.

2. Name which data access methodology was optimized for ODBC data.

3. What does the SqlConnection object do?

4. Why would you use a SqlCommand object?

5. What does the DataAdapter object do?

6. What does a DataSet object do?

Quiz Answers

1. DAO, RDO, OLEDB, ADO, and ADO.NET.

2. RDO.

3. It provides you with a consistent connection to data.

4. It enables you to execute commands that retrieve or update data.

5. It acts as a liaison between the permanent data store and the in-memory data store, enabling you to fully separate the DataSet from its underlying data store.

6. A powerful in-memory database that enables you to store and update relational or hierarchical data.

Activities

Write ADO code that retrieves data from the AdventureWorks table called Person.Contact. Have it display the FirstName, LastName, EmailAddress, and Phone in a text box. Write code to add a contact. Don't forget that you need to populate all fields that will not accept Nulls. Finally, write code to delete the contact that you just added.

HOUR 16

Using VB to Design SQL Server Stored Procedures

Just as you can execute a stored procedure written in T-SQL, you can also execute a stored procedure written in Visual Basic .NET. You'll probably agree that writing business logic in Visual Basic .NET is easier than writing it in T-SQL. As you'll see, the process of setting up a stored procedure written in Visual Basic .NET is somewhat more complicated than that of T-SQL. Fortunately, after you get the hang of it, it's not bad at all. In this hour you'll learn

- ► How to execute a simple Visual Basic .NET stored procedure
- ► How to declare and work with variables
- ► How to control the flow of the stored procedures that you create
- ► How to work with input and output parameters
- ► How to use stored procedures to modify data

Executing a Simple Stored Procedure

The stored procedure found in Listing 16.1 first opens a connection. It then creates a SQLCommand object that selects the last name, first name, email address, and hire date from the Contact table joined with the Employee table, ordering the result set by last name combined with first name. It uses the open connection (conn) to connect to data. The ExecuteReader command executes the SQL statement contained in the Command object, returning the result to the SqlDataReader object (rdr). Finally, the code sends the SqlDataReader object, via a pipe, back to SQL Server. You can find this code in the FirstSQLCLRClassVB solution, located on the sample code disk. The code is contained in the class called FirstSQLCLRVB.

By the Way

> To follow along with the example, create a project called `FirstSQLCLRClassVB` and a class called `FirstSQLCLRVB`.

LISTING 16.1   A Procedure That Lists Employees by Last Name and First Name

```
Public Shared Function ListEmployees() as Integer
    Dim conn As SqlConnection
    Dim cmd As SqlCommand
    Dim rdr As SqlDataReader

    SqlContext.Pipe.Send("Current Contacts as of: " & _
                            System.DateTime.Now.ToString() & _
                            "\n")
    conn = New SqlConnection("context connection=true")
    conn.Open()

    cmd = New SqlCommand("SELECT Person.Contact.LastName, " & _
        "Person.Contact.FirstName, Person.Contact.EmailAddress, " & _
        "HumanResources.Employee.HireDate FROM Person.Contact " & _
        "Inner Join HumanResources.Employee On " & _
        "Person.Contact.ContactID = HumanResources.Employee.ContactID " & _
        "ORDER BY LastName, FirstName", conn)
    rdr = cmd.ExecuteReader()
    SqlContext.Pipe.Send(rdr)
    Return 0
End Function
```

By the Way

> The code module containing the code in this chapter includes two `Imports` statements. These `Imports` statements look like this:
>
> ```
> Imports System.Data.SqlClient
> Imports Microsoft.SqlServer.Server
> ```
>
> Using these `Imports` statements enables you to shorten the code that you write. For example, you can shorten the code `Dim conn as System.Data.SqlClient.SQLConnection` to `Dim conn as SQLConnection`.

You must place the function in a Visual Basic 2005 class, and then build the solution to create a DLL. After you create the DLL you are ready for the next step. The next step is to register the assembly in SQL Server Management Studio Express. You do this with the code found in Listing 16.2.

LISTING 16.2 Registering the Assembly in SQL Server Management Studio Express

```
Use AdventureWorks
Go
CREATE ASSEMBLY [FirstSQLCLRClassVB]
FROM 'c:\Alisonsbook\firstsqlclrclassvb\bin\release\firstsqlclrclassvb.dll'
WITH PERMISSION_SET = SAFE
```

You simply create a new query in SQL Server Management Studio express, and paste this code found in Listing 16.2 into the query. You need to modify only the location of the DLL. Figure 16.1 shows Management Studio before executing the query. No assemblies are yet available. Figure 16.2 shows Management Studio after the query has been executed successfully. Note that the assembly is listed under the Assemblies node.

After you have registered the assembly, you are ready to add any of its functions as stored procedures within SQL Server. The code found in Listing 16.3 accomplishes this task.

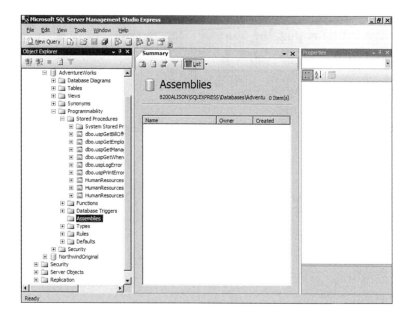

FIGURE 16.1
Before you execute the query, no assemblies are available.

FIGURE 16.2
After the query
is executed, the
assembly is
listed under the
Assemblies
node.

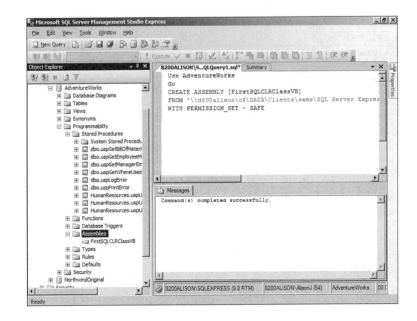

LISTING 16.3   Creating the Stored Procedure Called FirstListEmployees

```
CREATE PROCEDURE FirstListEmployeesVB
AS
EXTERNAL NAME
FirstSQLCLRClassVB.[FirstSQLCLRClassVB.FirstSQLCLRVB].ListEmployees
```

After the code in Listing 16.3 is executed, the stored procedure appears in the list of
stored procedures available within the database (see Figure 16.3). You execute the
stored procedure as you would any stored procedure (see Listing 16.4).

LISTING 16.4   Executing the Stored Procedure Called
FirstListEmployees

```
use Adventureworks
Go
exec FirstListEmployeesVB
```

By the
Way

If you receive an error message indicating that Execution of user code in
the .NET Framework is disabled, run the stored procedure sp_configure
'clr enabled', 1 and then reconfigure.

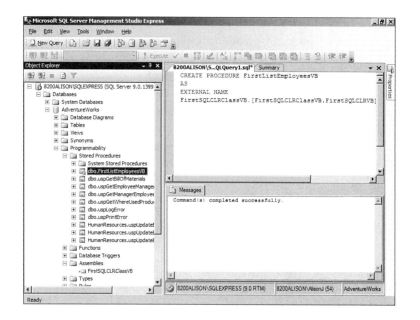

FIGURE 16.3
After you create the procedure, it is available in the list of stored procedures available within the database.

As shown in Listing 16.1, the stored procedure returns a SQLDataReader with the last name, first name, email address and hire date from the Contact table joined with the Employee table, ordering the result set by last name combined with first name. The results appear in Figure 16.4.

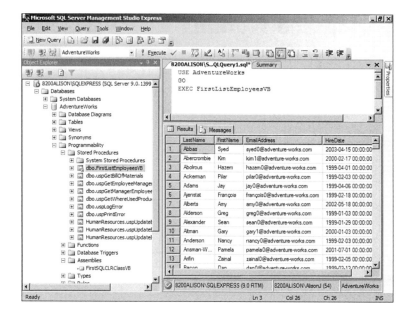

FIGURE 16.4
The stored procedure returns data to SQL Server Management Studio Express.

When you add a .NET stored procedure within the SQL Server Management Studio Express environment, you cannot modify it within SQL Server. Instead, you must return to Visual Studio .NET to make any changes to the stored procedure. This is evident in Figure 16.5. Notice that Modify is unavailable.

FIGURE 16.5
You cannot modify a .NET stored procedure from within the SQL Server Management Studio Express environment.

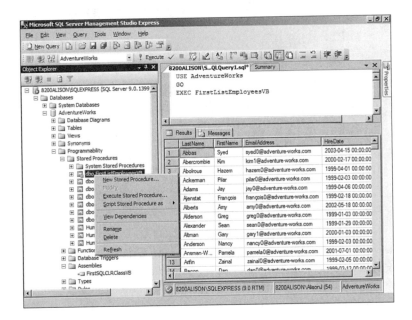

Declaring and Working with Variables

It is often necessary for your stored procedures to contain variables. This enables them to behave differently in different situations. Listing 16.5 provides an example. It receives a string parameter called orderBy. It then uses that parameter as a variable to determine the order by which the records appear in the output.

LISTING 16.5   A Stored Procedure That Uses a Variable

```
Public Shared Function ListEmployeesWithVariable _
    (ByVal orderBy As String) as Integer

    Dim conn As SqlConnection
    Dim cmd As SqlCommand
    Dim rdr As SqlDataReader

    SqlContext.Pipe.Send("Current Contacts as of: " & _
        System.DateTime.Now.ToString() + "\n")

    conn = New SqlConnection("context connection=true")
```

LISTING 16.5   Continued

```
  conn.Open()

  cmd = New SqlCommand("SELECT Person.Contact.LastName, " & _
      "Person.Contact.FirstName, Person.Contact.EmailAddress, " & _
      "HumanResources.Employee.HireDate " & _
      "FROM Person.Contact " & _
      "Inner Join HumanResources.Employee " & _
      "On Person.Contact.ContactID = HumanResources.Employee.ContactID " & _
      "ORDER BY " + orderBy.ToString(), conn)
  rdr = cmd.ExecuteReader()
  SqlContext.Pipe.Send(rdr)
  Return 0
End Function
```

Because the assembly was created earlier, there is no need to take that step again. It is necessary that you define the stored procedure within SQL Server Management Studio Express. The code in Listing 16.6 accomplishes this task. Notice that the code creates a SQL Server procedure called ListEmployeesUsingVariablesVB, based on the .NET procedure called ListEmployeesWithVariable.

> You must rebuild your project before creating the procedure in SQL Server Management Studio Express.

By the Way

LISTING 16.6   Creating the Stored Procedure Called
SecondListEmployees

```
CREATE PROCEDURE ListEmployeesUsingVariablesVB
(@OrderBy NVarChar(20))
AS
EXTERNAL NAME FirstSQLCLRClassVB.[FirstSQLCLRClassVB.FirstSQLCLRVB].
    ListEmployeesWithVariable
```

> You must add the code to the class module and then rebuild the assembly before you can run this code in Management Studio.

By the Way

You must pass the SecondListEmployees stored procedure a parameter when you execute it (see Listing 16.7). The stored procedure uses the parameter to determine the order of the output. The results of passing LastName and FirstName as parameters appear in Figure 16.7.

LISTING 16.7   Executing the Stored Procedure Called
ListEmployeesUsingVariables

```
use Adventureworks
Go
exec ListEmployeesUsingVariablesVB 'HireDate'
GO
Exec ListEmployeesUsingVariablesVB 'LastName, FirstName'
```

FIGURE 16.6
After parameters are passed to the stored procedure, the output appears in the specified order.

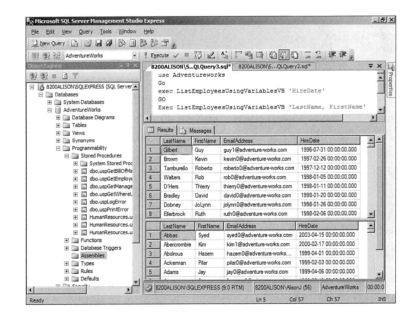

Controlling Program Flow

It is important to be able to determine the logical flow within a stored procedure. For example, you may want to evaluate the information passed into the stored procedure and respond differently depending on what information is passed. Listing 16.8 provides an example. It receives two parameters: one called chooseFieldsToUse, and the other called chooseOrderBy. The chooseFieldsToUse parameter is an integer variable used to indicate the fields that the procedure will display in the output. The chooseOrderBy parameter is also an integer variable used to indicate the order in which the stored procedure will display the output.

After a connection is opened, the stored procedure begins to build a string variable. The string variable begins with the keyword Select. The stored procedure then uses the keywords SELECT CASE to evaluate what was passed in as the chooseFieldsToUse parameter. If it was 1, the procedure concatenates LastName,

FirstName, EmailAddress, and HireDate onto the existing string. If it was 2, the procedure concatenates LastName, FirstName, Title, and Birthdate onto the existing
string. Finally, if it was 3, it concatenates LastName, FirstName, MaritalStatus, and
Gender onto the string. Now that the string contains the fields used in the SQL statement, the code concatenates the FROM statement onto the existing string. In the final
step of building the SQL statement, the stored procedure uses an If statement to
determine the order in which the output will appear. The stored procedure uses the
ExecuteReader method of the SqlCommand object to execute the SQL statement,
returning the results to a SQLDataReader object. The SQLDataReader object is then
returned to SQL Server.

LISTING 16.8   The Select Case **Command Used to Control the Flow
of a Stored Procedure**

```
Public Shared Function ControllingProgramFlow _
    (ByVal chooseFieldsToUse As Integer, _
    ByVal chooseOrderBy As Integer) as Integer

    Dim conn As SqlConnection
    Dim cmd As SqlCommand
    Dim rdr As SqlDataReader

    SqlContext.Pipe.Send("Current Contacts as of: " & _
        System.DateTime.Now.ToString() + "\n")

    conn = New SqlConnection("context connection=true")

    conn.Open()

    Dim sql As String = "Select "

    'First way to control flow of program, switch...case code block.
    Select Case chooseFieldsToUse

        Case 1
            sql += "Person.Contact.LastName, Person.Contact.FirstName, " & _
            "Person.Contact.EmailAddress, HumanResources.Employee.HireDate"

        Case 2
            sql += "Person.Contact.LastName, Person.Contact.FirstName, " & _
            "HumanResources.Employee.Title, HumanResources.Employee.BirthDate"

        Case 3
            sql += "Person.Contact.LastName, Person.Contact.FirstName, " & _
            "HumanResources.Employee.MaritalStatus, " & _
            HumanResources.Employee.Gender"
    End Select

    sql += " FROM Person.Contact Inner Join HumanResources.Employee " & _
    " On Person.Contact.ContactID = HumanResources.Employee.ContactID ORDER BY "

    'Another way, using the if...else code block.
    If (chooseOrderBy = 1) Then
```

LISTING 16.8   Continued

```
        sql += "LastName, FirstName"
    Else
        sql += "HireDate"
    End If

    cmd = New SqlCommand(sql, conn)
    rdr = cmd.ExecuteReader()
    SqlContext.Pipe.Send(rdr)
    Return 0
End Function
```

Before executing the stored procedure, you must define it within SQL Server
Management Studio Express. The code in Listing 16.9 accomplishes this task. It creates a procedure called ControlFieldsAndOrderByVB based on the .NET function
called ControllingProgramFlow.

**LISTING 16.9   Adding the ControlFieldsAndOrderBy Procedure to
SQL Server**

```
Use Adventureworks
Go
CREATE PROCEDURE ControlFieldsAndOrderByVB(@FieldsToUse int, @OrderBy int)
AS
EXTERNAL NAME
FirstSQLCLRClassVB.[FirstSQLCLRClassVB.FirstSQLCLRVB].ControllingProgramFlow
```

**By the
Way**

> Each time that you add a procedure to a class you need to rebuild the assembly
> and reregister it. To reregister an assembly you must first drop the stored proce-
> dures in the existing assembly and then drop the existing assembly. You can then
> reregister the assembly as you did when you first created it.

Now that you have defined the stored procedure to SQL Server, you are ready to execute it. Listing 16.10 provides two examples. The first displays LastName, FirstName,
EmailAddress, and HireDate ordered by HireDate. The second displays LastName,
FirstName, MaritalStatus, and Gender ordered by LastName and FirstName. Figure
16.7 shows the ControlFieldsAndOrderByVB stored procedure first with 1 and 2
passed as parameters, and then with 3 and 1 passed as parameters.

**LISTING 16.10   Executing the procedure called
ControlFieldsAndOrderByVB**

```
Use AdventureWorks
Go
Exec ControlFieldsAndOrderByVB 1,2
Go
Exec ControlFieldsAndOrderByVB 3,1
```

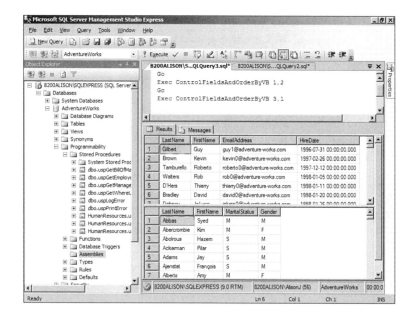

FIGURE 16.7
The output appears with different fields and in different orders.

Working with Parameters

Some stored procedures receive and return parameters. When a stored procedure receives a parameter, we refer to it as an *input parameter*. When a stored procedure returns a parameter, we refer to it as an *output parameter*. The following two sections illustrate the use of input parameters and output parameters.

Input Parameters

As mentioned, input parameters are used to supply information to a stored procedure. The code in Listing 16.11 illustrates this process. As with the other examples, it first opens a connection. The code then instantiates a SQL command object. The key to this example is the SQL statement used when the command object is instantiated. Notice that the SQL statement contains a Where clause that compares the LastName field to @LastName, using the open connection. The next line of code adds @LastName as a parameter to the parameters collection of the command object. After the code adds the parameter, it then sets its value to the value that was passed to the function (searchLastName). Finally, the ExecuteReader method uses the command object, along with its input parameter, to return the specified fields with the designated Where clause. An example of the output appears in Figure 16.8.

LISTING 16.11   A Stored Procedure That Receives Input Parameters

```
Public Shared Function ListEmployeesUsingInputParameter _
    (ByVal searchLastName As String)

    Dim conn As SqlConnection
    Dim cmd As SqlCommand
    Dim rdr As SqlDataReader

    SqlContext.Pipe.Send("Current Contacts as of: " & _
                    System.DateTime.Now.ToString() & _
                    "\n")
    conn = New SqlConnection("context connection=true")

    conn.Open()
    cmd = New SqlCommand("SELECT Person.Contact.LastName, " & _
        "Person.Contact.FirstName, Person.Contact.EmailAddress, " & _
        "HumanResources.Employee.HireDate " & _
        "FROM Person.Contact Inner Join HumanResources.Employee " & _
        "On Person.Contact.ContactID = HumanResources.Employee.ContactID " & _
        "Where Person.Contact.LastName Like @LastName", conn)
    cmd.Parameters.Add("@LastName", SqlDbType.NVarChar)
    cmd.Parameters(0).Value = searchLastName

    rdr = cmd.ExecuteReader()
    SqlContext.Pipe.Send(rdr)
    Return 0
End Function
```

As usual, you must first create the stored procedure within SQL Server Management Studio Express before you can execute it. Because of the use of the input parameter, this process is slightly different than in the other examples. Listing 16.12 provides an example. Note that when you declare the stored procedure, you declare the name of the parameter and its type.

LISTING 16.12   Creating a Stored Procedure That Receives Input Parameters

```
Use AdventureWorks
Go
CREATE PROCEDURE ListEmployeesUsingInputParameterVB(@lastName NVarChar(50))
AS
EXTERNAL NAME FirstSQLCLRClassVB.[FirstSQLCLRClassVB.FirstSQLCLRVB].
    ListEmployeesUsingInputParameter
```

To execute the stored procedure, you must pass the designated parameter(s). Listing 16.13 provides a couple of examples. It first passes the letter B along with a wildcard character. This returns all records where the contents of the LastName field begin with B. The stored procedure then executes again with the letter C and the same wildcard. Figure 16.8 shows the results of executing the stored procedure.

LISTING 16.13 Executing a Stored Procedure That Receives Input Parameters

```
Use AdventureWorks
Go
Exec ListEmployeesUsingInputParameterVB 'B%'
Go
Exec ListEmployeesUsingInputParameterVB 'C%'
```

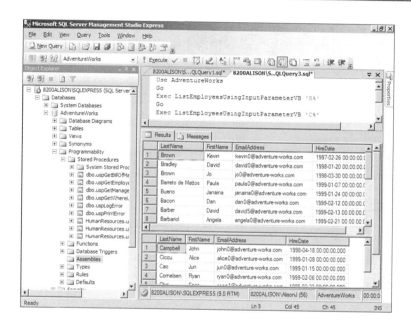

FIGURE 16.8
The output appears with specified last names.

Working with Output Parameters

Working with output parameters is similar to working with input parameters. The difference is that SQL Server returns information from the stored procedure rather than the stored procedure receiving something. Listing 16.14 provides an example. Using an IF statement to control the logical flow of the stored procedure, the code within the stored procedure builds a string containing a SQL Select statement. This SQL statement varies depending on the contents of the ProductNumber field passed into the function. The code then instantiates a SqlCommand object, using the SQL statement just built. The code then adds three parameters and sets their values. The first two are input parameters and contain the values passed into the function. The third parameter is an output parameter and contains the value of @MyMessage, set in the IF statement. Finally, the ExecuteReader method executes the stored procedure, sending the results to SQL Server.

LISTING 16.14   A Stored Procedure That Receives Output Parameters

```
Public Shared Function ListEmployeesUsingOutputParameter _
    (ByVal productNumber As String, ByVal color As String)
    as Integer

    Dim conn As SqlConnection
    Dim cmd As SqlCommand
    Dim rdr As SqlDataReader

    conn = New SqlConnection("context connection=true")

    conn.Open()

    Dim sql As String = "IF @ProductNumber IS Null"
    sql += "    BEGIN"
    sql += "        SELECT Name FROM Production.Product WHERE Color = @Color"
    sql += "        SELECT @MyMessage = 'No Product Number'"
    sql += "    END "
    sql += "ELSE"
    sql += "    BEGIN"
    sql += "        SELECT Name FROM Production.Product " & _
        "WHERE ProductNumber = @ProductNumber"
    sql += "        SELECT @MyMessage = 'Product Number Supplied'"
    sql += "    END "
    sql += "SELECT @MyMessage"


        cmd = New SqlCommand(sql, conn)

        cmd.Parameters.Add("@ProductNumber", SqlDbType.VarChar,20)
        cmd.Parameters(0).Value = productNumber
        cmd.Parameters.Add("@Color", SqlDbType.VarChar,20)
        cmd.Parameters(1).Value = color
        cmd.Parameters.Add("@MyMessage", SqlDbType.VarChar,30)
        cmd.Parameters(2).Direction = System.Data.ParameterDirection.Output

        rdr = cmd.ExecuteReader()
        SqlContext.Pipe.Send(rdr)

        Return 0
    End Function
```

Once again, you must add the stored procedure before executing it (see Listing 16.15). Notice that the declaration includes only the input parameters. It is not necessary to declare the output parameters.

LISTING 16.15   Adding a Stored Procedure That Receives Input Parameters

```
Use AdventureWorks
Go
CREATE PROCEDURE ListEmployeesUsingOutputParameterVB
    (@productNumber NVarChar(25), @color NVarChar(15))
```

LISTING 16.15 Continued

```
AS
EXTERNAL NAME
FirstSQLCLRClassVB.[FirstSQLCLRClassVB.FirstSQLCLRVB].ListEmployeesUsingOutputPa
rameter
```

When you execute the stored procedure, you must pass the appropriate input parameters. In other words, they must be the proper data type. Listing 16.16 provides two examples. The first receives Null and Black as input parameters. To view the output parameters, you must select Query, Results, Results to Text from the SQL Server Management Studio Express menu. After you scroll below the output from the SELECT statement, the results appear in Figure 16.9.

LISTING 16.16 Executing a Stored Procedure That Returns Output Parameters

```
Use AdventureWorks
Go
Exec ListEmployeesUsingOutputParameterVB NULL, "Black"
Go
Exec ListEmployeesUsingOutputParameterVB 'BA-8327', NULL
```

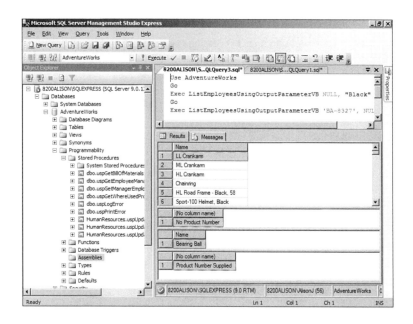

FIGURE 16.9
The result of executing a stored procedure with an output parameter.

Modifying Data with Stored Procedures

Not only can you use Visual Basic 2005 stored procedures to retrieve data, you can use them to insert, update, and delete data as well. The sections that follow illustrate this process.

Using Stored Procedures to Insert Data

You will often want to use a stored procedure to insert data. The function in Listing 16.17 provides an example. It receives two parameters: departmentName and groupName. The code instantiates and opens a connection. It then builds a SQL INSERT statement that inserts into the HumanResources.Department table the values passed into the function. Next, the code instantiates a SqlCommand object, passing it the SQL statement and the open connection. Finally, it uses the ExecuteNonQuery method of the SqlCommand object to execute the SQL statement.

LISTING 16.17   A Stored Procedure That Inserts Data

```
Public Shared Function InsertingData(ByVal departmentName As String, _
    ByVal groupName As String)

    Dim conn As SqlConnection
    Dim cmd As SqlCommand

    conn = New SqlConnection("context connection=true")

    conn.Open()

    Dim sql As String = "INSERT INTO HumanResources.Department " & _
        "(Name, GroupName) VALUES ('" & departmentName.ToString() & _
        "', '" & groupName.ToString() & "')"

    cmd = New SqlCommand(sql, conn)
    cmd.ExecuteNonQuery()

    Return 0
End Function
```

As with all the other examples, you must first add the stored procedure to SQL Server Management Studio Express before you can execute it. Listing 16.18 provides the necessary code.

LISTING 16.18   Inserting a Stored Procedure That Inserts Data

```
Use AdventureWorks
Go
CREATE PROCEDURE InsertingDataVB(@departmentName NVarChar(50),
    @groupName NVarChar(50))
```

LISTING 16.18   Continued

```
AS
EXTERNAL NAME
FirstSQLCLRClassVB.[FirstSQLCLRClassVB.FirstSQLCLRVB].InsertingData
```

To execute the stored procedure, you simply pass it the necessary parameters. Listing 16.19 provides an example. Figure 16.10 shows the results of executing the query.

LISTING 16.19   Executing a Stored Procedure That Inserts Data

```
Use AdventureWorks
Go
Exec InsertingDataVB 'Widget Creation', 'Manufacturing'
```

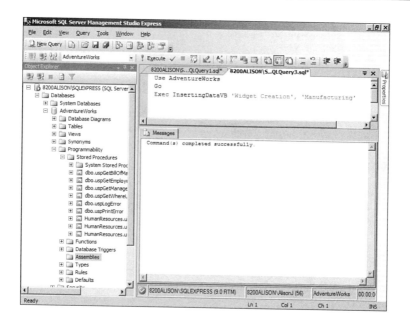

FIGURE 16.10
The result of executing a stored procedure that inserts data.

Using Stored Procedures to Update Data

Of course, in addition to using a stored procedure to insert data, you also will want to use a stored procedure to update data. Listing 16.20 provides an example. Like the INSERT example, it receives two input parameters. After opening a connection it builds a SQL UPDATE statement. Notice that the UPDATE statement contains a WHERE clause. The WHERE clause determines what record(s) the stored procedure will update.

Again, the code uses the ExecuteNonQuery method of the SQLCommand object to execute the update statement.

LISTING 16.20   A Stored Procedure That Updates Data

```
Public Shared Function UpdatingData(ByVal departmentName As String, _
    ByVal groupName As String) as Integer
    Dim conn As SqlConnection
    Dim cmd As SqlCommand

    conn = New SqlConnection("context connection=true")

    conn.Open()

    Dim sql As String = "UPDATE HumanResources.Department SET " & _
        "GroupName = '" + groupName.ToString() & "' WHERE Name = '" & _
        departmentName.ToString() + "'"

    cmd = New SqlCommand(sql, conn)
    cmd.ExecuteNonQuery()

    Return 0
End Function
```

The code in Listing 16.21 declares the stored procedure to SQL Server Management Studio Express. Notice that it receives two parameters.

LISTING 16.21   Declaring a Stored Procedure That Updates Data

```
Use AdventureWorks
Go
CREATE PROCEDURE UpdatingDataVB(@departmentNameVB NVarChar(50),
    @groupName NVarChar(50))
AS
EXTERNAL NAME FirstSQLCLRClassVB.[FirstSQLCLRClassVB.FirstSQLCLRVB].UpdatingData
```

To execute the stored procedure, simply pass the two parameters (see Listing 16.22). The results appear in Figure 16.11.

LISTING 16.22   Executing a Stored Procedure That Updates Data

```
Use AdventureWorks
Go
Exec UpdatingDataVB 'Widget Creation', 'Changed to New Group'
```

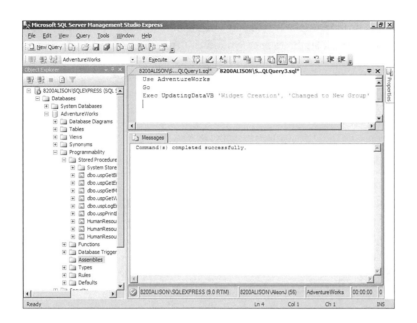

FIGURE 16.11
The result of executing a stored procedure updates data.

Using Stored Procedures to Delete Data

You can also use stored procedures to delete data. Listing 16.23 provides an example. It receives a parameter containing a department name. After opening a connection, it builds a SQL DELETE statement with a WHERE clause containing the department name that came in as a parameter. It instantiates the SqlCommand object, using the SQL statement and the connection as parameters. Finally, it uses the ExecuteNonQuery method of the SqlCommand object to execute the DELETE statement.

LISTING 16.23   A Stored Procedure That Deletes Data

```
Public Shared Function DeletingData(ByVal departmentName As String)


    Dim conn As SqlConnection
    Dim cmd As SqlCommand

    conn = New SqlConnection("context connection=true")

    conn.Open()

    Dim sql As String = "DELETE FROM HumanResources.Department " & _
        "WHERE Name = '" + departmentName.ToString() + "'"

    cmd = New SqlCommand(sql, conn)
    cmd.ExecuteNonQuery()
    Return 0
End Function
```

As with the other example, before you can execute the stored procedure within SQL Server Management Studio Express, you must first declare it. Listing 16.24 provides an example.

LISTING 16.24   Declaring a Stored Procedure That Deletes Data

```
Use AdventureWorks
Go
CREATE PROCEDURE DeletingDataVB(@departmentName NVarChar(50))
AS
EXTERNAL NAME FirstSQLCLRClassVB.[FirstSQLCLRClassVB.FirstSQLCLRVB].DeletingData
```

Finally, to execute the stored procedure, you simply pass it any required parameters (see Listing 16.25). SQL Server executes the SQL statement. The results appear in Figure 16.12.

LISTING 16.25   Executing a Stored Procedure That Deletes Data

```
Use AdventureWorks
Go
Exec DeletingDataVB 'Widget Creation'
```

FIGURE 16.12
The result of executing a stored procedure that updates data.

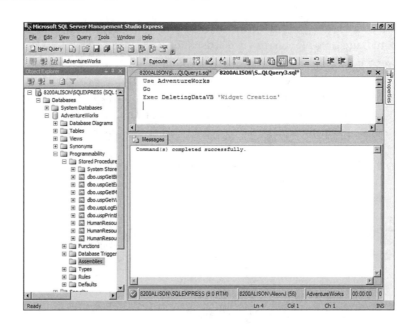

Summary

It is generally easier to write business logic in Visual Basic 2005 than it is in T-SQL. It is therefore important that you understand how to build procedures within Visual Studio 2005 and execute them from within SQL Server. In this hour you learned how to write, declare, and execute stored procedures written in the Visual Basic .NET language.

Q&A

Q. *Discuss the process of building and executing a Visual Basic .NET stored procedure.*

A. You must first write the stored procedure in the Visual Basic .NET language within a Visual Studio .NET class. You then build the project. You must then declare the stored procedure within SQL Server Management Studio Express. Finally, you can execute it just as you would any other stored procedure.

Q. *Explain what logical flow is within a stored procedure.*

A. Logical flow is when you want to react differently within a stored procedure depending on certain situations. For example, you may want to respond in a special manner if a parameter is passed in as NULL.

Q. *Describe the purpose of output parameters.*

A. Output parameters enable you to supply information back to the calling program about what happened within the stored procedure.

Workshop

Quiz

1. Name the object that you use to return data to SQL Server.

2. What keywords do you use when controlling the flow?

3. Output parameters do not display in Grid View (true/false).

4. What syntax do you use to add a parameter to a stored procedure?

5. You use the keyword EDIT when updating data within a stored procedure (true/false).

6. What is the method that you use to execute a SQL statement that does not return data (it inserts, updates, or deletes instead)?

Quiz Answers

1. `SqlDataReader`.

2. `Switch` and `If`.

3. False. They will only display in Text view.

4. `cmd.parameters.add`.

5. False. You use the keyword UPDATE.

6. `ExecuteNonQuery`.

Activities

Create, build, declare, and execute a stored procedure that retrieves data from the Production.Product table. Return the contents of the ProductID, Name, ProductNumber, Color, ReorderPoint, and ListPrice in the result set. Create, build, declare, and execute another stored procedure that receives one input parameter and returns one output parameter. The input parameter is an int, and will contain the ProductID. The procedure will evaluate the reorder point for that product. If it is less than 500, the output parameter will contain the text "Low Reorder Point." Otherwise, the output parameter will contain the text "High Reorder Point." Practice executing the stored procedure, passing it different ProductID values.

HOUR 17

Visual Basic .NET Special Topics

You can use some special techniques to write more robust and powerful stored procedures. In this hour you'll learn

- ▶ How to work with temporary tables
- ▶ How to add error handling to your stored procedures
- ▶ How to use transaction processing within your stored procedures

Working with Temporary Tables

Temporary tables can be useful in certain situations. When you need them they are invaluable. A temporary table can contain data from heterogeneous data sources (even a text file). Using temporary tables, you have access to methods that facilitate data access and retrieval. These methods enable you to sort, filter, index, and select a table's rows.

The stored procedure found in Listing 17.1 first opens a connection. It then builds a string. The string first defines the structure of a temporary table. You know that the table is temporary because of the pound sign (#) preceding the table name. The string then contains an INSERT INTO statement that inserts into the temporary table the results of selecting data from the Person.Contact table. Finally, the SQL statement selects the contents of the LastName and FirstName fields from the temporary table, ordering the results by LastName and FirstName.

After building the string, the code instantiates a command object, passing it the SQL statement along with a reference to the open connection. The ExecuteReader method of the command object executes the SQL statement contained in the command object, returning the result to the SqlDataReader object (rdr). Finally, the code sends the SqlDataReader object, via a pipe, back to SQL Server. If you had selected data from the Person.Contact table, because no sort was applied, the data would have appeared in ContactID order. Because you selected the data from the temporary table, ordering the results by LastName combined with FirstName, the data appears in the specified order. You can find this code in the `FirstSQLCLRClassVB` solution, located on the sample code disk. The code is contained in the class called `FirstSQLCLRVB`.

LISTING 17.1   A Procedure That Uses a Temporary Table

```
Public Shared Function UsingTemporaryTables() as Integer

        Dim conn As SqlConnection = New _
            SqlConnection("context connection=true")

        conn.Open()

        Dim sql As String = "CREATE TABLE #TempContacts"
        sql += "            (ContactID int NOT NULL PRIMARY KEY, "
        sql += "            LastName varchar(50), "
        sql += "            FirstName varchar(50))"
        sql += "  INSERT INTO #TempContacts "
        sql += "  (ContactID, LastName, FirstName) "
        sql += "  SELECT Person.Contact.ContactID, "
        sql += "  Person.Contact.LastName, "
        sql += "  Person.Contact.FirstName From Person.Contact"
        sql += "  SELECT LastName, FirstName FROM #TempContacts " & _
            "ORDER BY LastName, FirstName"


        Dim cmd As SqlCommand = New SqlCommand(sql, conn)

        Dim rdr As SqlDataReader = cmd.ExecuteReader()
        SqlContext.Pipe.Send(rdr)
        Return 0
    End Function
```

You must place the function in a Visual Basic .NET class, and then build the solution to create a DLL. After you create the DLL you are ready for the next step. If you have not yet registered the `FirstSQLCLRClassVB.dll`, the next step is to register the assembly in SQL Server Management Studio Express. This process was covered in Hour 16.

If you try to register an assembly, and it is already registered, you get an error. You must first delete the assembly from within Management Studio and then reregister it. Before you can delete an assembly, you must first delete all the stored procedures within it. In summary, when you update a DLL, you must go through the process of deleting the stored procedures, deleting the assembly, adding the assembly, and adding the stored procedures. You can easily use a SQL script to help you with this process. Note that if available, the assembly is listed under the Assemblies node (see Figure 17.1) .

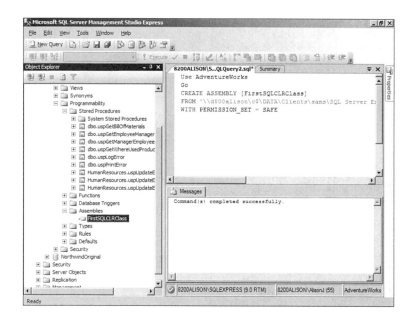

FIGURE 17.1
After the query
is executed, the
assembly is
listed under the
Assemblies
node.

After you have ensured that the assembly is registered, you are ready to add any of
its functions as stored procedures within SQL Server. The code found in Listing 17.2
accomplishes this task.

LISTING 17.2   Creating the Stored Procedure Called `TemporaryTables`

```
CREATE PROCEDURE TemporaryTables
AS
EXTERNAL NAME
    FirstSQLCLRClassVB.[FirstSQLCLRClassVB.FirstSQLCLRVB].UsingTemporaryTables
```

You execute the stored procedure as you would any stored procedure (see Listing
17.3).

LISTING 17.3   Executing the Stored Procedure Called
`FirstListEmployees`

```
use Adventureworks
Go
exec TemporaryTables
```

As shown previously in Listing 17.1, the stored procedure returns a `SQLDataReader`
with the last name and first name from the Contact table, ordering the result set by
last name combined with first name. The results appear in Figure 17.2.

FIGURE 17.2
The stored pro-
cedure returns
data sorted by
last name and
first name.

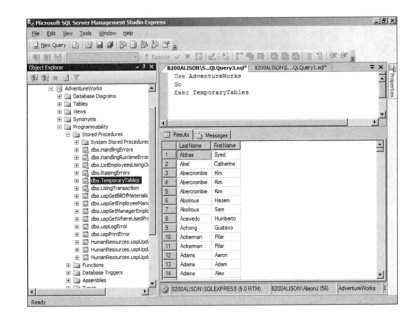

Including Error Handling in the Stored Procedures that You Build

All stored procedures should contain error handling. In this way *you* control what happens when an error occurs. In Listing 17.4 the code first evaluates the groupName parameter to determine whether it is Null. If it is Null, the code sends the text Group Name must be filled in. back to SQL Server. Otherwise, the code instanti-ates a new connection. It opens the connection, then builds a string containing a SQL IF statement. The statement evaluates the DepartmentName parameter. If it is Null, the statement builds a SELECT statement, selecting the text No Department Name and DepartmentID = 0. Otherwise (Department Name Not Null), the code builds an INSERT INTO statement that inserts data into the HumanResources.Department table and a SELECT statement that selects the mes-sage Success and the DepartmentID of @@Identity. @@Identity is a system vari-able that contains the primary key value of the last inserted row. Finally, the code instantiates a command object, setting its parameters to the parameter values passed into the stored procedure. It uses the execute method of the command object to execute the stored procedure, sending the results back to SQL Server.

LISTING 17.4 A Stored Procedure Containing Error Handling

```
Public Shared Function HandlingRuntimeErrors(ByVal departmentName As String, _
        ByVal groupName As String)

        If groupName = "" Then
            'Error handled in Visual Basic .NET
            SqlContext.Pipe.Send("Group Name must be filled in.")
        Else

            Dim conn As SqlConnection =
                New SqlConnection("context connection=true")

            conn.Open()
            'Error handled in T-SQL
            Dim sql As String = "IF @DepartmentName Is Null "
            sql += "    BEGIN "
            sql += "        SELECT Message = 'No Department Name', "
            sql += "        DepartmentID = 0"
            sql += "    END "
            sql += "ELSE "
            sql += "    BEGIN "
            sql += "        INSERT INTO "
            sql += "        HumanResources.Department(Name, GroupName) "
            sql += "        VALUES (@DepartmentName, @GroupName) "
            sql += "        SELECT Message = "
            sql += "        'Success', DepartmentID = @@Identity "
            sql += "    END "

            Dim cmd = New SqlCommand(sql, conn)
            cmd.Parameters.Add(New SqlParameter _
                ("@DepartmentName", System.Data.SqlDbType.VarChar, 50))
            cmd.Parameters(0).Value = departmentName
            cmd.Parameters.Add(New SqlParameter _
                ("@GroupName", System.Data.SqlDbType.VarChar, 50))
            cmd.Parameters(1).Value = groupName

            Dim rdr As SqlDataReader = cmd.ExecuteReader()
            SqlContext.Pipe.Send(rdr)

        End If
        Return 0

    End Function
```

Because the assembly was created earlier, there is no need to take that step again. It is necessary that you define the stored procedure within SQL Server Management Studio Express. The code in Listing 17.5 accomplishes this task. Notice that the code creates a SQL Server procedure called HandlingErrors based on the .NET procedure called HandlingRuntimeErrors.

> If you are building the samples yourself, rather than executing the sample code, you must unregister and reregister the component so that it can see the new procedure. The process of registering a component is covered in Hour 16. It is important to note that before you can unregister the component, you must first delete any stored procedures associated with it. You must then use the CREATE PROCEDURE statement to re-establish the stored procedures within management studio.

LISTING 17.5   Creating the Stored Procedure Called SecondListEmployees

```
CREATE PROCEDURE HandlingErrors
(@DepartmentName NVarChar(20), @GroupName NVarChar(2))
AS
EXTERNAL NAME
FirstSQLCLRClassVB.[FirstSQLCLRClassVB.FirstSQLCLRVB].HandlingRuntimeErrors
```

You must pass the HandlingErrors stored procedure two parameters when you execute it (see Listing 17.6). The first is the department name, and the second is the group name. The results of passing DVD Department and Null as parameters the first time, and then Null and Manufacturing as parameters the second time, appear in Figure 17.3 and Figure 17.4.

LISTING 17.6   Executing the Stored Procedure Called HandlingErrors

```
Use AdventureWorks
Go
Exec HandlingErrors 'DVD Department', Null
Go
Exec HandlingErrors Null, 'Manufacturing'
```

Notice that whereas the Send method sends the specified *text* to the Messages pane (see Figure 17.3), it sends the DataReader object to the Results pane (see Figure 17.4).

Sometimes you may actually want to raise errors in your code. You may want to do this to simulate an error condition in your application, or to treat a user error like a system error, passing it through your standard error handler. Listing 17.7 provides an example. The procedure receives two parameters, departmentName and groupName. It instantiates and opens a connection. It then builds a SQL statement that inserts data into the HumanResources.Department table, using the parameter values passed to the procedure. Next it sets DepartmentID equal to the value of @@Identity, the system variable containing the primary key value of the last inserted row. After the procedure builds the SQL statement, it declares and instantiates a command object. It then adds parameters to the command object, setting their values to the values passed in as parameters to the procedure. Next it uses the

ExecuteAndSend method of the SqlContext.Pipe object, passing it the command object, to return the results of the SQL statement to SQL Server. The difference between this procedure and the HandlingErrors procedure lies in the Catch block. If an error occurs, the code uses the Send method of the SqlContext.Pipe object to send a custom error message back to SQL Server.

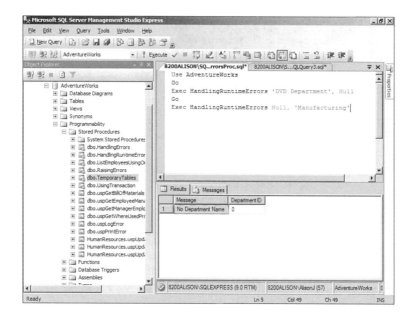

FIGURE 17.3
After parameters are passed to the stored procedure, the output appears with appropriate errors on the Results tab.

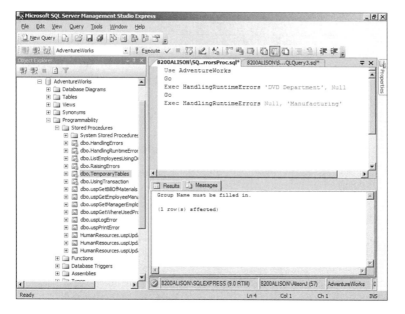

FIGURE 17.4
After parameters are passed to the stored procedure, the output appears with appropriate errors on the Messages tab.

LISTING 17.7   Sending a Custom Error Message to SQL Server

```
Public Shared Function RaisingErrors(ByVal departmentName As String, _
    ByVal groupName As String) As Integer

    Try

        Dim conn As SqlConnection = New SqlConnection("context connection=true")

        conn.Open()
        Dim sql As String = "SET NOCOUNT ON INSERT INTO "
        sql += "HumanResources.Department(Name, GroupName) VALUES "
        sql += "(@DepartmentName, @GroupName) "
        sql += "SELECT DepartmentID = @@Identity"

        Dim cmd As SqlCommand = New SqlCommand(sql, conn)
        cmd.Parameters.Add(New SqlParameter("@DepartmentName", _
            System.Data.SqlDbType.VarChar, 50))
        cmd.Parameters(0).Value = departmentName
        cmd.Parameters.Add(New SqlParameter("@GroupName", _
            System.Data.SqlDbType.VarChar, 50))
        cmd.Parameters(1).Value = groupName

        SqlContext.Pipe.ExecuteAndSend(cmd)

    Catch ex As Exception

        'This error will get sent, rather than the other,
        'to suppress this, comment out the next line.
        SqlContext.Pipe.Send("An exception occurred during the " & _
        "execution of RaisingErrors " + ex.ToString())

    End Try

    Return 0

End Function
```

Before you execute the stored procedure, you must define it within SQL Server
Management Studio Express. The code in Listing 17.8 accomplishes this task. It
creates a procedure called RaisingErrors based on the .NET function called
RaisingErrors.

**LISTING 17.8   Adding the Procedure Called RaisingErrors to
SQL Server**

```
Use AdventureWorks
Go
CREATE PROCEDURE RaisingErrors(@departmentName NVarChar(50), @groupName
NVarChar(50))
AS
EXTERNAL NAME
FirstSQLCLRClassVB.[FirstSQLCLRClassVB.FirstSQLCLRVB].RaisingErrors
```

Now that you have defined the stored procedure to SQL Server, you are ready to execute it. Listing 17.9 provides an example. It passed Widget Department and Null as parameters to the stored procedure. Figure 17.5 shows the resulting error message. Notice that the highlighted text contains the text that the procedure sent when it raised the error.

LISTING 17.9 **Executing the Procedure Called** RaisingErrors

```
Use AdventureWorks
Go
Exec RaisingErrors 'DVD Department', Null
```

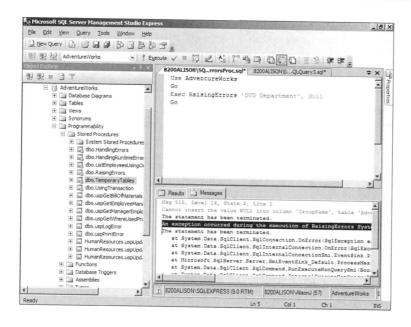

FIGURE 17.5
The output appears with the custom error message.

Using Transactions to Protect Your Data

Sometimes you want to ensure that a series of statements execute completely or not at all. For example, if you were performing a bank transaction you would want to ensure that both the debit and credit occurred before committing the data. Transactions can help you solve this dilemma. Listing 17.10 provides an example.

The code begins by using a try...catch block to establish error handling. It then declares and instantiates a connection object. It opens the connection and then begins to build a SQL string. The SQL string first declares three variables:

@DepartmentID, @LocalError, and @LocalRows. The code then adds a BEGIN TRANSACTION statement to the SQL string. From this point on, everything that follows is part of a transaction. Next the code adds an INSERT INTO statement to the SQL statement, inserting the parameter values into the appropriate fields in the HumanResources.Department table. The code immediately tests to see whether an error occurred by testing the values of the system variables @@Error and @@Rowcount. @@Error contains the number of the error that occurred, and @@Rowcount contains the number of rows affected by the SQL statement that immediately precedes it.

After the error number and the number of rows affected have been captured, the code evaluates them to determine whether their values are indicative of problems. A non-zero error number means that an error occurred. Zero rows affected also means that an error occurred. If @LocalError is non-zero or @LocalRows is zero, a ROLLBACK TRANSACTION occurs. The ROLLBACK TRANSACTION obliterates any processing that occurred since the BEGIN TRANSACTION statement. An END statement then terminates processing. Otherwise, the code attempts to commit the transaction. It sets the DepartmentID equal to the value of the system variable @@Identity. It sets the value of Error equal to zero and the value of NumRows equal to @LocalRows.

After the SQL statement is built, it is time to execute it. The code declares and instantiates a command object. It then adds two parameters to the command object, one for departmentName and one for groupName. The code uses the ExecuteAndSend method of the SQLContext.Pipe object to execute the SQL statement, returning the results to SQL Server.

If an error occurs during processing, execution jumps to the Catch block. The Catch block sends the message Transaction Rolled Back to SQL Server. If no error occurs, the COMMIT TRAN statement commits the data to disk.

LISTING 17.10   A Stored Procedure That Receives Input Parameters

```
Public Shared Function UsingTransaction(ByVal departmentName As String, _
    ByVal groupName As String) As Integer

    Try
        Dim conn As SqlConnection = _
            New SqlConnection("context connection=true")

        conn.Open()
        Dim sql As String = "SET NOCOUNT ON "
        sql += "DECLARE @DepartmentID int, @LocalError int, @LocalRows int "
        sql += "BEGIN TRANSACTION "
        sql += "INSERT INTO HumanResources.Department(Name, GroupName) "
        sql += "VALUES (@DepartmentName, @GroupName) "
        sql += "SELECT @LocalError = @@Error, @LocalRows = @@RowCount "
        sql += "IF NOT @LocalError = 0 or @LocalRows = 0 "
```

LISTING 17.10   Continued

```
sql += "   BEGIN "
sql += "       ROLLBACK TRANSACTION "
sql += "           SELECT DepartmentID = Null, Error = @LocalError, "
sql += "NumRows = @LocalRows "
sql += "   END "
sql += "ELSE "
sql += "   BEGIN "
sql += "       COMMIT TRAN "
sql += "           SELECT @DepartmentID = @@Identity "
sql += "           SELECT DepartmentID = @DepartmentID, Error = 0, "
sql += "           NumRows = @LocalRows "
sql += "   END "

Dim cmd As SqlCommand = New SqlCommand(sql, conn)
cmd.Parameters.Add(New SqlParameter _
    ("@DepartmentName", System.Data.SqlDbType.VarChar, 50))
cmd.Parameters(0).Value = departmentName
cmd.Parameters.Add(New SqlParameter("@GroupName", _
    System.Data.SqlDbType.VarChar, 50))
cmd.Parameters(1).Value = groupName
  SqlContext.Pipe.ExecuteAndSend(cmd)

Catch ex As Exception

    'This error will get sent, rather than the other,
    'to suppress this, comment out the next line.
    SqlContext.Pipe.Send("Transaction Rolled Back")

End Try

Return 0

End Function
```

As usual, you must first create the stored procedure within SQL Server Management Studio Express before you can execute it. Listing 17.11 provides an example. Note that when you declare the stored procedure, you declare the name of the parameter and its type.

LISTING 17.11   Creating a Stored Procedure That Contains Transactions

```
Use AdventureWorks
Go
CREATE PROCEDURE UsingTransaction(@departmentName NVarChar(50), @groupName
NVarChar(50))
AS
EXTERNAL NAME
FirstSQLCLRClassVB.[FirstSQLCLRClassVB.FirstSQLCLRVB].UsingTransaction
```

To execute the stored procedure, you must pass the designated parameter(s). Listing 17.12 provides an example. It first passes 'Toy Creation' and 'Manufacturing' to the stored procedure. This should successfully insert a row into the HumanResources.Department table (see Figure 17.6). If you execute the stored procedure a second time you will get an error and the code will roll back the transaction (see Figure 17.7). The table does not allow duplicate department names.

LISTING 17.12 Executing a Stored Procedure That Receives Input Parameters

```
Use AdventureWorks
Go
Exec UsingTransaction 'Toy Creation', 'Manufacturing'
```

FIGURE 17.6
The stored procedure executes successfully.

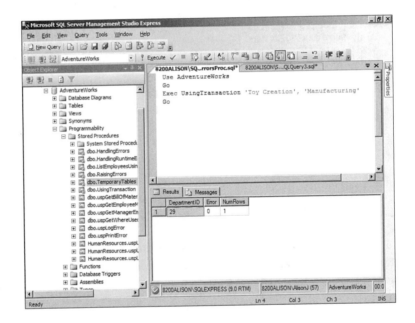

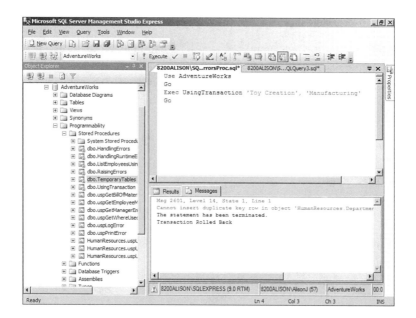

FIGURE 17.7
The stored pro-
cedure executes
with an error
and the transac-
tion is rolled
back.

Summary

Several techniques can help to make the stored procedures that you write more powerful and robust. These techniques include the use of temporary tables, error handling, and transaction processing in the stored procedures that you build. In this
hour you learned these three invaluable techniques.

Q&A

Q. *Explain why you might want to use a temporary table.*

A. Temporary tables enable you to perform operations on data as if that data
were structured differently than it actually is. For example, using temporary
tables, you can join two tables, have the result go to a temporary table, sort
the results, and then send the results back to SQL Server. The temporary table
is in memory only, so its structure does not have to be stored anywhere.

Q. *Explain why error handling is useful.*

A. Without error handling, you get the default error handling associated with
Visual Basic .NET. This default error handling is probably not what you want.
Using custom error handling you can control exactly what happens when an
error occurs.

Q. *Give an example of where transaction processing may be useful.*

A. Transaction processing would be helpful, for example, for an airline ticket pro-cessing system. If processing is interrupted during the booking of a flight, you would not want a partial transaction to be entered into the system. Using transaction processing, you ensure that the entire transaction is completed or the processing that has occurred is rolled back.

Workshop

Quiz

1. What character do you use to indicate that you are working with a temporary table?

2. Explain @@IDENTITY.

3. What is the name of the system variable that returns the number of rows affected by a SQL statement?

4. What does @@ERROR do?

5. An error number of zero means that an error occurred (true/false).

6. What keywords do you use when things go wrong and you want to discard any changes that have been made?

Quiz Answers

1. #.

2. It returns the key value of the most recently inserted row.

3. @@ROWCOUNT.

4. It returns the error number associated with the previous line of code.

5. False. Any non-zero number means that an error occurred.

6. ROLLBACK TRANSACTION.

Activities

Create, build, declare, and execute a stored procedure that inserts data into the Purchasing.Vendor table. Make sure that you write code to insert data into all the columns because all but one of the fields is required. Add error handling and transaction processing to the stored procedure. Make sure that one row is affected and that no error occurs before committing the transaction. Return an error message back to SQL Server when an error occurs.

HOUR 18

Using C# to Design SQL Server Stored Procedures

Just as you can execute a stored procedure written in VB, you can also execute a stored procedure written in C#. As you'll see, the process is identical. It's only the language that's different. In this hour you'll learn

- ▶ How to execute a simple stored procedure
- ▶ How to declare and work with variables
- ▶ How to control the flow of the stored procedures that you create
- ▶ How to work with input and output parameters
- ▶ How to use stored procedures to modify data

> The examples in this hour can be run with the Express edition of C#. **By the** Way

Executing a Simple Stored Procedure

> You will notice that this hour is almost identical to Hour 16. The intention is to show you how the exact same examples are implemented in the Visual Basic .NET language as well as the C# language. **By the** Way

The stored procedure found in Listing 18.1 first opens a connection. It then creates a SQLCommand object that selects the last name, first name, email address, and hire date from the Contact table joined with the Employee table, ordering the result set by last name combined with first name. It uses the open connection (conn) to connect to data. The ExecuteReader command executes the SQL statement contained in the Command object, returning the result to the SqlDataReader object (rdr). Finally, the code sends the

SqlDataReader object, via a pipe, back to SQL Server. You can find this code in the FirstSQLCLRClass solution, located on the sample code disk. The code is contained in the class called FirstSQLCLR.

LISTING 18.1   A Procedure That Lists Employees by Last Name and First Name

```
public static void ListEmployees()
{
    SqlContext.Pipe.Send("Current Contacts as of: " +
                        System.DateTime.Now.ToString() + "\n");
    using (SqlConnection conn =
        new SqlConnection("context connection=true"))
    {
        conn.Open();
        SqlCommand cmd = new SqlCommand(
            "SELECT Person.Contact.LastName, Person.Contact.FirstName, " +
            "Person.Contact.EmailAddress, HumanResources.Employee.HireDate " +
            "FROM Person.Contact Inner Join HumanResources.Employee " +
            "On Person.Contact.ContactID = HumanResources.Employee.ContactID " +
            "ORDER BY LastName, FirstName", conn);
        SqlDataReader rdr = cmd.ExecuteReader();
        SqlContext.Pipe.Send(rdr);
    }
}
```

You must place the function in a C# class, and then build the solution to create a DLL. After you create the DLL you are ready for the next step. The next step is to register the assembly in SQL Server Management Studio Express. You do this with the code found in Listing 18.2.

LISTING 18.2   Registering the Assembly in SQL Server Management Studio Express

```
Use AdventureWorks
Go
CREATE ASSEMBLY [FirstSQLCLRClass]
FROM 'c:\Alisonsbook\firstsqlclrclass\bin\release\firstsqlclrclass.dll'
WITH PERMISSION_SET = SAFE
```

You simply create a new query in SQL Server Management Studio express, and paste this code found in Listing 18.2 into the query. You will need to modify only the location of the DLL. Figure 18.1 shows Management Studio before the query is executed. No assemblies are yet available. Figure 18.2 shows Management Studio after the query has executed successfully. Note that the assembly is listed under the Assemblies node.

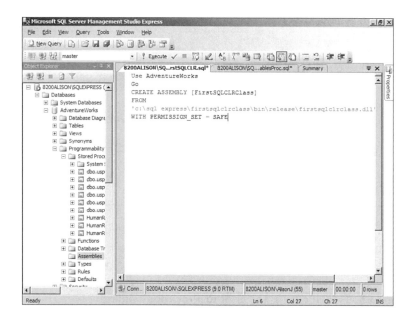

FIGURE 18.1
Before you execute the query, no assemblies are available.

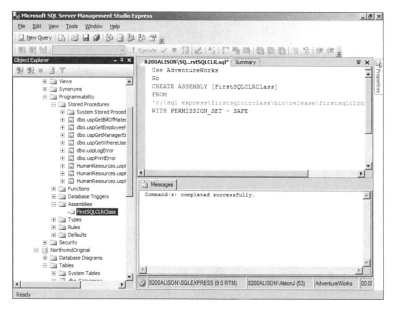

FIGURE 18.2
After executing the query, the assembly is listed under the Assemblies node.

After you have registered the assembly, you are ready to add any of its functions as stored procedures within SQL Server. The code found in Listing 18.3 accomplishes this task.

LISTING 18.3   Creating the Stored Procedure Called FirstListEmployees

```
CREATE PROCEDURE FirstListEmployees
AS
EXTERNAL NAME FirstSQLCLRClass.[FirstSQLCLRClass.FirstSQLCLR].ListEmployees
```

By the Way

> You may find that the EXTERNAL NAME syntax used here does not work. If that is the case, use the following syntax:
>
> FirstSQLCLRClass.FirsSQLCLR.ListEmployees
>
> You will notice that this is the syntax used for all the C# figures in this hour and in Hour 19.

After the code in Listing 18.3 has executed, the stored procedure appears in the list of stored procedures available within the database (see Figure 18.3). You execute the stored procedure as you would any stored procedure (see Listing 18.4) .

LISTING 18.4   Executing the Stored Procedure Called FirstListEmployees

```
use Adventureworks
Go
exec FirstListEmployees
```

FIGURE 18.3
After you create the procedure, it appears in the list of stored procedures available within the database.

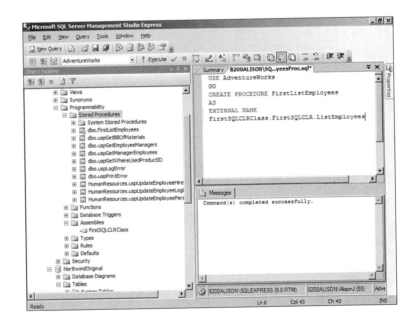

As shown in Listing 18.1, the stored procedure returns a SQLDataReader with the last name, first name, email address, and hire date from the Contact table joined with the Employee table, ordering the result set by last name combined with first name. The results appear in Figure 18.4.

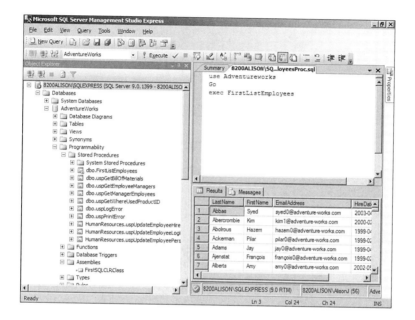

FIGURE 18.4
The stored procedure returns data to SQL Server Management Studio Express.

When you add a .NET stored procedure within the SQL Server Management Studio Express environment, you cannot modify it within SQL Server. Instead, you must return to Visual Studio 2005 to make any changes to the stored procedure. This is evident in Figure 18.5. Notice that Modify is unavailable.

FIGURE 18.5
You cannot modify a .NET stored procedure from within the SQL Server Management Studio Express environment.

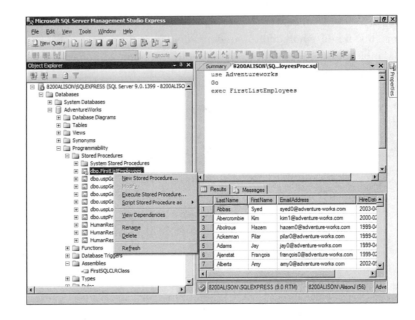

Declaring and Working with Variables

It is often necessary for your stored procedures to contain variables. This enables them to behave differently in different situations. Listing 18.5 provides an example. It receives a string parameter called orderBy. It then uses that parameter as a variable to determine the order by which the records appear in the output.

LISTING 18.5   A Stored Procedure That Uses a Variable

```
public static void ListEmployeesWithVariable
    (System.Data.SqlTypes.SqlString orderBy)
{
    SqlContext.Pipe.Send("Current Contacts as of: " +
                         System.DateTime.Now.ToString() + "\n");
    using (SqlConnection conn =
        new SqlConnection("context connection=true"))
    {
        conn.Open();
        SqlCommand cmd = new SqlCommand
            ("SELECT Person.Contact.LastName, Person.Contact.FirstName, " +
            "Person.Contact.EmailAddress, HumanResources.Employee.HireDate " +
            "FROM Person.Contact Inner Join HumanResources.Employee " +
            "On Person.Contact.ContactID = HumanResources.Employee.ContactID " +
            "ORDER BY " + orderBy.ToString(), conn);
        SqlDataReader rdr = cmd.ExecuteReader();
        SqlContext.Pipe.Send(rdr);
    }
```

Because the assembly was created earlier, there is no need to take that step again. It is necessary that you define the stored procedure within SQL Server Management Studio Express. The code in Listing 18.6 accomplishes this task. Notice that the code creates a SQL Server procedure called ListEmployeesUsingVariables based on the .NET procedure called ListEmployeesWithVariable.

If you are creating all the examples yourself, you need to first rebuild the solution. You must then unregister and reregister the assembly in Management Studio Express so that it can see the new procedure. It is important to note that you cannot unregister the assembly until you delete all its stored procedures from the list of stored procedures in Management Studio Express. If you are using the sample code provided with this book, it is not necessary for you to take any of these steps.

LISTING 18.6   Creating the Stored Procedure Called
ListEmployeesUsingVariables

```
CREATE PROCEDURE ListEmployeesUsingVariables
(@OrderBy NVarChar(20))
AS
EXTERNAL NAME
FirstSQLCLRClass.[FirstSQLCLRClass.FirstSQLCLR].ListEmployeesWithVariable
```

You must pass the ListEmployeesUsingVariables stored procedure a parameter when you execute it (see Listing 18.7). The stored procedure uses the parameter to determine the order of the output. The results of passing LastName and FirstName as parameters appear in Figure 18.6.

LISTING 18.7   Executing the Stored Procedure Called
ListEmployeesUsingVariables

```
use Adventureworks
Go
exec ListEmployeesUsingVariables 'HireDate'
GO
Exec ListEmployeesUsingVariables 'LastName'
```

FIGURE 18.6
After parameters are passed to the stored procedure, the output appears in the specified order.

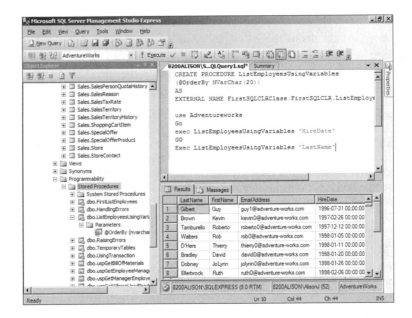

Controlling Program Flow

It is important to be able to determine the logical flow within a stored procedure. For example, you may want to evaluate the information passed into the stored procedure and respond differently, depending on what information is passed. Listing 18.8 provides an example. It receives two parameters; one called chooseFieldsToUse, and the other called chooseOrderBy. The chooseFieldsToUse parameter is an integer variable used to indicate the fields that the procedure will display in the output. The chooseOrderBy parameter is also an integer variable used to indicate the order in which the stored procedure will display the output.

After opening a connection, the stored procedure begins to build a string variable. The string variable begins with the keyword Select. The stored procedure then uses the keyword switch to evaluate what was passed in as the chooseFieldsToUse parameter. If it was 1, the procedure concatenates LastName, FirstName, EmailAddress, and HireDate onto the existing string. If it was 2, the procedure concatenates LastName, FirstName, Title, and Birthdate onto the existing string. Finally, if it was 3, it concatenates LastName, FirstName, MaritalStatus, and Gender onto the string. Now that the string contains the fields used in the SQL statement, the code concatenates the FROM statement onto the existing string. In the final step of building the SQL statement, the stored procedure uses an if statement to determine the order in which the output will appear. The stored procedure uses the

ExecuteReader method of the SqlCommand object to execute the SQL statement, returning the results to a SQLDataReader object. The SQLDataReader object is then returned to SQL Server.

LISTING 18.8   Using the switch Command to Control the Flow of a Stored Procedure

```
public static void
    ControllingProgramFlow(System.Data.SqlTypes.SqlInt32
    chooseFieldsToUse, System.Data.SqlTypes.SqlInt32
    chooseOrderBy)
{
    SqlContext.Pipe.Send
        ("Current Contacts as of: " +
            System.DateTime.Now.ToString() + "\n");
    using (SqlConnection conn =
        new SqlConnection("context connection=true"))
    {
        conn.Open();

        string sql = "Select ";

        // First way to control flow of program,
        // switch...case code block.
        switch((int) chooseFieldsToUse)
        {
            case 1:
                sql += "Person.Contact.LastName,
                Person.Contact.FirstName,
                Person.Contact.EmailAddress,
                HumanResources.Employee.HireDate";
                break;

            case 2:
                sql += "Person.Contact.LastName,
                Person.Contact.FirstName,
                HumanResources.Employee.Title,
                HumanResources.Employee.BirthDate";
                break;

            case 3:
                sql += "Person.Contact.LastName,
                Person.Contact.FirstName,
                HumanResources.Employee.MaritalStatus,
                HumanResources.Employee.Gender";
                break;
        }
        sql += " FROM Person.Contact
            Inner Join HumanResources.Employee
            On Person.Contact.ContactID =
            HumanResources.Employee.ContactID ORDER BY ";

        // Another way, using the if...else code block.
        if(chooseOrderBy == 1)
            sql += "LastName, FirstName";
        else
```

LISTING 18.8   Continued

```
        sql += "HireDate";
    SqlCommand cmd = new SqlCommand(sql, conn);
    SqlDataReader rdr = cmd.ExecuteReader();
    SqlContext.Pipe.Send(rdr);
  }
}
```

Before executing the stored procedure, you must define it within SQL Server
Management Studio Express. The code in Listing 18.9 accomplishes this task. It creates a procedure called ControlFieldsAndOrderBy, based on the .NET function
called ControllingProgramFlow.

LISTING 18.9   Adding the Procedure Called
ControlFieldsAndOrderBy **to SQL Server**

```
Use Adventureworks
Go
CREATE PROCEDURE ControlFieldsAndOrderBy(@FieldsToUse int, @OrderBy int)
AS
EXTERNAL NAME
FirstSQLCLRClass.[FirstSQLCLRClass.FirstSQLCLR].ControllingProgramFlow
```

Now that you have defined the stored procedure to SQL Server, you are ready to execute it. Listing 18.10 provides two examples. The first displays LastName, FirstName,
EmailAddress, and HireDate ordered by HireDate. The second displays LastName,
FirstName, MaritalStatus, and Gender ordered by LastName and FirstName. Figure
18.7 shows the ControlFieldsAndOrderBy stored procedure first with 1 and 2
passed as parameters, and then 3 and 1 passed as parameters.

LISTING 18.10   Executing the Procedure Called
ControlFieldsAndOrderBy

```
Use AdventureWorks
Go
Exec ControlFieldsAndOrderBy 1,2
Go
Exec ControlFieldsAndOrderBy 3,1
```

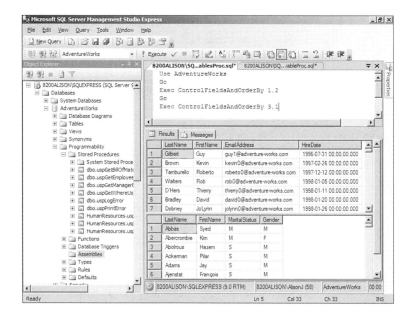

FIGURE 18.7
The output appears with different fields and in different orders.

Working with Parameters

Some stored procedures receive and return parameters. When a stored procedure receives a parameter, we refer to it as an *input parameter*. When a stored procedure returns a parameter, we refer to it as an *output parameter*. The following two sections illustrate the use of input parameters and output parameters.

Input Parameters

As mentioned, input parameters are used to supply information to a stored procedure. The code in Listing 18.11 illustrates this process. As with the other examples, it first opens a connection. The code then instantiates a SqlCommand object. The key to this example is the SQL statement used when instantiating the command object. Notice that the SQL statement contains a Where clause that compares the LastName field to @LastName, using the open connection. The next line of code adds @LastName as a parameter to the parameters collection of the command object. After the code adds the parameter, it then sets its value to the value that was passed to the function (searchLastName). Finally, the ExecuteReader method uses the command object, along with its input parameter, to return the specified fields with the designated Where clause. An example of the output appears in Figure 18.8.

LISTING 18.11   A Stored Procedure That Receives Input Parameters

```
public static void ListEmployeesUsingInputParameter
    (System.Data.SqlTypes.SqlString searchLastName)
{
    SqlContext.Pipe.Send("Current Contacts as of: " +
                          System.DateTime.Now.ToString() + "\n");
    using (SqlConnection conn = new SqlConnection
        ("context connection=true"))
    {
        conn.Open();
        SqlCommand cmd = new SqlCommand
            ("SELECT Person.Contact.LastName, " +
            "Person.Contact.FirstName, Person.Contact.EmailAddress, " +
            "HumanResources.Employee.HireDate " +
            "FROM Person.Contact Inner Join HumanResources.Employee " +
            "On Person.Contact.ContactID = HumanResources.Employee.ContactID " +
            "Where Person.Contact.LastName Like @LastName", conn);
        cmd.Parameters.Add(new SqlParameter
            ("@LastName",System.Data.SqlDbType.NVarChar, 2));
        cmd.Parameters[0].Value = searchLastName;

        SqlDataReader rdr = cmd.ExecuteReader();
        SqlContext.Pipe.Send(rdr);
    }
}
```

As usual, you must first create the stored procedure within SQL Server Management Studio Express before you can execute it. Because of the use of the input parameter, this process is slightly different than in the other examples. Listing 18.12 provides an example. Note that when you declare the stored procedure, you declare the name of the parameter and its type.

LISTING 18.12   Creating a Stored Procedure That Receives Input Parameters

```
Use AdventureWorks
Go
CREATE PROCEDURE ListEmployeesUsingInputParameter(@lastName NVarChar(50))
AS
EXTERNAL NAME
 FirstSQLCLRClass.[FirstSQLCLRClass.FirstSQLCLR].
ListEmployeesUsingInputParameter
```

To execute the stored procedure, you must pass the designated parameter(s). Listing 18.13 provides a couple of examples. It first passes the letter B along with a wildcard character. This returns all records where the contents of the LastName field begin with B. The stored procedure then executes again with the letter C and the same wildcard. Figure 18.8 shows the results of executing the stored procedure.

LISTING 18.13   Executing a Stored Procedure That Receives Input Parameters

```
Use AdventureWorks
Go
Exec ListEmployeesUsingInputParameter 'B%'
Go
Exec ListEmployeesUsingInputParameter 'C%'
```

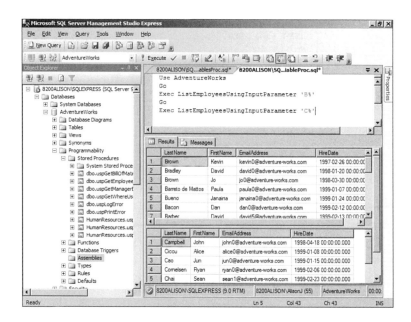

FIGURE 18.8
The output appears with specified last names.

Working with Output Parameters

Working with output parameters is similar to working with input parameters. The difference is that SQL Server returns information from the stored procedure rather than the stored procedure receiving something. Listing 18.14 provides an example. Using an IF statement to control the logical flow of the stored procedure, the code within the stored procedure builds a string containing a SQL Select statement. This SQL statement varies depending on the contents of the ProductNumber field passed into the function. The code then instantiates a SqlCommand object, using the SQL statement just built. The code then adds three parameters and sets their values. The first two are input parameters and contain the values passed into the function. The third parameter is an output parameter and contains the value of @MyMessage, set in the IF statement. Finally, the ExecuteReader method executes the stored procedure, sending the results to SQL Server.

LISTING 18.14   A Stored Procedure That Receives Output Parameters

```
public static void ListEmployeesUsingOutputParameter
    (System.Data.SqlTypes.SqlString productNumber,
    System.Data.SqlTypes.SqlString color)
{
    using (SqlConnection conn = new SqlConnection
        ("context connection=true"))
    {
        conn.Open();
        string sql = "IF @ProductNumber IS Null";
    sql += "    BEGIN";
    sql += "        SELECT Name FROM Production.Product " +
        "WHERE Color = @Color";
        sql += "        SELECT @MyMessage = 'No Product Number'";
        sql += "    END ";
        sql += "ELSE";
        sql += "    BEGIN";
            sql += "        SELECT Name FROM Production.Product " +
            "WHERE ProductNumber = @ProductNumber";
        sql += "        SELECT @MyMessage = 'Product Number Supplied'";
        sql += "    END ";
        sql += "SELECT @MyMessage";

        SqlCommand cmd = new SqlCommand(sql, conn);

        cmd.Parameters.Add(new SqlParameter
            ("@ProductNumber", System.Data.SqlDbType.VarChar, 25));
        cmd.Parameters[0].Value = productNumber;
        cmd.Parameters.Add(new SqlParameter
            ("@Color", System.Data.SqlDbType.VarChar, 15));
        cmd.Parameters[1].Value = color;
        cmd.Parameters.Add(new SqlParameter
            ("@MyMessage", System.Data.SqlDbType.VarChar, 50));
        cmd.Parameters[2].Direction =
            System.Data.ParameterDirection.Output;

        SqlDataReader rdr = cmd.ExecuteReader();
        SqlContext.Pipe.Send(rdr);
    }
}
```

Once again you must add the stored procedure before executing it (see Listing
18.15). Notice that the declaration includes only the input parameters. It is not necessary to declare the output parameters.

**LISTING 18.15   Adding a Stored Procedure That Receives Input
Parameters**

```
Use AdventureWorks
Go
CREATE PROCEDURE ListEmployeesUsingOutputParameter
    (@productNumber NVarChar(25), @color NVarChar(15))
AS
EXTERNAL NAME
    FirstSQLCLRClass.[FirstSQLCLRClass.FirstSQLCLR].
    ListEmployeesUsingOutputParameter
```

When you execute the stored procedure, you must pass the appropriate input parameters. In other words, they must be the proper data type. Listing 18.16 provides two examples. The first receives Null and Black as input parameters. To view the output parameters, you must select Query, Results, Results to Text from the SQL Server Management Studio Express menu. After you scroll below the output from the SELECT statement, the results appear in Figure 18.9.

LISTING 18.16 Executing a Stored Procedure That Returns Output Parameters

```
Use AdventureWorks
Go
Exec ListEmployeesUsingOutputParameter NULL, "Black"
Go
Exec ListEmployeesUsingOutputParameter 'BA-8327', NULL
```

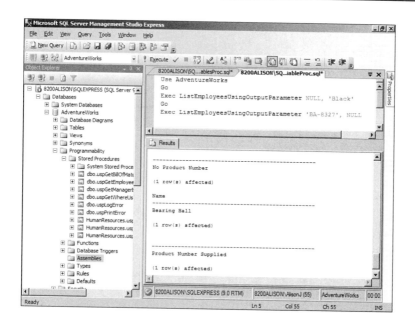

FIGURE 18.9
The result of executing a stored procedure with an output parameter.

Modifying Data with Stored Procedures

Not only can you use C# stored procedures to retrieve data, you can use them to insert, update, and delete data as well. The sections that follow illustrate this process.

Using Stored Procedures to Insert Data

You will often want to use a stored procedure to insert data. The function in Listing 18.17 provides an example. It receives two parameters: departmentName and groupName. The code instantiates and opens a connection. It then builds a SQL INSERT statement that inserts into the HumanResources.Department table the values passed into the function. Next, the code instantiates a SqlCommand object, passing it the SQL statement and the open connection. Finally, it uses the ExecuteNonQuery method of the SqlCommand object to execute the SQL statement.

LISTING 18.17   A Stored Procedure That Inserts Data

```
public static void InsertingData
    (System.Data.SqlTypes.SqlString departmentName,
        System.Data.SqlTypes.SqlString groupName)
{
    using (SqlConnection conn =
        new SqlConnection("context connection=true"))
    {
        conn.Open();
        string sql =
                string sql = "INSERT INTO HumanResources.Department" +
                    "(Name, GroupName) VALUES ('" +
                    departmentName.ToString() + "', '" +
                    groupName.ToString() +  "')";

        SqlCommand cmd = new SqlCommand(sql, conn);
        cmd.ExecuteNonQuery();
    }
}
```

As with all the other examples, you must first add the stored procedure to SQL Server Management Studio Express before you can execute it. Listing 18.18 provides the necessary code.

LISTING 18.18   Inserting a Stored Procedure That Inserts Data

```
Use AdventureWorks
Go
CREATE PROCEDURE InsertingData(@departmentName NVarChar(50), @groupName
NVarChar(50))
AS
EXTERNAL NAME FirstSQLCLRClass.[FirstSQLCLRClass.FirstSQLCLR].InsertingData
```

To execute the stored procedure, you simply pass it the necessary parameters. Listing 18.19 provides an example. Figure 18.10 shows the results of executing the query.

LISTING 18.19   Executing a Stored Procedure That Inserts Data

```
Use AdventureWorks
Go
Exec InsertingData 'Widget Creation', 'Manufacturing'
```

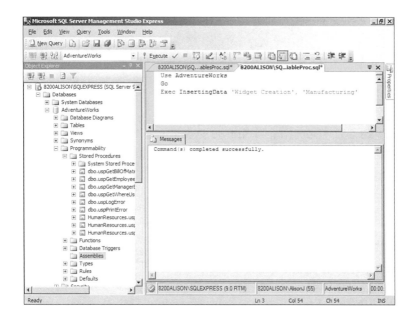

FIGURE 18.10
The result of executing a stored procedure that inserts data.

Using Stored Procedures to Update Data

Of course, in addition to using a stored procedure to insert data, you also will want to use a stored procedure to update data. Listing 18.20 provides an example. Like the insert example, it receives two input parameters. After opening a connection it builds a SQL UPDATE statement. Notice that the UPDATE statement contains a WHERE clause. The WHERE clause determines what record(s) the stored procedure will update. Again, the code uses the ExecuteNonQuery method of the SqlCommand object to execute the update statement.

LISTING 18.20   A Stored Procedure That Updates Data

```
public static void UpdatingData
    (System.Data.SqlTypes.SqlString departmentName,
    System.Data.SqlTypes.SqlString groupName)
{
    using (SqlConnection conn =
        new SqlConnection("context connection=true"))
    {
        conn.Open();
         string sql =
```

LISTING 18.20   Continued

```
        "UPDATE HumanResources.Department SET GroupName = '"
        + groupName.ToString() +
        "' WHERE Name = '" +
        departmentName.ToString() + "'";
    SqlCommand cmd = new SqlCommand(sql, conn);
    cmd.ExecuteNonQuery();
  }
}
```

The code in Listing 18.21 declares the stored procedure to SQL Server Management Studio Express. Notice that it receives two parameters.

LISTING 18.21   Declaring a Stored Procedure That Updates Data

```
Use AdventureWorks
Go
CREATE PROCEDURE UpdatingData
(@departmentName NVarChar(50), @groupName NVarChar(50))
AS
EXTERNAL NAME FirstSQLCLRClass.[FirstSQLCLRClass.FirstSQLCLR].UpdatingData
```

To execute the stored procedure, simply pass the two parameters (see Listing 18.22). The results appear in Figure 18.11.

LISTING 18.22   Executing a Stored Procedure That Updates Data

```
Use AdventureWorks
Go
Exec UpdatingData 'Widget Creation', 'Change to New Group'
```

Using Stored Procedures to Delete Data

You can also use stored procedures to delete data. Listing 18.23 provides an example. It receives a parameter containing a department name. After opening a connection, it builds a SQL DELETE statement with a WHERE clause containing the department name that came in as a parameter. It instantiates the SqlCommand object, using the SQL statement and the connection as parameters. Finally, it uses the ExecuteNonQuery method of the SqlCommand object to execute the DELETE statement.

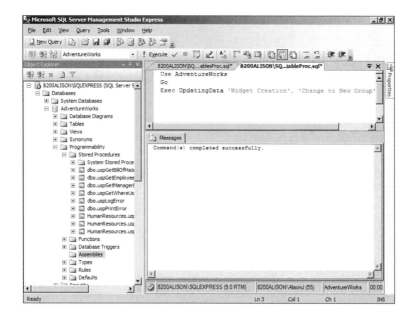

FIGURE 18.11
The result of
executing a
stored proce-
dure that
updates data.

LISTING 18.23   A Stored Procedure That Deletes Data

```
public static void DeletingData
    (System.Data.SqlTypes.SqlString departmentName)
{
    using (SqlConnection conn =
        new SqlConnection("context connection=true"))
    {
        conn.Open();
        string sql =
            "DELETE FROM HumanResources.Department WHERE Name = '" +
                departmentName.ToString() + "'";
        SqlCommand cmd = new SqlCommand(sql, conn);
        cmd.ExecuteNonQuery();
    }
}
```

As with the other example, before you can execute the stored procedure within SQL
Server Management Studio Express, you must first declare it. Listing 18.24 provides
an example.

LISTING 18.24   Declaring a Stored Procedure That Deletes Data

```
Use AdventureWorks
Go
CREATE PROCEDURE DeletingData(@departmentName NVarChar(50))
AS
EXTERNAL NAME FirstSQLCLRClass.[FirstSQLCLRClass.FirstSQLCLR].DeletingData
```

Finally, to execute the stored procedure, you simply pass it any required parameters (see Listing 18.25). SQL Server executes the SQL statement. The results appear in Figure 18.12.

LISTING 18.25   Executing a Stored Procedure That Deletes Data

```
Use AdventureWorks
Go
Exec DeletingData 'Widget Creation'
```

FIGURE 18.12
The result of executing a stored procedure that updates data.

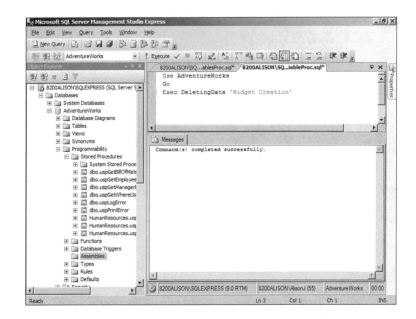

Summary

It is generally easier to write business logic in C# than it is in T-SQL. It is therefore important that you understand how to build procedures within Visual Studio 2005 and execute them from within SQL Server. In this hour you learned how to write, declare, and execute C# stored procedures.

Q&A

Q. *Discuss the process of building and executing a C# stored procedure.*

A. You must first write the stored procedure in the C# language within a Visual Studio 2005 class. You then build the project. You must then declare the stored procedure within SQL Server Management Studio Express. Finally, you can execute it just as you would any other stored procedure.

Q. *Explain what the keyword* `Switch` *does.*

A. The keyword `Switch` enables you to evaluate a variable and test its value against several conditions, executing the appropriate code based on the satisfied condition.

Q. *Describe the purpose of input parameters.*

A. *Input parameters enable you to supply information to a stored procedure.*

Workshop

Quiz

1. You can modify a SQL Server stored procedure from within SQL Server Management Studio Express (true/false).

2. You must reregister an assembly after you add functions to a C# class so that you can add those functions to Management Studio (true/false).

3. Name three T-SQL statements that you can use when modifying data with a stored procedure.

4. Why do you generally use a WHERE clause in an UPDATE statement?

5. It is common to provide a WHERE clause when using an INSERT statement (true/false).

6. What is the method that you use to execute a SQL statement that does not return data (it inserts, updates, or deletes instead)?

Quiz Answers

1. False.

2. True.

3. INSERT, UPDATE, and DELETE.

4. To determine which rows the stored procedure will update.

5. False. You use the keyword WHERE with UPDATE and DELETE statements.

6. ExecuteNonQuery.

Activities

Create, build, declare, and execute a stored procedure that retrieves data from the Sales.SpecialOffer table. Return the contents of the SpecialOfferID, Description, Discountpct, Type, Quantity, StartDate, and Endate in the result set. Create, build, declare, and execute another stored procedure that receives one input parameter and returns one output parameter. The input parameter is an int, and will contain the SpecialOrderID. The procedure will evaluate the discount percent for that special offer. If it is less than .3, the output parameter will contain the text "Low Discount." Otherwise, the output parameter will contain the text "High Discount." Practice executing the stored procedure, passing it different SpecialOfferID values.

HOUR 19

C# Special Topics

Just as there are special techniques available in Visual Basic .NET, these same techniques are available with C#. Using these techniques you can write more robust and powerful stored procedures. In this hour you'll learn:

- ▶ How to work with temporary tables
- ▶ How to add error handling to your stored procedures
- ▶ How to use transaction processing within your stored procedures

Working with Temporary Tables

> The code and text in this hour are very similar to the code and text found in Hour 17. The intention is to show you the similarities and differences between the Visual Basic .NET examples and the C# examples.

By the Way

Temporary tables can be useful in certain situations. When you need them they are invaluable. They can contain data from heterogeneous data sources (even a text file). Using temporary tables, you have access to methods that facilitate data access and retrieval. These methods enable you to sort, filter, index, and select their rows.

The stored procedure found in Listing 19.1 first opens a connection. It then builds a string. The string first defines the structure of a temporary table. You know that the table is temporary because of the pound sign (#) preceding the table name. The string then contains an INSERT INTO statement that inserts into the temporary table the results of selecting data from the Person.Contact table. Finally, the SQL statement selects the contents of the LastName and FirstName fields from the temporary table, ordering the results by LastName and FirstName.

After building the string, the code instantiates a command object, passing it the SQL statement along with a reference to the open connection. The `ExecuteReader` method of the command object executes the SQL statement contained in the command object, returning the result to the `SqlDataReader` object (rdr). Finally, the code sends the `SqlDataReader` object, via a pipe, back to SQL Server. If you had selected data from the Person.Contact table, because no sort was applied, the data would have appeared in ContactID order. Because you selected the data from the temporary table, ordering the results by LastName combined with FirstName, the data appears in the specified order. You can find this code in the FirstSQLCLRClass solution, located on the sample code disk. The code is contained in the class called FirstSQLCLR.

LISTING 19.1   A Procedure That Uses a Temporary Table

```
public static void UsingTemporaryTables()
{
    using (SqlConnection conn =
        new SqlConnection("context connection=true"))
    {
        conn.Open();
        string sql = "CREATE TABLE #TempContacts";
        sql += "         (ContactID int NOT NULL PRIMARY KEY, ";
        sql += "         LastName varchar(50),";
        sql += "         FirstName varchar(50))";
        sql += "  INSERT INTO #TempContacts ";
        sql += "  (ContactID, LastName, FirstName) ";
        sql += "  SELECT Person.Contact.ContactID, ";
        sql += "  Person.Contact.LastName, Person.Contact.FirstName ";
        sql += "  FROM Person.Contact";
        sql += "  SELECT LastName, FirstName ";
        sql += "  FROM #TempContacts ORDER BY LastName, FirstName";


        SqlCommand cmd = new SqlCommand(sql, conn);
        SqlDataReader rdr = cmd.ExecuteReader();
        SqlContext.Pipe.Send(rdr);
    }
}
```

You must place the function in a C# class, and then build the solution to create a DLL. After you create the DLL you are ready for the next step. If you have not yet registered the `firstsqlclrclass.dll`, the next step is to register the assembly in SQL Server Management Studio Express. This process was covered in Hour 17.

If you try to register an assembly, and it is already registered, you get an error. You must first delete the assembly and then reregister it. Before you can delete an assembly, you must first delete all the stored procedures within it. In summary, when you update a DLL, you must go through the process of deleting the stored procedures, deleting the assembly, adding the assembly, and adding the stored procedures. You can easily use a SQL script to help you with this process. Note that if available, the assembly is listed under the Assemblies node (see Figure 19.1).

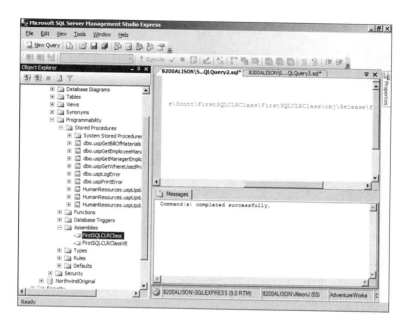

FIGURE 19.1
After the query has executed, the assembly is listed under the Assemblies node.

After you have ensured that the assembly is registered, you are ready to add any of its functions as stored procedures within SQL Server. The code found in Listing 19.2 accomplishes this task.

LISTING 19.2   Creating the Stored Procedure Called TemporaryTables

```
CREATE PROCEDURE TemporaryTables
AS
EXTERNAL NAME
FirstSQLCLRClass.[FirstSQLCLRClass.FirstSQLCLR].UsingTemporaryTables
```

You may find the EXTERNAL NAME syntax used here does not work. If that is the case, use the following syntax: FirstSQLCLRClass.FirsSQLCLR. UsingTemporaryTables

You execute the stored procedure as you would any stored procedure (see Listing 19.3).

LISTING 19.3   Executing the Stored Procedure Called
FirstListEmployees

```
use Adventureworks
Go
exec TemporaryTables
```

As shown in Listing 19.1, the stored procedure returns a SQLDataReader with the last name and first name from the Contact table, ordering the result set by last name combined with first name. The results appear in Figure 19.2.

FIGURE 19.2
The stored procedure returns data sorted by last name and first name.

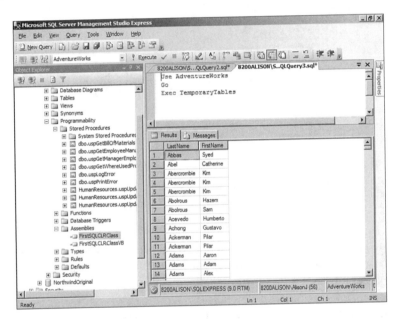

Including Error Handling in the Stored Procedures That You Build

All stored procedures should contain error handling. In this way *you* control what happens when an error occurs. In Listing 19.4 the code first evaluates the groupName parameter to determine whether it is Null. If it is Null, the code sends the text Group Name must be filled in. back to SQL Server. Otherwise the code instantiates a new connection. It opens the connection. Next it builds a string containing a SQL IF statement. The statement evaluates the DepartmentName parameter. If it is Null, it builds a SELECT statement, selecting the text No Department Name and DepartmentID = 0. Otherwise (Department Name Not Null) the code builds an

INSERT INTO statement that inserts data into the HumanResources.Department table and a SELECT statement that selects the message Success and the DepartmentID of @@Identity. @@Identity is a system variable that contains the primary key value of the last inserted row. Finally, the code instantiates a command object, setting its parameters to the parameter values passed into the stored procedure. It uses the execute method of the command object to execute the stored procedure, sending the results back to SQL Server.

LISTING 19.4   A Stored Procedure Containing Error Handling

```
public static void HandlingRuntimeErrors
    (System.Data.SqlTypes.SqlString departmentName,
    System.Data.SqlTypes.SqlString groupName)
{
    if (groupName.IsNull)
        // Error handled in C#
        SqlContext.Pipe.Send("Group Name must be filled in.");
    else
    {
        using (SqlConnection conn =
            new SqlConnection("context connection=true"))
        {
            conn.Open();
            // Error handled in T-SQL
            string sql = "IF @DepartmentName Is Null ";
            sql += "    BEGIN ";
            sql += "        SELECT Message = 'No Department Name', ";
            sql += "        DepartmentID = 0";
            sql += "    END ";
            sql += "ELSE ";
            sql += "    BEGIN ";
            sql += "        INSERT INTO HumanResources.Department";
            sql += "        (Name, GroupName) VALUES ;
            sql += "        (@DepartmentName, @GroupName) ";
            sql += "        SELECT Message = 'Success', ;
            sql += "        DepartmentID = @@Identity ";
            sql += "    END ";

            SqlCommand cmd = new SqlCommand(sql, conn);
            cmd.Parameters.Add(new SqlParameter
                ("@DepartmentName", System.Data.SqlDbType.VarChar, 50));
            cmd.Parameters[0].Value = departmentName;
            cmd.Parameters.Add(new SqlParameter
                ("@GroupName", System.Data.SqlDbType.VarChar, 50));
            cmd.Parameters[1].Value = groupName;
            SqlDataReader rdr = cmd.ExecuteReader();
            SqlContext.Pipe.Send(rdr);
        }
    }
}
```

Because the assembly was created earlier, there is no need to take that step again. It is necessary that you define the stored procedure within SQL Server Management

Studio Express. The code in Listing 19.5 accomplishes this task. Notice that the code creates a SQL Server procedure called HandlingErrors based on the .NET procedure called HandlingRuntimeErrors.

By the Way

If you are creating all the examples yourself, you need to first rebuild the solution. You must then unregister and reregister the assembly in Management Studio Express so that it can see the new procedure. It is important to note that you will not be able to unregister the assembly until you delete all its stored procedures from the list of stored procedures in Management Studio Express. If you are using the sample code provided with this book, it will not be necessary for you to take any of these steps.

LISTING 19.5   Creating the Stored Procedure Called SecondListEmployees

```
CREATE PROCEDURE HandlingErrors
(@DepartmentName NVarChar(20), @GroupName NVarChar(2))
AS
EXTERNAL NAME
FirstSQLCLRClass.[FirstSQLCLRClass.FirstSQLCLR].HandlingRuntimeErrors
```

You must pass the HandlingErrors stored procedure two parameters when you execute it (see Listing 19.6). The first is the department name, and the second is the group name. The results of passing Widget Department and Null as parameters the first time, and then Null and Manufacturing as parameters the second time appear in Figure 19.3 and Figure 19.4.

LISTING 19.6   Executing the Stored Procedure Called HandlingErrors

```
Use AdventureWorks
Go
Exec HandlingErrors 'Widget Department', Null
Go
Exec HandlingErrors Null, 'Manufacturing'
```

Notice that whereas the Send method sends the specified *text* to the Messages pane (see Figure 19.3), it sends the DataReader object to the Results pane (see Figure 19.4).

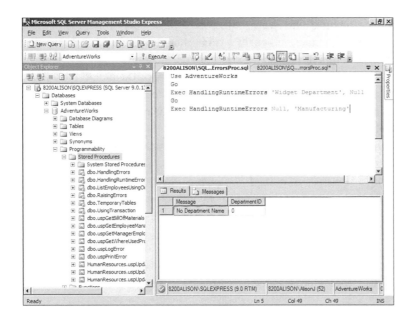

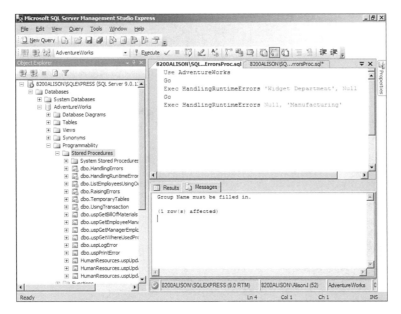

Sometimes you may actually want to raise errors in your code. You may want to do this to simulate an error condition in your application, or to treat a user error like a system error, passing it through your standard error handler. Listing 19.7 provides an example. The procedure receives two parameters, departmentName and groupName. It instantiates and opens a connection. It then builds a SQL statement that inserts data into the HumanResources.Department table, using the parameter values passed to the procedure. Next it sets DepartmentID equal to the value of @@Identity, the system variable containing the primary key value of the last inserted row. After the procedure builds the SQL statement, it declares and instantiates a command object. It then adds parameters to the command object, setting their values to the values passed in as parameters to the procedure. Next it uses the ExecuteAndSend method of the SqlContext.Pipe object, passing it the command object, to return the results of the SQL statement to SQL Server. The difference between this procedure and the HandlingErrors procedure lies in the Catch block. If an error occurs, the code uses the Send method of the SqlContext.Pipe object to send a custom error message back to SQL Server.

LISTING 19.7   Sending a Custom Error Message to SQL Server

```
public static void RaisingErrors
    (System.Data.SqlTypes.SqlString departmentName,
    System.Data.SqlTypes.SqlString groupName)
{
    try
    {
        using (SqlConnection conn =
            new SqlConnection("context connection=true"))
        {
            conn.Open();
            string sql = "SET NOCOUNT ON ";
            sql += "INSERT INTO HumanResources.Department(Name, GroupName) ";
            sql += "VALUES (@DepartmentName, @GroupName) ";
            sql += "SELECT DepartmentID = @@Identity";

            SqlCommand cmd = new SqlCommand(sql, conn);
            cmd.Parameters.Add(new SqlParameter("@DepartmentName",
                System.Data.SqlDbType.VarChar, 50));
            cmd.Parameters[0].Value = departmentName;
            cmd.Parameters.Add(new SqlParameter("@GroupName",
                System.Data.SqlDbType.VarChar, 50));
            cmd.Parameters[1].Value = groupName;
            SqlContext.Pipe.ExecuteAndSend(cmd);
        }
    }
    catch (Exception ex)
    {
        // This error will get sent, rather than the other,
        // to suppress this, comment out the next line.
        SqlContext.Pipe.Send
        ("An exception occurred during the execution of RaisingErrors " +
        ex.ToString());

    }
```

Before executing the stored procedure, you must define it within SQL Server Management Studio Express. The code in Listing 19.8 accomplishes this task. It creates a procedure called `RaisingErrors`, based on the .NET function called `RaisingErrors`.

LISTING 19.8 Adding the Procedure Called `RaisingErrors` to SQL Server

```
Use AdventureWorks
Go
CREATE PROCEDURE RaisingErrors(@departmentName NVarChar(50), @groupName
NVarChar(50))
AS
EXTERNAL NAME FirstSQLCLRClass.[FirstSQLCLRClass.FirstSQLCLR].RaisingErrors
```

Now that you have defined the stored procedure to SQL Server, you are ready to execute it. Listing 19.9 provides an example. It passed `Widget Department` and `Null` as parameters to the stored procedure. Figure 19.5 shows the resulting error message. Notice that the highlighted text contains the text that the procedure sent when it raised the error.

LISTING 19.9 Executing the Procedure Called `RaisingErrors`

```
Use AdventureWorks
Go
Exec RaisingErrors 'Widget Department', Null
```

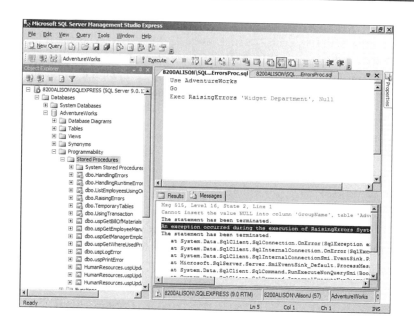

FIGURE 19.5
The output appears with the custom error message.

Using Transactions to Protect Your Data

Sometimes you want to ensure that a series of statements execute completely or not at all. For example, if you were performing a bank transaction, you would want to ensure that both the debit and credit occurred before committing the data. Transactions can help you solve this dilemma. Listing 19.10 provides an example.

The code begins by using a try...catch block to establish error handling. It then declares and instantiates a connection object. It opens the connection and then begins to build a SQL string. The SQL string first declares three variables: @DepartmentID, @LocalError, and @LocalRows. The code then adds a BEGIN TRANSACTION statement to the SQL string. From this point on, everything that follows is part of a transaction. Next the code adds an INSERT INTO statement to the SQL statement, inserting the parameter values into the appropriate fields in the HumanResources.Department table. The code immediately tests to see whether an error occurred by testing the values of the system variables @@Error and @@Rowcount. @@Error contains the number of the error that occurred, and @@Rowcount contains the number of rows affected by the SQL statement that immediately precedes it.

After the error number and the number of rows affected have been captured, the code evaluates them to determine whether their values are indicative of problems. A non-zero error number means that an error occurred. Zero rows affected also means that an error occurred. If @LocalError is non-zero or @LocalRows is zero, a ROLLBACK TRANSACTION occurs. The ROLLBACK TRANSACTION obliterates any processing that occurred since the BEGIN TRANSACTION statement. An END statement then terminates processing. Otherwise, the code attempts to commit the transaction. It sets the DepartmentID equal to the value of the system variable @@Identity. It sets the value of Error equal to zero and the value of NumRows equal to @LocalRows.

After the SQL statement is built, it is time to execute it. The code declares and instantiates a command object. It then adds two parameters to the command object, one for departmentName and one for groupName. The code uses the ExecuteAndSend method of the SQLContext.Pipe object to execute the SQL statement, returning the results to SQL Server.

If an error occurs during processing, execution jumps to the Catch block. The Catch block sends the message Transaction Rolled Back to SQL Server. If no error occurs, the COMMIT TRAN statement commits the data to disk.

LISTING 19.10   A Stored Procedure That Receives Input Parameters

```
public static void UsingTransaction
    (System.Data.SqlTypes.SqlString departmentName,
    System.Data.SqlTypes.SqlString groupName)
{
    try
    {
        using (SqlConnection conn = new SqlConnection
            ("context connection=true"))
        {
            conn.Open();
            string sql = "SET NOCOUNT ON ";
            sql += "DECLARE @DepartmentID int, @LocalError int, @LocalRows int
";

            sql += "BEGIN TRANSACTION ";
            sql += "INSERT INTO HumanResources.Department(Name, GroupName) ";
            sql += "VALUES (@DepartmentName, @GroupName) ";
            sql += "SELECT @LocalError = @@Error, @LocalRows = @@RowCount ";
            sql += "IF NOT @LocalError = 0 or @LocalRows = 0 ";
            sql += "    BEGIN ";
            sql += "        ROLLBACK TRANSACTION ";
            sql += "        SELECT DepartmentID = Null, Error = @LocalError, ";
            sql += "        NumRows = @LocalRows ";
            sql += "    END ";
            sql += "ELSE ";
            sql += "    BEGIN ";
            sql += "        COMMIT TRAN ";
            sql += "      SELECT @DepartmentID = @@Identity ";
            sql += "        SELECT DepartmentID = @DepartmentID, ";
            sql += "        Error = 0, NumRows = @LocalRows ";
            sql += "    END ";

            SqlCommand cmd = new SqlCommand(sql, conn);
            cmd.Parameters.Add(new SqlParameter("@DepartmentName",
                System.Data.SqlDbType.VarChar, 50));
            cmd.Parameters[0].Value = departmentName;
            cmd.Parameters.Add(new SqlParameter("@GroupName",
                System.Data.SqlDbType.VarChar, 50));
            cmd.Parameters[1].Value = groupName;

            SqlContext.Pipe.ExecuteAndSend(cmd);

        }
    }
    catch (Exception ex)
    {
        // This error will get sent, rather than the other,
        // to suppress this, comment out the next line.
        SqlContext.Pipe.Send("Transaction Rolled Back");

    }

}
```

As usual, you must first create the stored procedure within SQL Server Management Studio Express before you can execute it. Listing 19.11 provides an example. Note that when you declare the stored procedure, you declare the name of the parameter and its type.

LISTING 19.11   Creating a Stored Procedure That Contains Transactions

```
Use AdventureWorks
Go
CREATE PROCEDURE UsingTransaction(@departmentName NVarChar(50), @groupName
NVarChar(50))
AS
EXTERNAL NAME FirstSQLCLRClass.[FirstSQLCLRClass.FirstSQLCLR].UsingTransaction
```

To execute the stored procedure, you must pass the designated parameter(s). Listing 19.12 provides an example. It first passes 'Bolt Creation' and 'Manufacturing' to the stored procedure. This should successfully insert a row into the HumanResources.Department table (see Figure 19.6). If you execute the stored procedure a second time, you will get an error and the code will roll back the transaction (see Figure 19.7). This is because the table does not allow duplicate department names.

LISTING 19.12   Executing a Stored Procedure That Receives Input Parameters

```
Use AdventureWorks
Go
Exec UsingTransaction 'Widget Creation', 'Manufacturing'
```

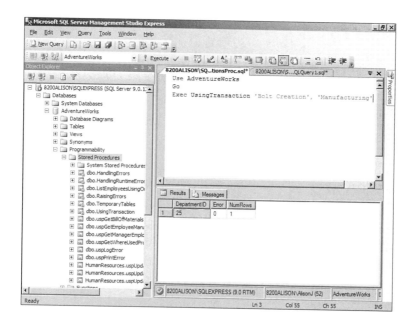

FIGURE 19.6
The stored procedure executes successfully.

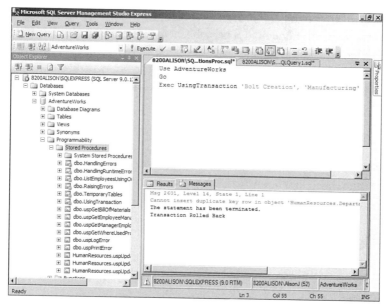

FIGURE 19.7
The stored procedure executes with an error and the transaction is rolled back.

Summary

Several techniques help to make the stored procedures that you write more powerful and robust. These techniques include the use of temporary tables, error handling, and transaction processing in the stored procedures that you build. In this hour you learned these three invaluable techniques.

Q&A

Q. *Explain why you might want to use a temporary table.*

A. Temporary tables enable you to perform operations on data as if that data were structured differently than it actually is. For example, using temporary tables, you can join two tables, have the result go to a temporary table, sort the results, and then send the results back to SQL Server. The temporary table is in memory only, so its structure does not have to be stored anywhere.

Q. *Explain why error handling is useful.*

A. Without error handling, you get the default error handling associated with C#. This default error handling is probably not what you want. With custom error handling you can control exactly what happens when an error occurs.

Q. *Give an example of where transaction processing may be useful.*

A. Transaction processing would be helpful, for example, for an airline ticket processing system. If processing is interrupted during the booking of a flight, you would not want a partial transaction to be entered into the system. Using transaction processing, you ensure that the entire transaction is completed or the processing that has occurred is rolled back.

Workshop

Quiz

1. What character do you use to indicate that you are working with a temporary table?

2. Explain @@IDENTITY.

3. What is the name of the system variable that returns the number of rows affected by a SQL statement?

4. What does @@ERROR do?

5. An error number of zero means that an error occurred (true/false).

6. What keywords do you use when things go wrong and you want to discard any changes that have been made?

Quiz Answers

1. #.

2. It returns the key value of the most recently inserted row.

3. @@ROWCOUNT.

4. It returns the error number associated with the previous line of code.

5. False. Any non-zero number means that an error occurred.

6. ROLLBACK TRANSACTION.

Activities

Create, build, declare, and execute a stored procedure that inserts data into the Purchasing.Vendor table. Make sure that you write code to insert data into all the columns because all but one of the fields is required. Add error handling and transaction processing to the stored procedure. Make sure that one row is affected and that no error occurred before committing the transaction. Return an error message back to SQL Server when an error occurs.

HOUR 20

Debugging the Stored Procedures That You Write

A good programmer is not necessarily one who can get things right the first time. To be fully effective as a .NET programmer, you need to master the art of debugging—the process of troubleshooting your application. Debugging involves locating and identifying problem areas within your code and is a mandatory step in the application-development process. Fortunately, the Visual Studio 2005 programming environment provides excellent tools to help you with the debugging process. Using the Visual Studio 2005 debugging tools, you can step through your code, setting watches and breakpoints as needed. In this hour you'll learn:

▶ How to harness the power of the Immediate window
▶ How to invoke the debugger
▶ How to use breakpoints to troubleshoot
▶ How to step through a stored procedure
▶ How to set the next statement to execute
▶ How to use the Calls window to determine program flow
▶ How to use the Locals window
▶ How to watch variables

Harnessing the Power of the Immediate Window

The Immediate window serves several purposes. It provides you with a great way to test .NET stored procedures, it enables you to inquire about and change the value of variables while your code is running, and it enables you to view the results of Debug.Print statements. To open the Immediate window while viewing programming code, do one of three things:

▶ Click the Immediate window tool on the Debug toolbar.

▶ Choose Debug, Windows, Immediate.

▶ Press Ctrl+G.

Figure 20.1 shows the Immediate window.

FIGURE 20.1
The Immediate window enables you to test functions and to inquire about and change the value of variables.

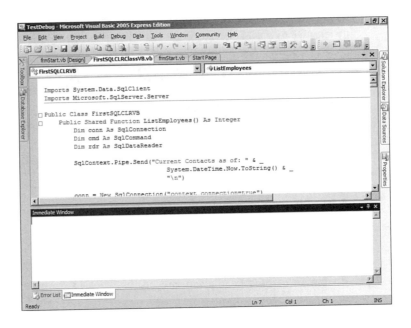

The Debug tools are available on a separate toolbar. To show the Debug toolbar, right-click any toolbar or menu bar and select Debug from the list of available toolbars.

By the Way

The Debug tools are available on a separate toolbar. To show the Debug toolbar, right-click any toolbar or menu bar and select Debug from the list of available toolbars.

Testing Values of Variables and Properties

The Immediate window enables you to test the values of variables and properties as your code executes. This can be quite enlightening as to what is actually happening within your code.

To practice with the Immediate window, you do not even need to be executing code. To invoke the Immediate window while in the .NET programming environment, press Ctrl+G. To see how this works, follow these steps:

1. Run the frmStart form from the TestDebug project on the accompanying CD-ROM.

2. Type a value into the text box on the form.

3. Click the Start command button. You are placed in Break mode. You will learn much more about Break mode later.

4. Press Ctrl+G to open and activate the Immediate window. The debugger places you within the Immediate window.

5. Type **?Forms.frmStart.txtTest.Text** and press Enter. The value of the text in the text box appears in the Immediate window.

6. Type **?Forms.frmStart.txtTest.Visible** and press Enter. The word True appears on the next line, indicating that the control is visible.

7. Type **?Forms.frmStart.txtTest.Enabled** and press Enter. The word True appears on the next line, indicating that the control is enabled.

Your screen should look like the one shown in Figure 20.2. You can continue to request the values of properties or variables within your .NET code.

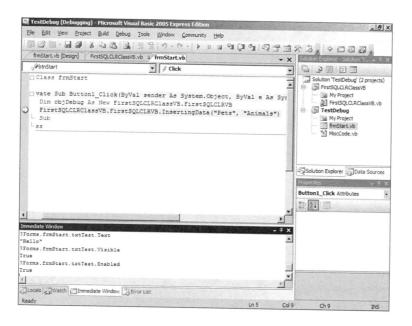

FIGURE 20.2
Using the Immediate window to test the values of properties.

Setting Values of Variables and Properties

Not only can you display things in the Immediate window, but you also can use the Immediate window to modify the values of variables and controls as your code executes. This feature becomes even more valuable when you realize that you can re-execute code within a procedure after changing the value of a variable. Here's how this process works:

1. Invoke the Immediate window, if necessary. Remember that you can do this by pressing Ctrl+G.

2. Type `Forms.frmStart.txtTest.Text` = `"Hello World"` in the immediate pane. Press Enter. The value in the text box changes to `"Hello World"`.

3. Type `Forms.frmStart.txtTest.Visible` = `False`. Press Enter. .NET hides the `txtTest` control on the `frmStart` form.

4. Type `Forms.frmStart.txtTest.Visible` = `True`. Press Enter. .NET shows the `txtTest` control on the `frmStart` form.

5. Type `Forms.frmStart.Text` = `"Form Caption"`. Press Enter. The caption of the form changes.

6. Press F5 to complete the code execution. The Immediate window and your form now look like those shown in Figures 20.3 and 20.4, respectively.

FIGURE 20.3
Setting the values of properties, using the Immediate window.

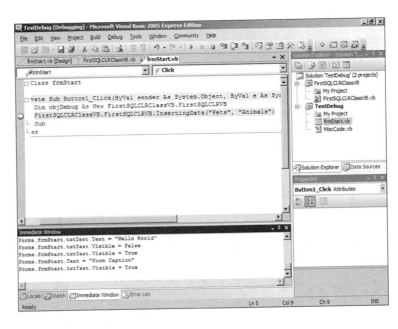

FIGURE 20.4
The results of
using the
Immediate
window to set
the values of
properties.

The Immediate window is an extremely valuable testing and debugging tool. The examples here barely begin to illustrate its power and flexibility.

> Changes you make to data while working in the Immediate window are permanent. On the other hand, changes you make to the properties of controls or the values of variables with the form are not permanent.
>
> Some people think that data changes made in the Immediate window are not permanent. In other words, if you modify the last name of a customer, some people believe that the change will not be permanent (but, of course, it is). Other people think that if they change the BackColor property of a control, the change will persist in the design environment (but, of course, it won't).

**Watch
Out!**

Practicing with the Built-In Functions

In addition to being able to test and set the values of properties and variables with the Immediate window, you can test any Visual Basic .NET or C# function. To do so, type the function and its arguments in the Immediate window, preceded by a question mark. This code returns the month of the current date, for example:

```
?datepart(DateInterval.Month, Today)
```

This tells you the date one month after today's date:

```
?dateadd(DateInterval.Month,1,Today)
```

This tells you how many days exist between the current date and the end of the millennium:

```
?datediff(DateInterval.Day,Today,#12/31/2999#)
```

Executing Subroutines, Functions, and Methods

In addition to enabling you to test any Visual Basic .NET or C# function, the Immediate window lets you test any user-defined subroutine, function, or method. This is a great way to debug your user-defined procedures. To see how this works, follow these steps:

1. Invoke the Immediate window if it is not already visible.

2. Type **?MiscCode.ReturnInitsFunc("Bill","Gates")**. This calls the user-defined function ReturnInitsFunc in the class called MiscCode, sending "Bill" as the first parameter and "Gates" as the second parameter. The value B.G. appears in the Immediate window. This is the return value from the function.

3. Type **Call MiscCode.ReturnInitsSub("Bill","Gates")**. This calls the user-defined subroutine ReturnInitsSub of the MiscCode class, sending "Bill" as the first parameter and "Gates" as the second parameter. The value B.G. appears in a message box.

Notice the difference between how you call a function and how you call a subroutine. Because the function returns a value, you must call it by using a question mark. On the other hand, when calling a subroutine, you use the Call keyword.

By the Way

> You also can call a subroutine from the Immediate window with this syntax:
> ```
> RoutineName(Parameter1, Parameter2, ....)
> ```

Invoking the Debugger

You can invoke the .NET debugger in several ways:

▶ Place a breakpoint in your code.

▶ Place a watch in your code.

▶ Press Ctrl+Break while the code is running.

▶ Insert a Stop statement in your code.

A *breakpoint* is an unconditional point at which you want to suspend code execution.

A *watch* is a condition under which you want to suspend code execution. You might want to suspend code execution when a counter variable reaches a specific value, for example.

A Stop statement is permanent. In fact, if you forget to remove Stop statements from your code, your application stops execution while the user is running it.

Using Breakpoints to Troubleshoot

As mentioned, a breakpoint is a point at which the debugger will unconditionally halt the execution of code. You can set multiple breakpoints in your code. You can add and remove breakpoints as your code executes.

A breakpoint enables you to halt your code execution at a suspicious area of code. This enables you to examine everything that is going on at that point in your code execution. By strategically placing breakpoints in your code, you quickly can execute sections of code that you already debugged, stopping only at problem areas.

To set a breakpoint, follow these steps:

1. Place your cursor on the line of code where you want to invoke the debugger.

2. You can insert a breakpoint in one of four ways:

   ▶ Press your F9 function key.

   ▶ Click in the gray margin area to the left of the line of the code that will contain the breakpoint.

   ▶ Click the Toggle Breakpoint button on the Debug toolbar.

   ▶ Choose Debug, Toggle Breakpoint.

   The line of code containing the breakpoint appears in a different color, and a dot appears, indicating the breakpoint.

3. Run the form containing the breakpoint. The debugger suspends execution just before executing the line of code where you placed the breakpoint. The statement that is about to execute appears in a contrasting color (the default is yellow).

Now that you have suspended your code, you can step through it one line at a time, change the value of variables, and view your call stack, among other things.

Keep in mind that a breakpoint is actually a toggle. If you want to remove a break-point, click in the gray margin area, press F9, or click Toggle Breakpoint on the Debug toolbar.

It is easiest to get to know the debugger by actually using it. The following example gives you hands-on experience in setting and stopping code execution at a break-point. The example is developed further later in the hour.

By the Way

> The sample code includes the example on the frmStart form that we have been working with. The code is invoked from the btnDebug command button and calls the class clsFuncs.

Start by creating a form called frmDebug that contains a command button called btnDebug. Give the button the caption Start Debug Process by setting its Text property. Place the following code in the Click event of the command button:

```
Sub btnDebug_Click ()
    Call clsFuncs.Sub1
End Sub
```

Create a class called clsFuncs. Enter three functions into the module:

```
Public Shared Sub Sub1()
    Dim intTemp As Integer

    intTemp = 10
    Debug.Print "We Are Now In Sub1()"
    Debug.Print intTemp
    Call Sub2
End Sub

Public Shared Sub Sub2 ()
    Dim strName As String

    strName = "Bill Gates"
    Debug.Print "We Are Now In Sub2()"
    Debug.Print strName
    Call Sub3

End Sub

Public Shared Sub Sub3 ()
    Debug.Print "We Are Now In Sub3()"
    MsgBox "Hi There From The Sub3() Sub Procedure"
End Sub
```

Now you should debug. Start by placing a breakpoint within the Click event of btnDebug on the line called Call clsFuncs.Sub1. Here are the steps:

1. Click anywhere on the line of code that says Call clsFuncs.Sub1.

2. Click in the gray margin area, press the F9 function key, click the Toggle Breakpoint button on the Debug toolbar, or choose Debug, Toggle Breakpoint. The line with the breakpoint turns a different color (red by default).

3. Run the application and click the Start Debug Process button. Execution suspends just before the line where you placed the breakpoint executes. The debugger displays the line that reads Call Sub1 in a different color (by default, yellow), indicating that it is about to execute that line. (See Figure 20.5.)

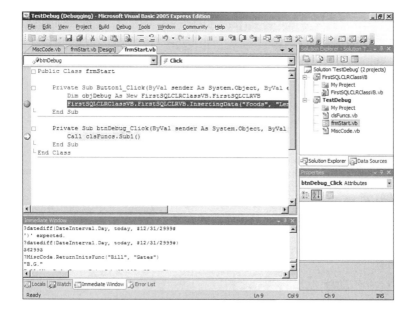

FIGURE 20.5
Code execution halted at a breakpoint.

Stepping Through Code

The .NET programming environment gives you three main options for stepping through your code. Each one is slightly different. The Step Into option enables you to step through each line of code within a subroutine or function, whereas the Step Over option executes a procedure without stepping through each line of code within it. The Step Out option runs all code in nested procedures and then returns you to the procedure that called the line of code where you are. Knowing the correct option to use to solve a particular problem is an acquired skill that comes with continued development experience.

Using Step Into

When you reach a breakpoint, you can continue executing your code one line at a time or continue execution until you reach another breakpoint. To step through your code one line at a time, click Step Into on the Debug toolbar, press F8, or choose Debug, Step Into.

The following example illustrates the process of stepping through your code, printing the values of variables to the Immediate window, and using the Immediate window to modify the values of variables.

You can continue the debug process from the breakpoint you set in the previous example. Step two times (press F8). You should find yourself within Sub1, about to execute the line of code intTemp = 10 (see Figure 20.6). Notice that the debugger did not stop on the line Dim intTemp As Integer. The debugger does not stop on variable declarations.

FIGURE 20.6
The Immediate window halted within Sub1.

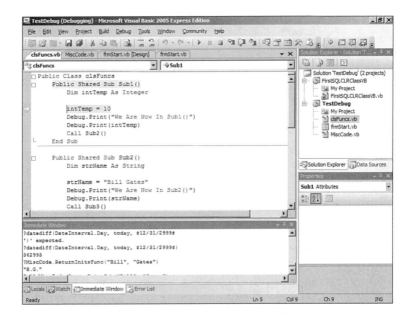

The code is about to print the Debug statements to the Immediate window. Take a look by opening the Immediate window. None of your code has printed anything to the Immediate window yet. Press F8 (step) three more times until you have executed the line `Debug.Print(intTemp)`. Your screen should look like Figure 20.7. Notice the results of the `Debug.Print` statements.

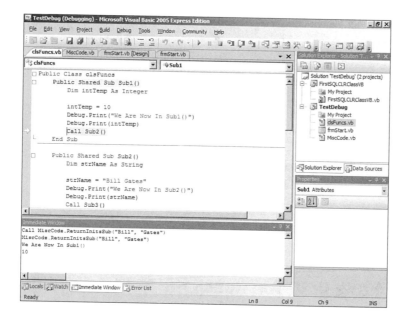

FIGURE 20.7
The Immediate window with entries generated by `Debug.Print` statements.

Now that you have seen how you can display variables and the results of expressions to the Immediate window, take a look at how you can use the Immediate window to modify values of variables and controls. Start by changing the value of `intTemp`. Click the Immediate window and type `intTemp = 50`. When you press Enter, you actually modify the value of `intTemp`. Type `?intTemp`, and you'll see that the debugger echoes back the value of 50. You also can see the value of `intTemp` in the Locals window. Notice in Figure 20.8 that the `intTemp` variable appears along with its value and type.

To invoke the Locals window, select Debug, Windows, Locals, or click the Locals button on the Debug toolbar.

By the Way

FIGURE 20.8
The Immediate
and Locals
windows after
the value of
intTemp has
been modified.

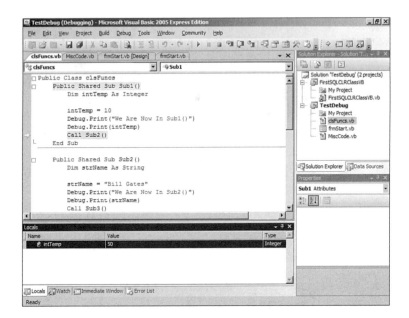

Executing Until You Reach the Next Breakpoint

Suppose that you have reached a breakpoint, but you realize that your problem is
farther down in the code execution. In fact, the problem is actually in a different
function. You might not want to continue to move one step at a time down to the
offending function. Use the Procedure drop-down menu to locate the questionable
function, and then set a breakpoint on the line where you want to continue stepping. You now are ready to continue code execution until the debugger reaches this
line. To do this, click Continue on the Debug toolbar, press F5, or choose Run,
Continue. Your code continues to execute, stopping at the next breakpoint. To see
how this works, continue the Debug process with the next example.

By the Way

> You also can opt to resume code execution to the point at which your cursor is
> located. To do this, select Run to Cursor from the Debug menu, or press Ctrl+F8.

Suppose that you realize your problem might be in Sub3. You do not want to continue to move one step at a time down to Sub3. No problem. Use the Procedure
drop-down menu to view Sub3, as shown in Figure 20.9. Set a breakpoint on the line
that reads Debug.Print("We Are Now In Sub3()"). You are ready to continue
code execution until the debugger reaches this line. Click Continue on the Debug
toolbar, press F5, or choose Run, Continue. Your code continues to execute, stopping

on the breakpoint you just set. Press F5 again. The code finishes executing. Return to the Form View window.

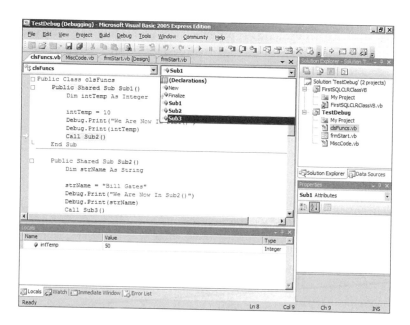

FIGURE 20.9
Using the Procedure drop-down menu to view another function.

Using Step Over

Sometimes you already have a subroutine fully tested and debugged. You want to continue stepping through the routine, but you don't want to watch the execution of subroutines. In this case, you use Step Over. To step over a subroutine or function, click Step Over on the Debug toolbar, press Shift+F8, or choose Debug, Step Over. The code within the subroutine or function you are stepping over executes, but you do not step through it. To experiment with the Step Over feature, follow the next example.

Click the open form and click the Start Debug Process button one more time. Because you did not remove the existing breakpoints, the debugger places you on the line of code that reads Call clsFuncs.Sub1(). Select Delete All Breakpoints from the Debug menu, or use the Ctrl+Shift+F9 keystroke combination to remove all breakpoints. Step (press F8) five times until you are about to execute the line Call Sub2. Suppose that you have tested Sub2 and Sub3 and know that they are not the cause of the problems in your code. With Sub2 highlighted as the next line that will execute, click Step Over on the toolbar. Notice that the debugger executes Sub2 and Sub3, but that you now are ready to continue stepping in Sub1. In this case, the debugger places you on the End Sub line immediately following the call to Sub2.

Using Step Out

You use the Step Out feature to step out of the procedure where you are and to return to the procedure that called the line of code where you are. You use this feature when you have accidentally stepped into a procedure that you realize you have fully tested. You want to execute all the code called by the procedure you are in and then step out to the calling procedure so that you can continue with the debugging process. To test how this works, follow this example.

1. Place a breakpoint on the call to Sub2.

2. Click the Reset button on the toolbar to halt code execution.

3. Activate the frmDebug form and click the Start Debug Process command button.

4. Step once to place yourself in the first line of Sub2.

5. Suppose that you realize you just stepped one step too far. You really intended to step over Sub2 and all the procedures it calls. No problem! Click the Step Out button to step out of Sub2 and return to the line following the line of code that called Sub2. In this case, you should find yourself on the End Sub statement of Sub1.

Setting the Next Statement to Execute

After you have stepped through your code, watched the logical flow, and modified some variables, you might want to re-execute the code beginning at a prior statement. The easiest way to do this is to click and drag the yellow arrow in the margin to the statement on which you want to continue execution. If you prefer, you can click anywhere in the line of code where you want to commence execution and then choose Debug, Set Next Statement. Regardless of the method you chose, notice that the contrasting color (usually yellow)—indicating the next line of code that the debugger will execute—is now placed over that statement. You then can step through the code by pressing F8, or you can continue normal code execution by pressing F5. The debugger enables you to set the next line it will execute within a procedure only. You can use this feature to re-execute lines of code or to skip over a problem line of code.

The following example walks you through the process of changing the value of a variable and then re-executing code after you have changed the value.

The preceding example left you at the last line of code (the End Sub statement) within Sub1. You want to change the value of intTemp and re-execute everything.

1. Go to the Immediate window and type `intTemp = 100`.

2. You need to set the next statement to print on the line that reads `Debug.Print("We Are Now in Sub1()")`. To do this, click and drag the yellow arrow from the End Sub statement to the `Debug.Print("We Are Now In Sub1()")` line. Notice the contrasting color (yellow), indicating that is the next statement of code that the debugger will execute.

3. Press F8 (step) two times. The code now executes with `intTemp` set to 100. Observe the Immediate window again. Notice how the results have changed.

Viewing the Call Stack

You have learned how to set breakpoints, step through and over code, use the Immediate window, set the next line to be executed, and continue to run until you reach the next breakpoint. When you reach a breakpoint, it often is important to see which functions the code called to bring you to this point. This is where the Calls feature can help.

To bring up the Call Stack window, click the Call Stack button on the toolbar or choose Debug, Windows, Call Stack. The window in Figure 20.10 appears. If you want to see the line of code that called a particular function or subroutine, double-click that particular function or click the function and then click Show. Although the debugger does not move your execution point to the calling function or subroutine, you can view the code within the procedure. If you want to continue your code execution, press F8. You move back to the procedure through which you were stepping, and the next line of code executes. If you press F5, your code executes until it reaches another breakpoint or watch. If you want to return to where you were without executing additional lines of code, choose Debug, Show Next Statement.

To test this process, perform the steps in the next example:

1. Click the Reset button to stop your code execution if you are still in Break mode.

2. Remove the breakpoint on the call to Sub2.

3. Move to the procedure called Sub3 in clsFuncs. Set a breakpoint on the line `Debug.Print("We Are Now in Sub3()")`.

4. Run the frmDebug form and click the command button. The debugger places you in Sub3 on the line where you set the breakpoint.

5. Bring up the Call Stack window by selecting Debug, Windows, Call Stack. If you want to see the line of code that called Sub2 from Sub1, double-click Sub1. Although the debugger does not move your execution point to Sub1, you can view the code within the procedure. To return to the next line of code to execute, choose Debug, Show Next Statement.

6. Press F5, and the rest of your code executes.

FIGURE 20.10
Viewing the stack with the Call Stack window.

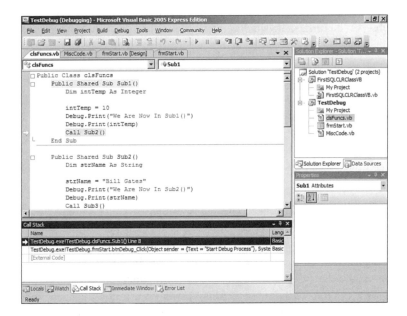

Working with the Locals Window

The Locals window enables you to see all the variables on the current stack frame and to view and modify their values. To access the Locals pane, click Locals on the toolbar, or select Debug, Windows, Locals. Three columns appear: Name, Value, and Type. The Name column shows you the variables, user-defined types, arrays, and other objects visible within the current procedure. The Value column displays the current value of a variable or expression. The Type column tells you what type of data a variable contains. The Locals window displays variables that contain hierarchical information—arrays, for example—with an Expand/Collapse button.

The information contained within the Locals window is dynamic. The debugger automatically updates it as it executes your code and as you move from routine to routine. Figure 20.11 illustrates how you can use the Locals window to view the variables available with the Sub2 subroutine. To try this example yourself, remove all existing breakpoints. Place a breakpoint in Sub2 on the line of code that reads Debug.Print(strName). Click Reset if you are still executing code, and click the Start Debug Process command button to execute code until the breakpoint. Click the Locals Window button on the Debug toolbar. View the contents of the variable strName.

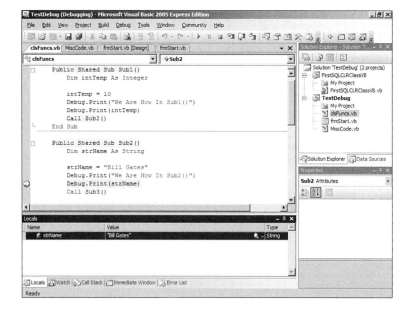

FIGURE 20.11
Viewing the
Locals window.

You can change the value of a variable in the Locals window, but you cannot change its name or type.

Working with Watch Expressions

Sometimes it is not enough to use the Immediate window to test the value of an expression or variable. You might want to keep a constant eye on the expression's value. After you add a Watch expression, it appears in the Watch window. As you'll see, you can create several types of watches.

Using Auto Data Tips

The quickest and easiest way to view the value contained within a variable is to use Auto Data Tips, which is an option for working with modules. This feature is available only when your code is in Break mode. While in Break mode, simply move your mouse over the variable or expression whose value you want to check. A tip appears with the current value.

Using a Quick Watch

A *quick watch* is the most basic type of watch. To add a quick watch, highlight the name of the variable or expression you want to watch, right-click, and select Quick Watch. The QuickWatch dialog box, shown in Figure 20.12, appears. You can click Add to add the expression as a permanent watch or choose Cancel to view the current value without adding it as a watch. If you click Add Watch and Close, a Watch window appears, like the one in Figure 20.13. The next section discusses this window in more detail.

FIGURE 20.12
The Quick Watch dialog box enables you to quickly view the value of a variable or add an expression as a permanent watch.

Adding a Watch Expression

As you saw, you can use a quick watch to add a Watch expression. You can also add a watch by right-clicking the variable and selecting Add Watch, or by clicking and dragging the variable to the Watch window.

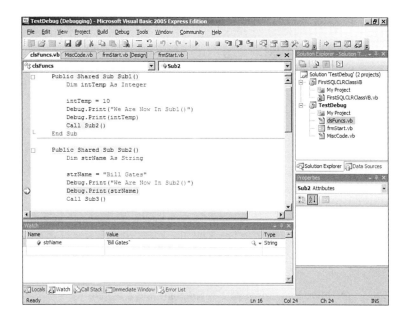

FIGURE 20.13
The Watches
window with
a Watch
expression.

The next example walks you through the process of adding a watch and viewing the Watch variable as you step through your code. It illustrates how a variable goes in and out of scope, and changes value, during code execution. To add a watch and then step through your code, follow these steps:

1. To begin, stop code execution if your code is running, and remove any breakpoints you have set.

2. Click within the strName variable in Sub2 and set a breakpoint on the line strName = "Bill Gates".

3. Run the frmDebug form and click the Command button.

4. Right-click strName and choose Add Watch.

5. View the Watches window and notice that strName has the value of Nothing.

6. Step one time and notice that strName is equal to Bill Gates.

7. Step three more times. Notice that although you are in the Sub3 routine, strName still has the value Bill Gates. This is because the variable is still in memory in the context of clsFuncs.Sub2.

9. Step four more times until you are back on the End Sub statement of Func2. The strName variable is still in context.

10. Step one more time. The strName variable is finally out of context because you have completed the execution of Sub2.

Summary

If programming were a perfect science, there would be no reason to use a debugger. Given the reality of the challenges of programming, though, a thorough under-standing of the use of the debugger is imperative. Fortunately, the .NET development environment provides an excellent tool to assist in the debugging process.

Q&A

Q. *Explain the difference between a breakpoint and a watch.*

A. A breakpoint is an unconditional point at which you want to suspend code execution, whereas a watch is a condition under which you want to suspend code execution.

Q. *Explain the difference between Step Into, Step Over, and Step Out.*

A. Step Into executes code one line at a time. You use Step Over to execute a subroutine or function without stepping through its code. Finally, you use Step Out to execute the remainder of a subroutine or function without stepping through its code. You return to the procedure that called the subroutine or function in which you were.

Q. *Explain the call stack.*

A. The call stack shows you which functions the code called to bring you to a specific point in code execution.

Workshop

Quiz

1. What keystroke combination do you use to activate the Immediate window?

2. What key do you press to set a breakpoint?

3. Changes that you make to data while debugging are only temporary (true/false).

4. Changes that you make to variables while debugging are only temporary (true/false).

5. What are the four ways that you can invoke the debugger?

6. What key do you use to step through code?

Quiz Answers

1. Ctrl+Break.

2. F9.

3. False. Changes that you make to data are permanent!

4. True.

5. Watch, Breakpoint, Stop Statement, Ctrl+Break.

6. F8.

Activities

Add a command button to initiate the process of stepping through the routine `DeletingData` in the `FirstSQLCLRVB` class of the `FirstSQLCLRClassVB` project. Modify the connection string to go against test data. Practice stepping through the routine.

PART III

Security and Administration

HOUR 21

SQL Server Authentication

Security is a very important aspect of a server database. It ensures that the data that you enter into the database is protected. In this hour you'll learn:

▶ The basics of security
▶ The types of authentication available
▶ How to create logins
▶ How to create roles

The Basics of Security

Security is necessary to prohibit access by unauthorized users and to ensure that authorized users have only the rights that you want them to have. SQL Server security is very robust and offers you several alternatives for your security model.

Let's begin by contrasting SQL Server security to that of a desktop database such as Microsoft Access. Access security is very limited and does not provide you with a lot of protection. You must grant read, write, and delete permissions to the users of an Access database for the network share on which the database resides. This makes the database vulnerable to hackers as well as the inadvertent actions of users (for example, accidentally moving or deleting a file). Furthermore, you cannot integrate Access security with the operating system. This means that users must log on to both the operating system and Microsoft Access. Furthermore, operating system features such as password aging, the logging of user activity, and the logging of invalid login attempts are all unavailable with Microsoft Access.

On the other hand, SQL Server offers a very robust and flexible security model. SQL Server 2005 security is tightly integrated with Windows security. This means that SQL Server can utilize the users and roles that you set up at the operating system level. Within SQL Server, you determine the rights that the users and roles have for the various SQL Server objects.

Not only are Windows users and roles available, but you can also take advantage of operating system features such as password expiration and the logging of login attempts and database activities.

We refer to the process of validating a user as *authentication*. We refer to the process of determining what a user can do as *permissions validation*. This hour covers authentication. The following hour covers permissions validation.

Types of Authentication Available

Authentication involves ensuring that a user is who he says he is. After SQL Server authenticates a user, the user can perform any actions specifically granted to his login, as well as actions granted to any roles of which the user is a member.

Two types of authentication exist:

▶ SQL Server and Windows (mixed authentication)

▶ Windows only

With SQL Server and Windows authentication, SQL Server supports both SQL Server and Windows logins. With Windows-only authentication, SQL Server supports only Windows logins. When you install SQL Server, you can configure the type of authentication that SQL Server will use. To modify the type of authentication that you want to use, follow these steps:

1. Launch SQL Server Management Studio Express.

2. Right-click the server whose authentication mode you want to modify and select Properties. The Server Properties dialog box appears.

3. Click the Security node.

4. Modify the Server authentication, as pictured in Figure 21.1.

Windows Only authentication has several advantages over SQL Server and Windows (Mixed) authentication. These advantages include:

▶ Requirement for the user to log on only once

▶ Central administration of logins

▶ Enforceable minimum password length

▶ Account lockout after unsuccessful login attempts

- More secure validation

- Encryption of passwords

- Auditing features

SQL Server and Windows (Mixed) authentication does have a few advantages over Windows Only authentication. They include:

- You can use SQL Server logins on the Windows 9x platform.

- SQL Server and Windows (Mixed) authentication enables you to support non-Windows users such as Novell users.

How to Create Logins

If you select Windows authentication, SQL Server assumes a trust relationship with your Windows server. It assumes that the user has already successfully logged in. Regardless of the authentication mode that you select, you must still create SQL Server logins.

Adding a Windows Login

To begin, we're going to take a look at the process of creating a Windows login. As you'll see, it is somewhat different from creating a SQL login. Follow these steps to create a Windows login.

   1. Click to expand the Security node for the server (see Figure 21.2).

FIGURE 21.2
To add a Windows login, click to expand the Security node for the server.

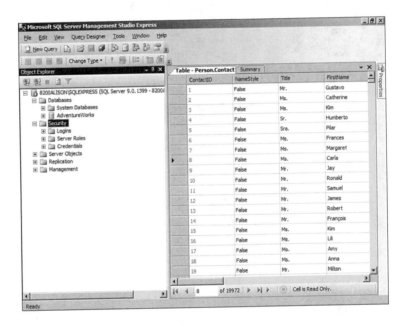

   2. Right-click Logins and select New Login. The Login Properties dialog box appears (see Figure 21.3).

   3. Type the name for the login, or click Search to locate the login.

   4. If you click Search, the Select User or Group dialog appears (see Figure 21.4). Make sure that the object type and location are correct, and then type the name of the user or group.

   5. Click Check Names to verify that the user or group exists.

   6. Click OK to close the Select User or Group dialog.

   7. Make sure that Windows authentication is selected.

   8. Specify the default database for the user (refer to Figure 21.3).

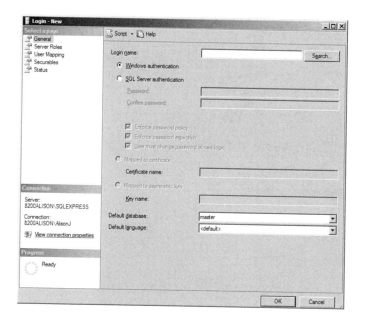

FIGURE 21.3
The Login Properties dialog box enables you to enter information about the new login.

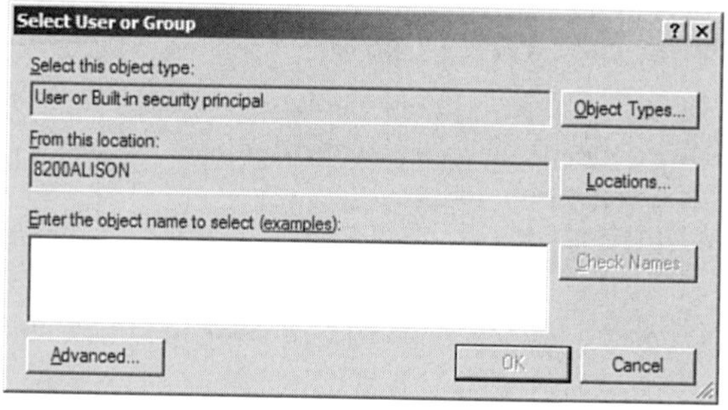

FIGURE 21.4
The Select User or Group dialog enables you to search for a login.

6. Click the Server Roles node to grant the user membership to server roles (see Figure 21.5).

7. Click the User Mapping tab to designate to which databases the user has rights. The "Granting Database Access to Logins" section of this hour covers database access.

8. Click OK to close the dialog box and add the user.

FIGURE 21.5
You use the
Server Roles
node to grant
the user mem-
bership to
server roles.

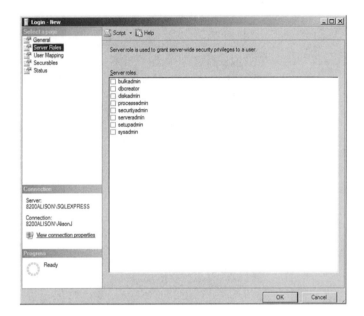

Adding a SQL Server Login

When adding a SQL Server login, you are adding a login that does not exist anywhere else. The login is independent of the operating system and its logins. Follow
these steps to create a SQL Server login:

1. Click to expand the Security node for the server.

2. Right-click Logins and select New Login. The Login Properties dialog box
   appears.

3. Type the name for the login.

4. Make sure that you select SQL Server authentication.

5. Type a password for the user (see Figure 21.6). This case-sensitive password
   can contain from 1 through 128 characters, including letters, symbols, and
   digits.

6. Confirm the password.

7. Specify the default database for the user.

8. Click the Server Roles node to grant the user membership to server roles.

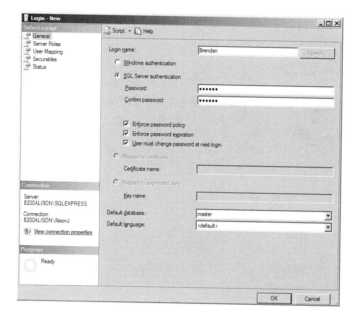

FIGURE 21.6
When using SQL
Server and
Windows
(Mixed) authen-
tication, the
SQL Server
Login Properties
dialog box
prompts you to
type a password
for the user.

9. Click the User Mapping node to designate to which databases the user has rights. The "Granting Database Access to Logins" section of this hour covers database access.

10. Click OK to close the dialog.

Granting Database Access to Logins

Whether you use Windows Only authentication or SQL Server authentication, you need to determine to which databases the user has rights and to which fixed database and user-defined database roles the user belongs. You can grant database access for a login when adding the login (see previous text). To grant database access for an existing login, follow these steps:

1. Click to expand the Security node for the server.

2. Click Logins in the left pane. The available logins appear in the right pane. Right-click the login that you want to affect and select Properties. The Login Properties dialog box appears.

3. Click to select the User Mapping node. The dialog box appears, as in Figure 21.7.

4. Click the Map check box next to each database to which you want the user to have access.

5. Click to select each database role (system- and user-defined) to which you want the user to belong.

6. Click OK to commit your changes.

FIGURE 21.7
The Database Access tab of the SQL Server Login Properties dialog box enables you to designate the databases to which you want the user to have access.

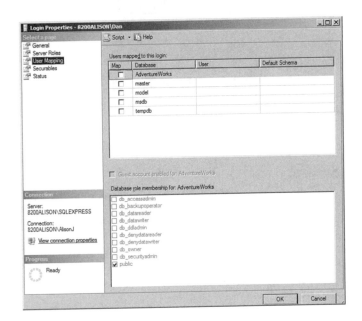

The SA Login

The SA Login is a special login within the SQL Server environment. If you install SQL Server in mixed mode (Windows and SQL Server authentication), the SA login has unlimited powers. With mixed-mode authentication, there is no way to modify or delete the SA account. It is therefore *imperative* that you assign a password to the SA account. Failure to do so renders any other security that you apply to the server futile.

How to Create Roles

Roles are the equivalent of Windows groups. You create roles and then grant users membership to those roles. Users who are members of a role inherit the permissions assigned to that role. The process of creating roles and assigning permissions to those roles greatly facilitates the process of administering security. Rather than having to assign specific rights to each user of a system, you can instead assign rights to groups of users.

Types of Roles

SQL Server offers four types of roles. These include:

▶ Fixed server roles

▶ Fixed database roles

▶ User-defined database roles

▶ Application roles

Each of these types of roles serves a specific purpose. Generally you will use several types of roles in combination. The sections that appear later in the hour discuss each type of role in detail.

Fixed Server Roles

Fixed server roles are built into SQL Server and are in no way user-definable (you cannot add them, modify them, or delete them). They enable their members to perform server-level administrative tasks. The fixed server roles include:

▶ **Bulk Insert Administrators (bulkadmin)**--Can execute bulk insert statements.

▶ **Database Creators (dbcreator)**--Can create and alter databases.

▶ **Disk Administrators (diskadmin)**--Can manage disk files.

▶ **Process Administrators (processadmin)**--Can manage SQL Server processes.

▶ **Security Administrators (securityadmin)**--Can manage server logins.

▶ **Server Administrators (serveradmin)**--Can configure server-wide settings.

▶ **Setup Administrators (setupadmin)**--Can install replication and can manage extended properties.

▶ **System Administrators (sysadmin)**--Can perform *any* activity on that SQL Server instance. This includes all activities of the other roles. In fact, if a user is a member of the sysadmin role, you cannot prohibit him from performing *any* tasks on the server.

Server roles greatly facilitate the process of managing security. They accomplish this by allowing you to compartmentalize the administrative tasks that users can perform and to grant them rights to perform only those specific tasks.

> When you install SQL Server, the installation process adds the Windows
> Administrators group to the sysadmin role. This means that all members of the
> Administrators group instantly become members of sysadmin. Fortunately, you can
> remove this mapping from Administrators to the sysadmin role. To remove the
> mapping, you must deny the Administrators group from logging on to the SQL
> Server. You then grant the individual users membership to the sysadmin role.

To assign a user to a fixed server role, follow these steps:

1. Expand the Security node until you can see the Server Roles subnode (see
   Figure 21.8) .

FIGURE 21.8
The Server
Roles subnode
of the Security
node enables
you to assign
users to a fixed
server role.

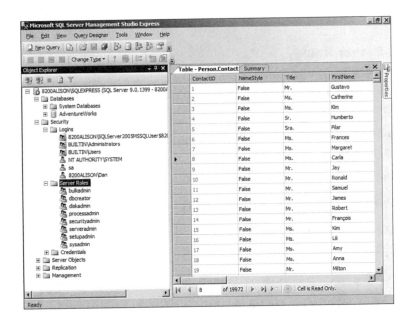

2. Right-click the role to which you want to grant users membership and select
   Properties. The Server Role Properties dialog box appears (see Figure 21.9).

3. Click Add to add a user to the role. The Select Logins dialog box appears (see
   Figure 21.10).

4. Click Browse to select the logins that you want to add. The Browse for Objects
   dialog appears (see Figure 21.11)

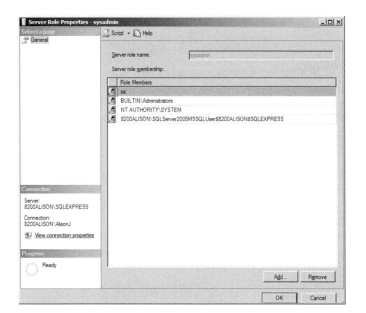

FIGURE 21.9
The Server Role Properties dialog box enables you to add users to a role.

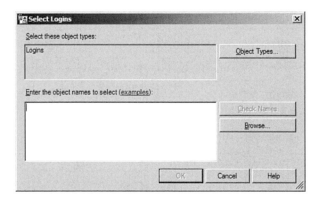

FIGURE 21.10
The Select Logins dialog box enables you to add logins to a role.

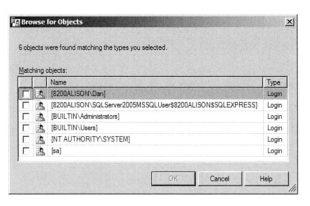

FIGURE 21.11
Browse for Objects dialog box enables you to select the users that you want to add to a role.

5. Click to check the objects you want to add to the role.

6. Click to close the Browse for Objects dialog.

7. Click OK. SQL Server adds the selected users to the role.

Fixed Database Roles

Whereas fixed server roles enable you to assign rights to users that apply at the server level, fixed database roles enable you to assign rights at the database level. Because fixed server roles apply at the server level, they are found under the Security node. Because fixed database roles apply at a database level, they are located under the specific database node of the database to which they apply.

As with fixed server roles, you cannot add, remove, or modify the rights granted to fixed database roles. Fixed database roles facilitate the process of assigning permissions for a database. The fixed database roles include:

▶ **db_accessadmin**--Can add and remove Windows 2000/Windows 2003 users and groups and SQL Server users for the database.

▶ **db_backupoperator**--Can back up the database.

▶ **db_datareader**--Can view data in all user tables in the database.

▶ **db_datawriter**--Can add, edit, and delete data in all user tables in the database.

▶ **db_ddladmin**--Can add, modify, and drop database objects.

▶ **db_denydatareader**--Cannot see any data in the database.

▶ **db_denydatawriter**--Cannot modify any data in the database.

▶ **db_owner**--Can perform the activities of any of the other roles. Can also perform all database maintenance and configuration tasks.

▶ **db_securityadmin**--Can manage role membership and statement and object permissions for the database.

To assign a user to a fixed database role, perform these steps:

1. Expand the Database node of the desired database until you can see the Roles subnode (see Figure 21.12).

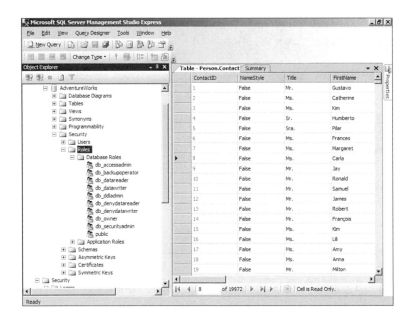

FIGURE 21.12
The Roles subnode of the Database node enables you to work with roles for that database.

2. Right-click the role to which you want to grant users membership and select Properties. The Database Role Properties dialog box appears (see Figure 21.13).

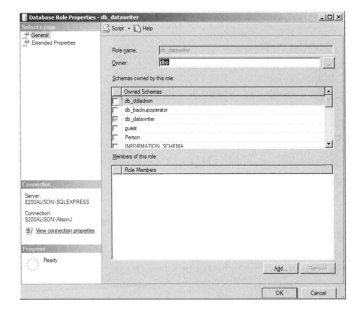

FIGURE 21.13
The Database Role Properties dialog box enables you to add users to a database role.

3. Click Add to add a user to the role. The Select Database User or Role dialog box appears (see Figure 21.14).

FIGURE 21.14
Select Database User or Role dialog box enables you to add users to a role.

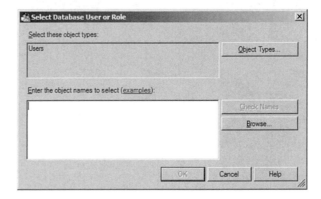

4. Click Browse. The Browse for Objects dialog appears (see Figure 21.15).

FIGURE 21.15
The Browse for Objects dialog box enables you to select the users that you want to add to a role.

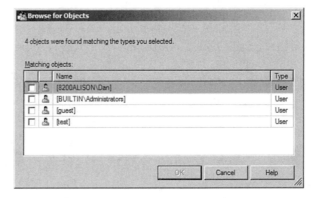

5. Click to select the logins that you want to add and click OK. Click OK to close the Select Database User or Role dialog. SQL Server adds the selected users to the role.

The Public role is a special built-in fixed database role. Every user is a member of it. When you grant a user access to a database, SQL Server adds the user to the Public database. You can't remove the Public role, nor can you remove users of a database from the Public role. Any rights that you grant to the Public role are automatically granted to all users of the database. The Public role therefore provides an excellent means of easily granting all users rights to a particular object. On the other hand, if you accidentally grant the Public role rights, those rights apply to all users of the database.

User-Defined Database Roles

At a database level, you are not limited to the predefined roles. In addition to the predefined roles, you can add your own roles. SQL Server offers two types of user-defined roles. They are

▶ **Standard role**--Custom role that you use to facilitate the task of assigning rights to users of the database.

▶ **Application role**--Role used by an application.

To create a user-defined role, follow these steps:

1. Expand the Database node of the desired database until you can see the Roles subnode (see Figure 21.16).

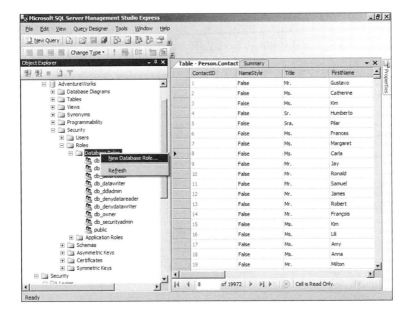

FIGURE 21.16
The Roles subnode of the Database node enables you to create and work with user-defined database roles.

2. Right-click the Roles subnode and select New and then New Database Role. The Database Role dialog box appears, prompting you to enter the name of the new role (see Figure 21.17).

FIGURE 21.17
The Database
Role dialog box
enables you to
enter the name
of the new role.

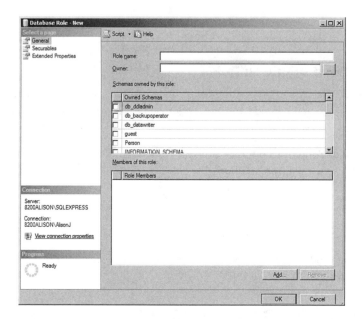

3. Type the name of the role in the Role name text box.

4. Designate the schemas owned by the role.

5. Click Add to add a user to the role. The Select Database User or Role dialog box appears.

6. Select the logins that you want to add (clicking Browse if necessary) and click OK. SQL Server adds the selected users to the role and the role to the database.

Ownership

It is important to understand what ownership is and what the implications of ownership are. SQL Server designates the creator of an object as its owner. The owner of an object has *full* permissions for that object. Furthermore, the name of the object is actually owner.objectname--for example, alexis.tblCustomers.

You cannot remove a user from a database as long as he owns objects within it. Ownership of an object is implied. This means that you cannot directly administer an object's owner.

There is a special user account (dbo)within each database. SQL Server maps the dbo to the sysadmin fixed server role. This means that if you are a member of the sysadmin group and you create an object, SQL Server flags the object as owned by dbo, not by you. You can refer to the object as dbo.objectname.

The sp_changeobjectowner system-stored procedure enables you to change an object's owner. Only members of the sysadmin fixed server role, the db_owner fixed database role, or a member of *both* the db_ddladmin and db_securityadmin fixed database roles can execute the sp_changeobjectowner stored procedure. It looks like this:

```
EXEC sp_changeobjectowner 'tblCustomers', 'Brendan'
```

When you change an object's owner, SQL Server drops all permissions for the object. To change the owner back to dbo, you must fully qualify the owner name and object name. The syntax looks like this:

```
EXEC sp_changeobjectowner 'Brendan.tblCustomers', 'dbo'
```

Summary

You can create the best application and database in the world, but if it is not properly secured, someone can easily sabotage it. In this hour you learned the basics of security. You learned about the types of authentication available, and about logins and roles. Hour 22, "SQL Server Permissions Validation," covers security in additional detail.

Q&A

Q. *Explain the difference between Windows Only authentication and SQL Server and Windows (Mixed) authentication.*

A. With Windows authentication the user does not need to log on to the server more than one time. Users you add to the SQL Server then gain the specified access to the server. With Windows authentication, you also get all the benefits of the operating system login process. For example, you can enforce minimum password length.

With SQL Server and Windows (Mixed) Authentication you can use SQL Server logins on the Windows 9x platform. You do not have to have organized Windows domains, and finally, SQL Server and Windows (Mixed) authentication enables you to support non-Windows users such as Novell users.

Q. *Explain the SA login and what it can do.*

A. The SA login is available only with Mixed Authentication. The SA login has unlimited powers! There is no way to modify or delete the SA account. It is therefore imperative that you assign a password to the SA account. Otherwise, any other security measures you take will be futile.

Q. *Explain the interaction between sysadmin and the Windows Administrators group.*

A. All members of the Windows Administrators group are added automatically to the sysadmin role upon installation of SQL Server. Remember that sysadmin is all-powerful in working with your server. Fortunately you can remove this mapping. You must first deny the Administrators group from logging on to the SQL Server. You then grant the individual users membership to the sysadmin role as required.

Workshop

Quiz

1. Name four types of roles.

2. The SA user is available with both SQL Server and Windows authentication (true/false).

3. Name some benefits of Windows authentication.

4. If a login exists in Windows and you want them to be able to access the SQL Server, you don't have to do anything special (true/false).

5. You find fixed database roles under the database node of the database with which they are associated (true/false).

6. What user is automatically the owner of an object?

7. Name the stored procedure that enables you to change an object's ownership.

Quiz Answers

1. Server, Database, User-Defined, Application.

2. False. Only with Mixed authentication.

3. Single login, password expiration, central administration, more secure validation, password encryption, account lockout after a certain number of
   attempts.

4. False. You still have to create them as a user in SQL Server.

5. True.

6. The user that creates the object.

7. `sp_changeobjectowner`.

Activities

Set up a server with Windows-Only authentication. Add three new logins. Grant
each login access to the AdventureWorks database. Assign one user to the Process
Administrator fixed server role. Assign another user to the db_datareader role of
AdventureWorks. Create a user-defined role as part of the AdventureWorks database.
Assign all three logins to that role

HOUR 22

SQL Server Permissions Validation

In the previous hour you learned about SQL Server authentication, the process of ensuring that only valid users work with your database. After users gain access to a database it is important that they have specific rights to objects within the database. In this hour you'll learn:

▶ The types of permissions available
▶ How to work with table permissions
▶ How to work with view permissions
▶ How to work with stored procedure permissions
▶ How to work with function permissions
▶ How to implement column-level security

The Types of Permissions Available

When a user logs in to the server, SQL Server first authenticates him to ensure that he is a valid user. SQL Server then grants the user permission to perform any task assigned to the user or to any roles of which the user is a member.

SQL Server offers three types of permissions. They include:

▶ **Object permissions**—Permissions set for objects such as tables and views. These include SELECT, INSERT, UPDATE, and DELETE permissions.

▶ **Statement permissions**—Permissions applied to statements such as the CREATE VIEW statement. These permissions define what rights the user has to the specified statement.

▶ **Inherited or implied permissions**—These permissions refer to rights that a user has to an object because he is a member of a role that has rights to that object, or because the user is the owner of the object.

Adding Database Users

If you want a user to have access to a database, you must first create a user account in the database. To do so, follow these steps:

1. Expand the Database node of the desired database until you can see the Users subnode (see Figure 22.1).

FIGURE 22.1
The Users subnode enables you to manage a database's users.

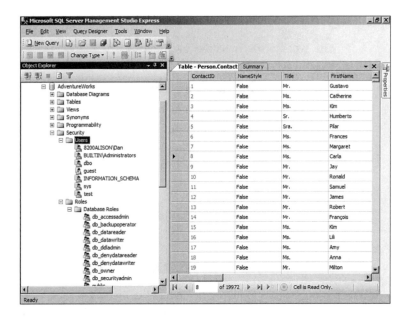

2. Right-click the Users sub-node and select New User. The Database User dialog box appears, prompting you to enter the login name of the new user (see Figure 22.2).

3. Type the login name, or click the Build button. If you click the Build button, the Select Login dialog appears (see Figure 21.3). Here you can type login names or click Browse. If you click Browse, the Browse for Objects dialog appears (see Figure 21.4).

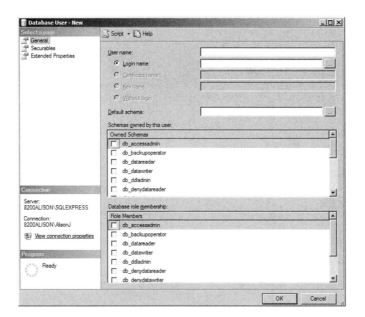

FIGURE 22.2
The Database User dialog prompts you to enter the new user's login name.

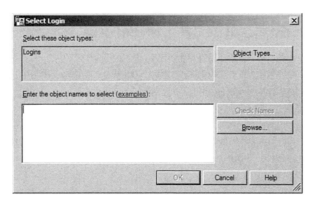

FIGURE 22.3
The Select Login dialog enables you to type login names.

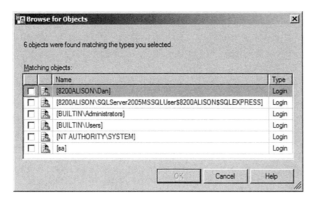

FIGURE 22.4
The Browse for Objects dialog enables you to select database users that you wish to add.

4. Click to select the database users you want to add.

5. Click OK to close the dialog box.

6. Click OK to close the Select Login dialog.

7. Click OK to close the Database User dialog and add the user(s).

Permission Statements

You can execute three different permission statements for the objects in your database. They include:

▶ **GRANT**—Grants permission.

▶ **WITH GRANT**—Allows the user or role to grant rights to other users or roles for the object.

▶ **DENY**—Revokes permission so that permission for that object cannot be inherited.

Administering Object Permissions

You can administer permissions for an object in one of two ways. The first way is via the object. This method shows you the rights for all users and roles for a particular object. It works like this:

1. Right-click the object and select Properties. The Properties dialog box appears.

2. Click to select the Permissions page. The rights established for the selected object appear (see Figure 22.5). Here you can assign users and roles rights for the object.

3. Click Add to begin the process. The Select Users or Roles dialog appears (see Figure 22.6).

4. Enter user and role names, or click Browse to select the users and roles to which you want to grant rights (see Figure 22.7) .

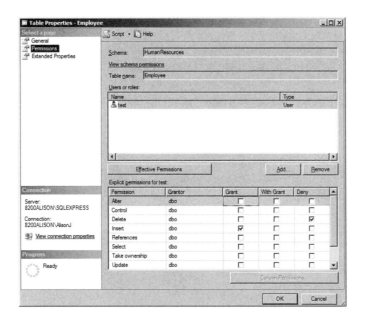

FIGURE 22.5
The Permissions page enables you to assign users and roles rights for the object.

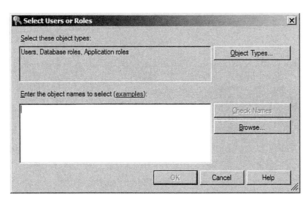

FIGURE 22.6
The Select Users or Roles dialog enables you to enter users or roles to which you want to designate permissions.

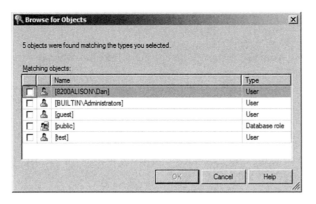

FIGURE 22.7
The Browse for Objects dialog enables you to select the users and roles to which you are setting rights.

5. Click OK to close the Browse for Objects dialog.

6. Click OK to close the Select Users or Roles dialog. The Permissions page of the Table Properties dialog should appear as in Figure 22.8.

FIGURE 22.8
The Permissions page after selecting the users and roles to which you want to assign rights.

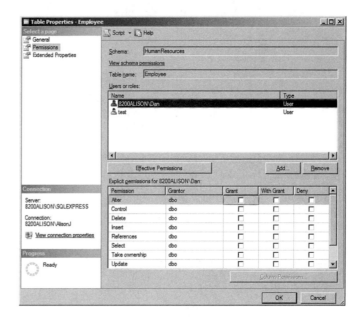

7. Select a user or role in the list of users and roles.

8. For each type of permission, designate whether you want to Grant, With Grant, or Deny permissions to the user or role, for that object. For example, in Figure 22.9, the user named Dan has been granted Insert rights to the Employee table, but has been denied Delete rights.

9. After granting all desired rights to all users and roles, click OK to close the Table Properties dialog. SQL Server applies the designated rights.

As an alternative, you can assign rights for all objects to a *database* user or role. Follow these steps:

1. Right-click the user or role and select Properties. The Database User dialog box appears.

2. Click to select the Securables page (see Figure 22.10). Here you can see a particular user or role and manage rights to all objects for the user or role.

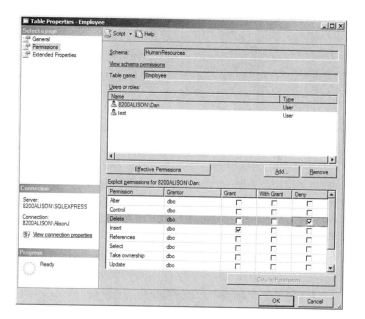

FIGURE 22.9
The Permissions page enables you to assign users and roles rights for the object.

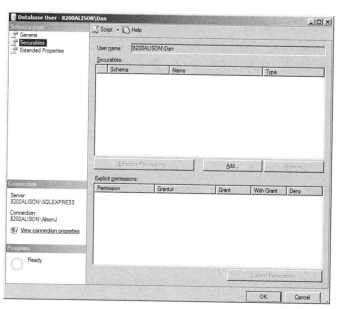

FIGURE 22.10
The Securables page enables you to select a user or role and then manage rights for its objects.

3. Click Add to add the objects that you want to secure. The Add Objects dialog appears (see Figure 22.11).

FIGURE 22.11
The Add Objects
dialog enables
you to desig-
nate the types
of objects you
want to secure.

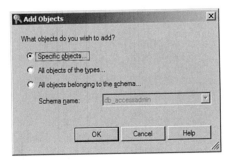

4. Indicate whether you want to secure specific objects, all objects of specific
   types (for example, tables), or all objects belonging to the schema. Make your
   selection and click OK.

5. If you click Specific Objects, the Select Objects dialog appears (see Figure 22.12).

FIGURE 22.12
The Select
Objects dialog
initiates the
process of
allowing you to
select the types
of objects you
want to secure.

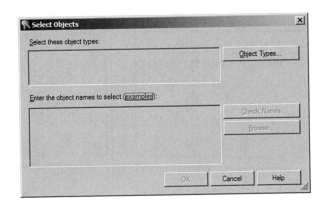

6. Click Object Types. The Select Object Types dialog appears (see Figure 22.13).

7. Click to select the types of objects you want to secure for that user. Click OK.

8. Click OK to return to the Select Objects dialog.

9. Click Browse to locate the object names you want to secure. The Browse
   for Objects dialog appears, showing only the selected types of objects (see
   Figure 22.14).

10. Select the objects you want to secure and click OK. The Select Objects dialog
    now appears as in Figure 22.15.

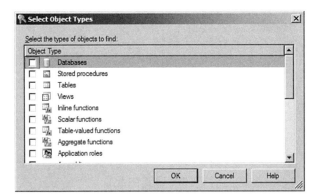

FIGURE 22.13
The Select Object Types dialog allows you to select the types of objects you wish to secure for that user or role.

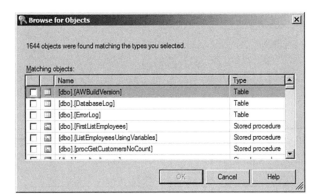

FIGURE 22.14
The Browse for Objects dialog shows you the selected types of objects.

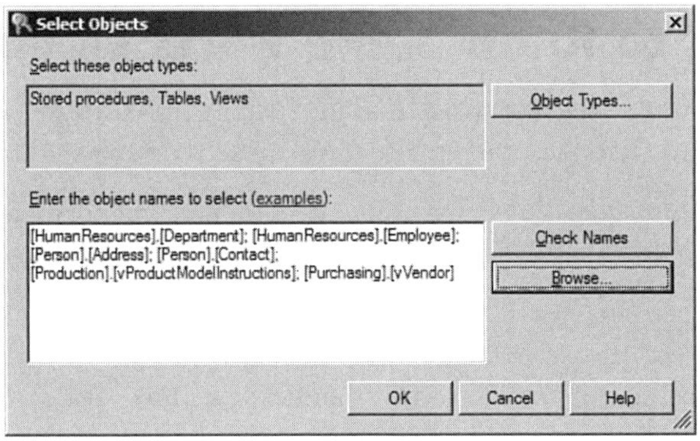

FIGURE 22.15
The Select Objects dialog appears with the types of objects you want to secure.

11. Click OK to close the Select Objects dialog. The Securables page of the Database User dialog appears as in Figure 22.16. You are ready to assign rights to the selected objects.

FIGURE 22.16
The Securables
page of the
Database User
dialog appears
with all the
objects you
want to secure.

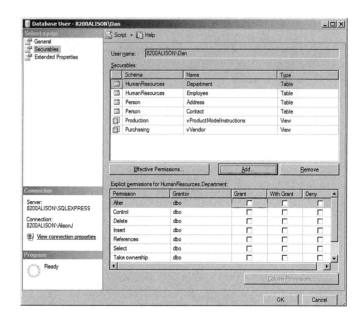

If you select all objects of the types in Step 4, the Select Object Types dialog
appears. Here you select the types of objects you want to find. You are then ready
to assign rights to the selected objects.

Getting to Know Table Permissions

You can grant ALTER, CONTROL, DELETE, INSERT, SELECT, TAKE OWNERSHIP, UPDATE,
and VIEW DEFINITION rights for a table. These are each described as follows:

▶ ALTER **permissions**—Allow the user to alter all properties of a table except
ownership. Include the capability to create, alter, and drop tables.

▶ CONTROL **permissions**—CONTROL permissions confer ownership-like capabilities
for an object. The user can administer the object (assign rights, and so on),
and has permission to all objects within it. For example, users who have
CONTROL permissions to a database can fully manage that database.

▶ DELETE **permissions**—Allow the user to delete table data.

▶ INSERT **permissions**—Allow the user to add data to the table.

▶ SELECT **permissions**—Allow the user to view the data in a table.

▶ TAKE OWNERSHIP **permissions**—Allow the user to take ownership of the table on which it is granted.

▶ UPDATE **permissions**—Allow the user to update the data in the table.

▶ VIEW DEFINITION **permissions**—Allow the user to access metadata for the table.

To assign permissions for a table, follow these steps:

1. Right-click the table for which you want to assign permissions and select Properties. The Table Properties dialog box appears.

2. Click the Permissions page. The Table Properties dialog box appears as in Figure 22.17.

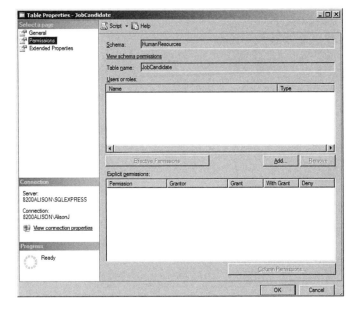

FIGURE 22.17
The Permissions page of the Table Properties dialog box before the users and roles to which you are assigning rights have been designated.

3. Click to Browse the users and roles to which you want to assign rights for that table. The Browse for Objects dialog appears.

4. Click to select the users and roles you want to affect.

5. Click OK. SQL Server returns you to the Select Users or Roles dialog.

6. Click OK to close the Select Users or Roles dialog and return to the Table
   Properties dialog. It should now appear as in Figure 22.18.

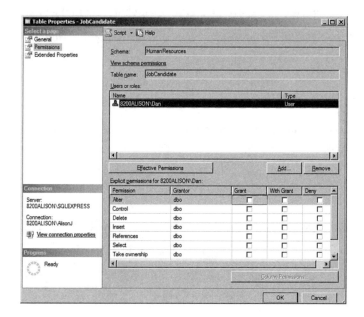

7. Click to Grant, With Grant, or Deny ALTER, CONTROL, DELETE, INSERT,
   REFERENCES, SELECT, TAKE OWNERSHIP, UPDATE, and VIEW DEFINITION rights
   as required.

8. Click OK when done. SQL Server applies the designated permissions.

EXEC permissions are not applicable to a table. They are applicable only for
stored procedures and are therefore covered in the section of this chapter entitled
"Stored Procedure Permissions."

Getting to Know View Permissions

Permissions for a view override those for the underlying tables. Using views, you can
very easily apply both row-level and column-level security. You can achieve column-
level security by limiting the columns included in the view. You can implement
row-level security by adding a WHERE clause to the view. Because the results of most

views are updateable, the process of applying security for a view is similar to that
for a table. Follow these steps:

1. Right-click the view for which you want to assign permissions for and select
    Properties. The View Properties dialog box appears.

2. Click the Permissions page of the View Properties dialog. The View Properties
    dialog box appears as in Figure 22.19.

3. Click Add the Users or Roles to add the users and roles who will gain rights to
    the view. The Select Users or Roles dialog appears.

4. Click Browse to designate the users and roles to which you want to assign
    rights. The Browse for Objects dialog appears.

5. Select the users and roles to which you want to assign rights for the view.

6. Click OK to close the Browse for Objects dialog.

7. Click OK to close the Select Users or Roles dialog. The Permissions tab of the
    View Properties dialog appears as in Figure 22.19.

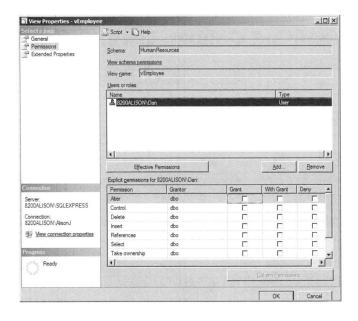

FIGURE 22.19
The Object
Properties
dialog box
enables you to
assign *ALTER*,
CONTROL,
DELETE, *INSERT*,
REFERENCES,
SELECT, *TAKE
OWNERSHIP*,
UPDATE, and
*VIEW
DEFINITION* per-
missions for a
View, as
required.

8. Click to assign ALTER, CONTROL, DELETE, INSERT, REFERENCES, SELECT, TAKE
    OWNERSHIP, UPDATE, and VIEW DEFINITION rights as required.

9. Click OK when finished.

Getting to Know Stored Procedure Permissions

As with rights for a view, rights assigned for a stored procedure override rights assigned for the underlying tables and views. This is the case as long as the stored procedure has the same owner as the tables referenced with it. Stored procedures have only five permissions: ALTER CONTROL, EXECUTE, TAKE OWNERSHIP, and VIEW DEFINITION. The most commonly assigned right, the EXECUTE right, determines whether the user or role can execute the stored procedure.

Getting to Know Function Permissions

As with rights assigned for views and stored procedures, rights assigned for a user-defined function that returns a table override rights assigned for the underlying tables and views. This is the case as long as the function has the same owner as the tables referenced with it. Functions have the same permissions as tables. The main limitation of functions is that they return read-only results

Implementing Column-Level Security

SQL Server 2005 Express enables you to assign column-level permissions easily for tables and views. Column-level permissions enable you to determine on a column-by-column basis whether the user has SELECT and UPDATE rights for that particular column. INSERT and DELETE rights cannot be assigned at a column level because they affect the entire row. To assign column-level permissions for tables and views, follow these steps:

1. Right-click the table for which you want to assign permissions and select Properties. The Table Properties dialog box appears.

2. Click the Permissions page to select it. The Permissions page of the dialog box appears.

3. Click Add to add the users and roles to which you want to apply column-level permissions. The Select Users or Roles dialog appears.

4. Click Browse to designate the users and roles to which you want to apply column-level permissions.

5. Click to select your choices.

6. Click OK to close the dialog box.

7. Click OK to close the Select Users or Roles dialog box.

8. Click to grant SELECT or UPDATE rights to the selected user or role for that table or view. The Column Permissions command button becomes enabled (see Figure 22.20) .

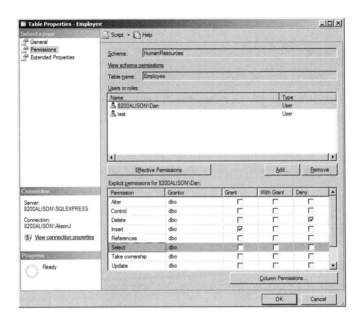

FIGURE 22.20
The Column Permissions command button becomes enabled after you grant SELECT or UPDATE rights to the selected user or role.

9. Click Column Permissions. The Column Permissions dialog box appears (see Figure 22.21). Indicate the SELECT or UPDATE rights for the individual columns as desired.

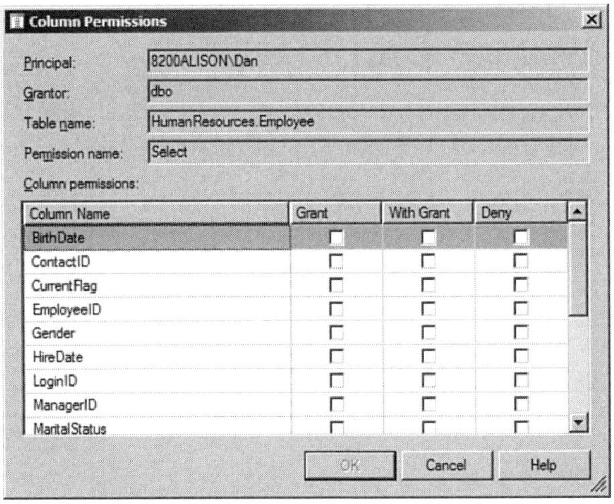

FIGURE 22.21
The Column Permissions dialog box lets you determine on a column-by-column basis whether the user has SELECT and UPDATE rights for that particular column.

10. Click OK to close the Column Permissions dialog box and return to the Table Properties dialog box.

11. Click OK to apply the permissions.

Summary

After a user gains access to a database, you must then determine what rights the user has to objects within the database. In this hour you learned about permissions validation, the process of determining what a user can do after gaining access to the database. You learned how to designate permissions for the various types of objects in the database, and you learned about the types of permissions available. Finally, you learned how to apply table and view security at a column-level.

Q&A

Q *Explain inherited permissions.*

A Inherited permissions refer to rights that a user has to an object because he is a member of a role that has rights to that object, or because he is the owner of the object.

Q *Explain the difference between* WITH GRANT *and* DENY *permissions.*

A WITH GRANT permissions revoke permission for an object unless that user is a member of a role that has rights to that object. DENY permissions revoke permission so that permission for an object cannot be inherited.

Q *Describe* CONTROL *permissions.*

A With CONTROL permissions the user or role has ownership-like capabilities for the object. The user can administer the object and has permission to all objects within it.

Workshop

Quiz

1. Name three types of permissions.

2. Name the permission statement that gives a user rights to an object.

3. Describe VIEW DEFINITION permissions.

4. Permissions for a view override those for the underlying table (true/false).

5. How can you implement row-level security with a view?

6. The results of views are not updateable (true/false).

7. What is the most commonly assigned right for a stored procedure?

Quiz Answers

1. Object, Statement, and Inherited, or Implied.

2. GRANT.

3. VIEW DEFINITION permissions allow the user to access metadata for the table.

4. True.

5. By using a WHERE clause.

6. False. The results of most views are updateable.

7. EXECUTE.

Activities

Add three roles to AdventureWorks. Named one staff, and another managers, and another systemadministrators. Apply permissions for the HumanResources. Department table in the AdventureWorks database. Give staff SELECT and INSERT rights to the table. Give management SELECT, INSERT, UPDATE, and DELETE rights to the table. Give systemadministrators CONTROL permissions for the table. Add three users, assigning each user to one of the three roles. Practice logging in as each user and note what you can do within the HumanResources.Department table.

Configuring, Maintaining, and Tuning SQL Server

The most attractive application can be extremely frustrating to use if its performance is less than acceptable. As a developer, you must take precautions to try to ensure that the SQL Server is as lean and efficient as possible. In this hour you'll learn about:

▶ How to select and tune your hardware
▶ How to configure and tune SQL Server
▶ How to maintain your databases
▶ How to maintain your tables and other objects

Selecting and Tuning Hardware

Your choice of hardware can greatly affect the performance of your server. Areas of particular concern are the amount of memory, processor speed, and hard disk configuration. The network architecture is also an important factor. The sections that follow cover the details of each of these items.

Memory—The More RAM, the Better!

SQL Server uses memory (RAM) to hold all data pages, index pages, and log records. It also uses memory to hold compiled queries and stored procedures. Needless to say, memory is vital to the server's performance.

Clients are always asking me how much memory they should purchase for their servers. My answer is, the more, the better. In fact, RAM is the best investment that you can make for your SQL Server. That aside, here are some guidelines. A bare minimum amount of RAM for any server is 256MB. SQL Server Express can take advantage of only 1GB of RAM! If your database requires more RAM than that, you will have to move to another version of SQL Server.

Optimizing Processor Power

Although it's not as important as RAM, more processing power never hurts. Unfortunately, SQL Express can take advantage of only one processor. If you need additional processing power, you should move to another version of SQL Server.

Optimizing Disk Performance

Because SQL Server stores all your data on disk, the type and layout of disks that you use are both important factors. Small Computer System Interface (SCSI) disks, as well as Serial Advanced Technology Enhancement (SATA and SATA II) drives, offer excellent performance for SQL Express. It is also effective to use multiple SCSI disks, each with its own disk controller. This enables SQL Server to distribute the workload across several disks and several controllers.

You can gain both performance benefits and fault tolerance benefits if the computer running SQL Server Express has at least two physical hard drives installed. By placing the database on one disk and the log file on the other, you gain a speed advantage over using just one disk for both the database and the log file. In addition, if the hard disk containing the database fails, you can replace that hard disk, restore the database from backup media, and then SQL Express plays back (from the log file) any transactions that occurred after the backup was made up to the point in time when the drive failed. If the disk that contains the log file fails, you can simply replace the failed drive. SQL Express will create a new log file, and the SQL Express database will still be perfectly intact.

You can use more sophisticated disk configurations for your SQL Express computer as well. For example, you can set up disk mirroring (also known as RAID Level 1 or just RAID 1). Disk mirroring requires two physical disks in which data is written identically to both disks simultaneously. RAID 1 can be configured with either hardware or software, but a hardware solution is generally faster and more reliable. Disk duplexing is also referred to as RAID 1. The only difference from disk mirroring is that duplexing employs two hard disk controllers—one controller for each physical disk. Disk duplexing eliminates the single point of failure that a single disk controller offers. If your SQL Server computer is configured with RAID 1, fault tolerance is already built in.

You may have heard of RAID 5, also known as disk striping with parity. RAID 5 requires a minimum of three physical disks and a maximum of 32 disks. Disk striping with parity enables you to have more available fault-tolerant disk space at a lower cost than disk mirroring or duplexing, in terms of the quantity of disks needed. RAID 1 uses up 50% of available disk space for fault tolerance; RAID 5 uses only 33% or less of available disk space because the parity information needed to restore an array when one disk fails is roughly equal to one disk in the array. For a RAID 5 array using three 100GB disks, the equivalent of one disk is used for parity information; the remaining two disks are used as available disk space (200GB would be available—a 33% reduction in total disk capacity). For RAID 1 (disk mirroring or duplexing), two 100GB disks give you only 100GB of available disk space—a 50% reduction in total disk capacity.

You may also have heard of RAID 0—disk striping. This uses no parity information and is therefore is not fault tolerant at all. You therefore should not use this disk configuration with SQL Server Express because it is used only for performance reasons.

Optimizing Network Performance

Both the network card in the SQL Server and the network bandwidth are important factors in your application's performance. The server should contain a 32- or 64-bit bus-mastering network card. You should use 1GB versus 100MB ethernet network cards whenever possible. You can also consider other fast networking technologies. The bottom line is that the best hardware and the best designed database do you no good on a slow, overtaxed network.

How to Configure and Tune SQL Server

If you do not configure the server properly, all the hardware in the world and the best designed database mean nothing. Processor options, memory options, I/O options, and query and index options all enable you to designate the most appropriate server configuration for you. Although most of the time you leave these options at their default values, it is useful to know what configuration options are available to you.

Memory Options

You can designate the minimum and maximum memory used by SQL Server. You can also specify the minimum memory allocated to each user for each query run. You should generally not modify any of the memory options. SQL Server does an excellent job of allocating and deallocating memory on its own. The only time you would want to modify these options is if you are running SQL Server on the same machine as another highly memory-intensive application, such as Microsoft Exchange Server. It's a good idea to run SQL Server on a dedicated machine where this is not a problem. If you must modify the SQL Server memory options, follow these steps:

1. Right-click the server you want to affect, and select Properties. The Server Properties dialog appears (see Figure 23.1).

FIGURE 23.1
The Server Properties dialog contains pages that enable you to modify various properties of your SQL Server.

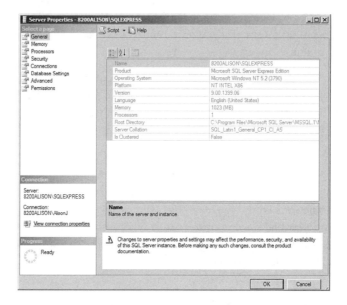

2. Click to select the Memory page (see Figure 23.2).

3. Modify the options as desired.

FIGURE 23.2
The Memory page of the SQL Server Properties dialog box enables you to set memory options.

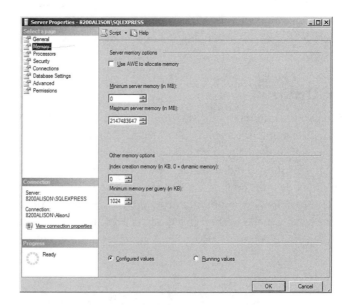

Processor Options

You can configure the way in which SQL Server uses your server's processors. The configuration options available include the following:

▶ You can configure the relative priority of the SQL Server process.

▶ You can determine which of the server's CPUs SQL Server will use.

▶ You can designate the total number of operating system threads that SQL Server can use on your computer.

▶ You can set the maximum number of CPUs used by parallel query operations.

To modify the processor-related properties, follow these steps:

1. Right-click the server you want to affect, and select Properties.

2. The Server Properties dialog appears.

3. Click to select the Processors page. The dialog appears as in Figure 23.3.

4. Modify the options as desired.

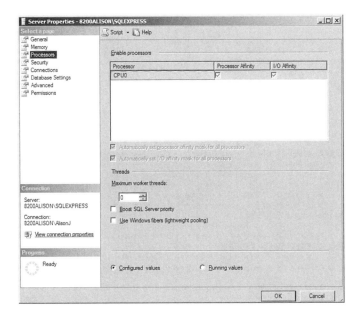

FIGURE 23.3
The Processors page of the Server Properties dialog enables you to modify processor-related properties of your SQL Server.

Security Options

You will usually work with Security options when establishing a SQL Server. Options available include what type of authentication you want on the server (Windows Authentication or SQL Server and Windows Authentication) and what type of login auditing you want to perform when user logins are unsuccessful.

To modify Security options for the server, follow these steps:

1. Right-click the server you want to affect, and select Properties.

2. The Server Properties dialog appears.

3. Click to select the Security page. The dialog appears as in Figure 23.4.

4. Modify the options as desired.

FIGURE 23.4
The Security page of the Server Properties dialog enables you to modify security-related properties of your SQL Server.

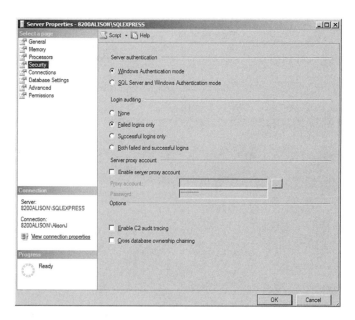

Connections Options

The Connections options enable you to determine the maximum number of concurrent connections that the server will allow, as well as whether the server will allow remote connections. Other options are available as well.

To modify Connections options for the server, follow these steps:

1. Right-click the server you want to affect, and select Properties.

2. The Server Properties dialog appears.

3. Click to select the Connections page. The dialog appears as in Figure 23.5.

4. Modify the options as desired.

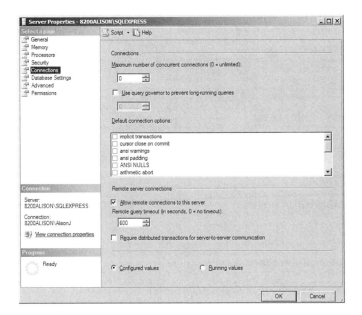

FIGURE 23.5
The Connections page of the Server Properties dialog enables you to modify connection-related properties of your SQL Server.

Database Settings Options

The Database Setting page of the Server Properties dialog enables you to alter settings that impact the databases on that server. For example, you can set the default locations for database and log files, and you can set the default index file factor.

To modify Database Settings options for the server, follow these steps:

1. Right-click the server you want to affect, and select Properties.

2. The Server Properties dialog appears.

3. Click to select the Database Settings page. The dialog appears as in Figure 23.6.

4. Modify the options as desired.

FIGURE 23.6
The Database
Settings page of
the Server
Properties dia-
log enables you
to modify data-
base-related
properties of
your SQL
Server.

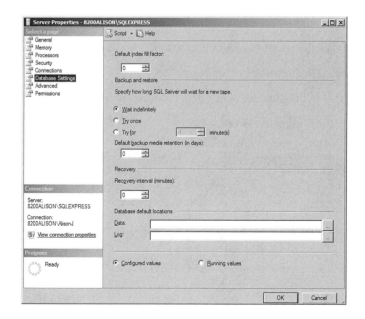

Advanced Options

The Advanced Options page of the Server Properties dialog enables you to configure
various server options. These include where triggers can fire other triggers, the two-
digit year cutoff, and much more.

To modify Advanced options for the server, follow these steps:

1. Right-click the server you want to affect, and select Properties.

2. The Server Properties dialog appears.

3. Click to select the Advanced page. The dialog appears as in Figure 23.7.

4. Modify the options as desired.

Permissions Options

The Permissions page of the Server Properties dialog enables you to modify permissions that relate to the server (not to a particular database). Here you can add and
remove logins and roles to and from the server. You can also Grant, With Grant,
and Deny server-related rights to logins and roles. Server-related rights include
whether the user or role can alter any database, whether the user or role can alter
any login, and much more.

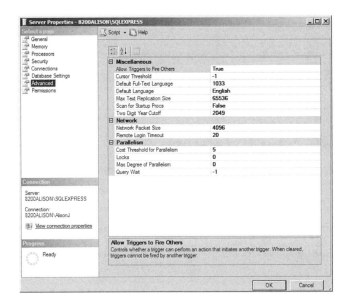

FIGURE 23.7
The Options page of the Server Properties dialog enables you to modify various properties of your SQL Server.

To modify Permissions options for the server, follow these steps:

1. Right-click the server you want to affect, and select Properties.

2. The Server Properties dialog appears.

3. Click to select the Permissions page. The dialog appears as in Figure 23.8.

4. Modify the options as desired.

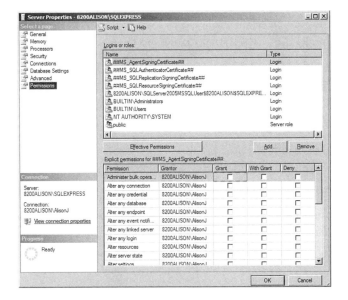

FIGURE 23.8
The Permissions page of the Server Properties dialog enables you to modify permission-related properties of your SQL Server.

How to Maintain Your Databases

If your data is important to you, it is imperative that you maintain your databases properly. Database maintenance generally includes backing up your database and auditing database access. It is also important that you understand how to restore a database in the case of a failure.

Backing Up Your Databases

Think of backing up your database like brushing your teeth. It is something that you don't think about; you just do it unequivocally each and every day, *without exception*! Two types of backups are available:

- **Full database backups**—Back up the entire database and portions of the log.

- **Differential database backups**—Back up data modified since the last backup.

You need to decide which backup option is appropriate for you. This depends on how much information is changed each day, as well as how critical the information is to you. For example, if the data is changed throughout the day and is mission-critical, you should perform a full database backup daily and then back up the transaction log hourly.

SQL Server offers three recovery models:

- **Full**—Offers full protection. With this option, you are able to restore all committed transactions. The database and the log are both backed up.

- **Bulk Logged**—Offers *minimal* data recovery. With this option, logging is minimal. You get the best performance and use the least amount of memory.

- **Simple**—In the case of failure, loses all data modified since the last backup. With this option, you can recover data only as of the last backup.

To select a recovery model, follow these steps:

1. Right-click the database for which you want to establish the recovery model and select Properties. The Database Properties dialog box appears.

2. Click the Options page.

3. Open the Recovery model drop-down list and select the appropriate recovery model (see Figure 23.9).

4. Click OK to close the Properties dialog box and save your changes.

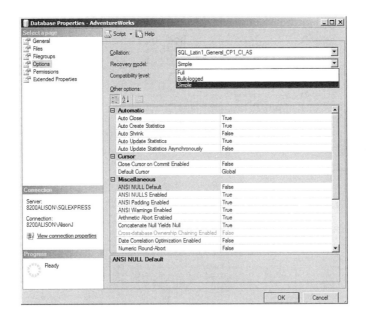

FIGURE 23.9
The Recovery model drop-down list on the Options page enables you to select the appropriate recovery model.

To perform a backup, follow these steps:

1. Right-click the database that you want to back up and select Tasks, Back Up. The Back Up Database dialog box appears (see Figure 23.10).

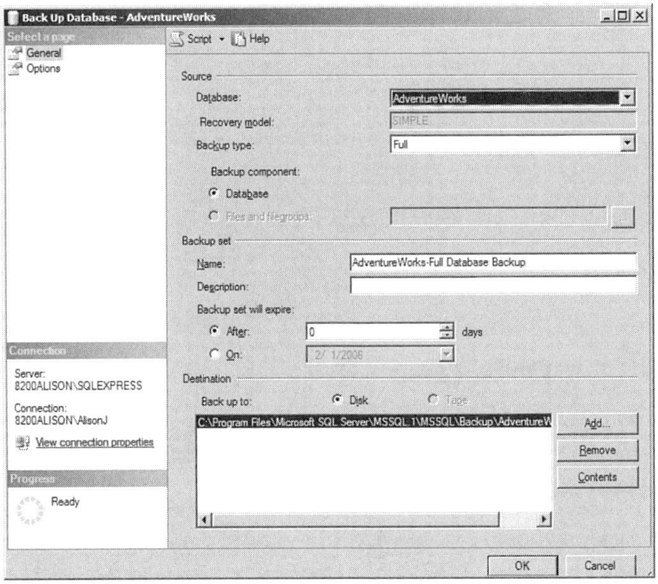

FIGURE 23.10
The Backup Database dialog box enables you to designate information about the backup.

2. Designate which database you want to back up, the name for the backup, and an optional description for the backup.

3. Use the Backup Type drop-down to indicate whether you want to perform a full or a differential backup.

4. Click Add or Remove to designate the filename and location for the backup.

5. Click the Options page to designate additional backup options (see Figure 23.11). For example, you can designate whether you want SQL Server to verify the backup on completion.

FIGURE 23.11
The Options page of the Backup Database dialog box enables you to designate additional backup options.

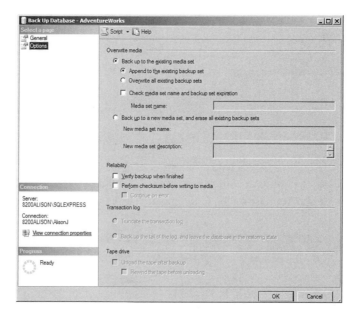

5. Designate whether you want to append to or overwrite the existing media.

6. Click OK to complete the process.

Restoring a Database

Restoring a database is similar to backing it up. You can restore a database to itself (overwrites the existing database), to another existing database, or to a new database. To restore a database, follow these steps:

1. Right-click the database that you want to restore and select Tasks, Restore, Database. The Restore Database dialog box appears (see Figure 23.12).

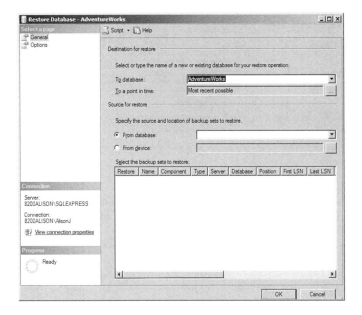

FIGURE 23.12
The Restore Database dialog box enables you to designate information about the restore process.

2. Designate whether you want to restore from a database or from a device.

3. If you click From Device and then click the Build button, the Specify Backup dialog box, shown in Figure 23.13, appears. Here you can designate the backup location.

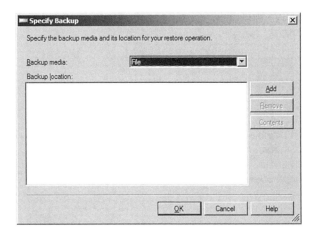

FIGURE 23.13
The Restore Database dialog box with From Device selected.

3. Click the Options page to designate the restore options (see Figure 23.14).

FIGURE 23.14
The Options
page of the
Restore
Database dialog
box enables you
to designate
additional
restore options.

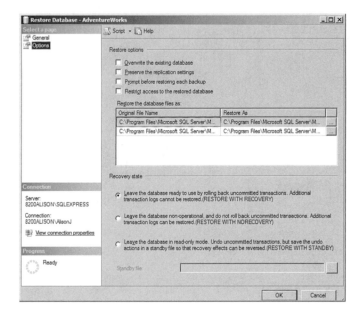

4. Designate whether you want to overwrite the existing database. If you do not select this option and you attempt to restore to an existing database, SQL Server returns an error.

5. Designate the logical and physical filenames for the database and the log file. If you are restoring from one machine to another and the machines have different directory structures, you need to change the physical filename to reflect the appropriate directory structure.

6. Indicate the recovery completion state.

7. Click OK to perform the restore process.

By the Way

It is important to be aware of who has rights to your database and what rights they have. You should periodically review users and their rights to ensure that only authorized individuals can access the database and that they can perform only the intended and necessary tasks.

How to Maintain Tables and Other Objects

You should perform certain audits periodically on the tables and other objects in your database. The main things that you should keep track of are the record count and who has access to an object.

Generally, the amount of data that a table should contain is fairly predictable. It's usually a good idea to keep an eye on the number of records in each table. If the number of records exceeds your limit, you should consider archiving the extra data.

Just as it is important to keep an eye on who has been granted access to the database, it is important to keep track of what permissions users and roles have for each object.

Summary

The best-designed system will fail to meet users' needs if it performs poorly. The first line of attack when attempting to optimize performance is to ensure that the hardware on which SQL Server runs is adequate for the job at hand. As soon as all the proper hardware is in place, you must determine that you have properly configured the SQL Server software. After you configure your hardware and the SQL Server software, you must make sure that you take all the steps to maintain the server properly. In case things go awry, you must implement and test a backup and restore procedure.

Q&A

Q. *Why is memory so important to a SQL Server?*

A. SQL Server uses memory to hold all data pages, index pages, and log records. It also uses memory to hold compiled queries and stored procedures.

Q. *Explain some of the security options available.*

A. Using the Security page of the Server Properties dialog, you can change the type of authentication that you want to allow (Windows only versus Windows and SQL Server). You can also determine what type of logging SQL Serve will perform when logins are unsuccessful.

Q. *Name and describe the three recovery models.*

A. The Full recovery model enables you to restore all committed transactions. With this option, SQL Server backs up both the database and the log file. With the Bulk Logged recovery model, logging is minimal. You get the best performance while using the least memory, but with the minimal recovery. The Simple recovery model loses all data since the last backup. With this model you can recover data only as of the last backup.

Workshop

Quiz

1. Name four things you can do to your hardware to improve performance of your SQL Server.

2. Using the Memory page of the Server Properties dialog, you can configure the relative priority of the SQL Server process (true/false).

3. Name two types of database backups.

4. Using the Processor options page of the Server Properties dialog, you can determine which of the server's CPUs SQL Server will use (true/false).

5. The Permissions page of the Server Properties dialog box enables you to modify database permissions (true/false).

Quiz Answers

1. More memory, more processors, RAID array, faster network.

2. False. Using the Processor options page of the Server Properties dialog, you can configure the relative priority of the SQL Server process.

3. Full database backups and differential database backups.

4. True.

5. False. The Permissions page of the Server Properties dialog box enables you to modify server-related permissions.

Activities

View the various pages of the Server Properties dialog. When you are finished, back up the AdventureWorks database. Then restore the database.

Performance Monitoring

It is important that you build SQL statements that will execute efficiently. Fortunately, SQL Server Management Studio Express provides you with the tools to analyze your SQL statements and ensure that you have built them as efficiently as possible. In this hour you'll learn about:

- ▶ How to execute queries in SQL Server Management Studio Express
- ▶ How to display and analyze the estimated execution plan for a query
- ▶ How to add indexes to allow queries to execute more efficiently
- ▶ How to set query options

Executing Queries in SQL Server Management Studio Express

SQL Server 2000 provided a tool called the Query Analyzer. This tool is now built into SQL Server Management Studio Express. You can use this tool to execute and analyze queries that you want to place in stored procedures and views. To execute a query, follow these steps:

1. Click the New Query button on the toolbar (see Figure 24.1). A new query window appears where you can type a SQL statement (see Figure 24.2).

2. Type the desired SQL statement (see Figure 24.3).

3. Click the Execute button on the toolbar to execute the query. The results appear as in Figure 24.4.

4. Click the Messages tab to view any messages associated with the execution of the query (see Figure 24.5).

FIGURE 24.1
Click the New
Query button on
the toolbar to
create a new
query.

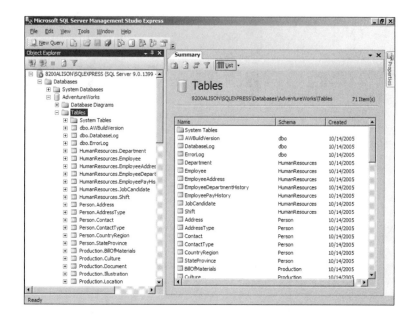

FIGURE 24.2
You use the
query window to
type the SQL
statement
you want to
execute.

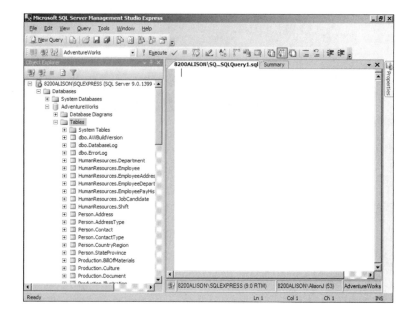

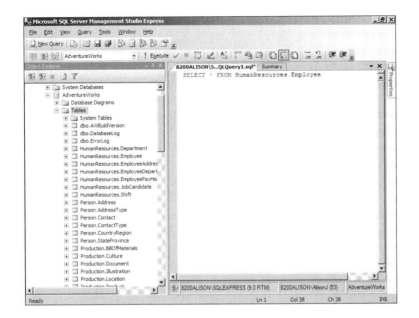

FIGURE 24.3
Type the desired SQL statement in the Query window.

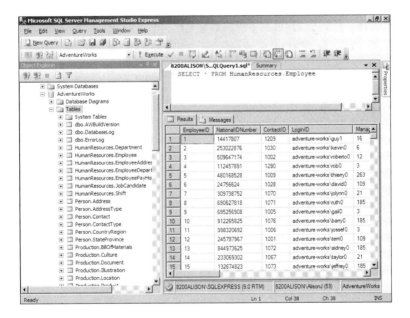

FIGURE 24.4
After executing the query, the results appear in the Results pane of the Query window.

FIGURE 24.5
The Messages
tab of the
Results pane
shows you any
messages asso-
ciated with the
execution of
the query.

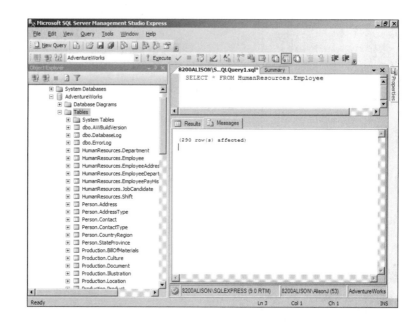

Displaying and Analyzing the Estimated Execution Plan for a Query

It's unlikely that you will just want to execute queries in SQL Server Management Studio Express. You also will want analyze those queries to see whether they are executing as efficiently as possible. To analyze a query, follow these steps:

1. Click the New Query button on the toolbar. A new query window appears where you can type a SQL statement.

2. Type the desired SQL statement.

3. Click Display Estimated Execution Plan. Your screen appears as in Figure 24.6.

4. Hover your mouse pointer over the various steps in the execution plan. You get more information about each step in the execution plan (see Figures 24.7 and 24.8).

5. If you want to display the execution plan each time that you execute the query, click the Include Actual Execution Plan button on the toolbar. The Execution Plan tab appears each time you execute the query (see Figure 24.9).

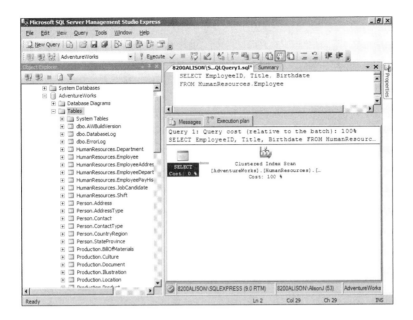

FIGURE 24.6
After clicking the Display Estimated Execution Plan toolbar button, you can see the execution plan for the query.

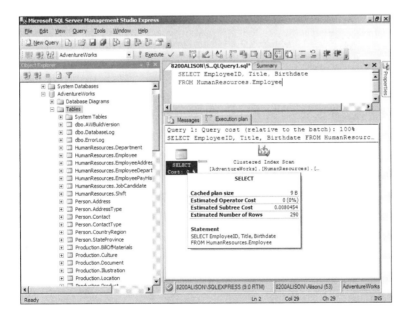

FIGURE 24.7
If you hover your mouse pointer over each step of the execution plan, you get information about that step in the execution plan.

FIGURE 24.8
Notice that in the example SQL Server Express is using a clustered index scan when executing the SQL statement.

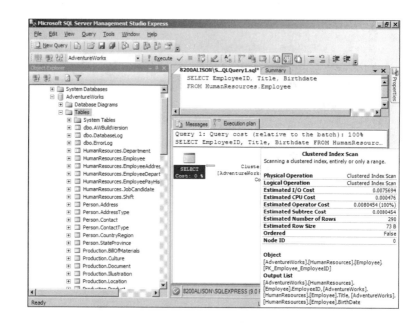

FIGURE 24.9
If you click the Include Actual Execution Plan button on the toolbar, the Execution Plan tab appears each time you execute the query.

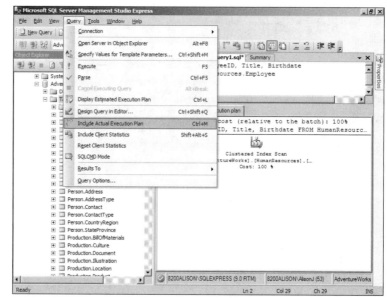

6. To include client statistics each time that you execute the query, click the Include Client Statistic button on the toolbar. After you execute the query, the Client Statistics tab appears as in Figure 24.10. Here you can receive valuable

statistical information about the execution of the query. For example, you can determine the number of round trips the client made to the server in executing the query.

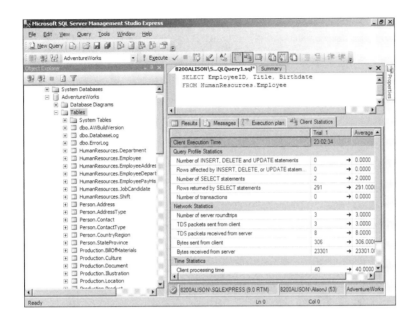

FIGURE 24.10
If you click the Include Client Statistics button on the toolbar, the Client Statistics tab appears each time that you run a query.

Adding Indexes to Enable Queries to Execute More Efficiently

The easiest way to improve the efficiency of the queries that you build is to add indexes to the underlying tables. You can view the results of your efforts easily by using the Execution Plan tab and the Client Statistics tab after the query has executed. Follow these steps:

1. Make sure that you have both the Include Actual Execution Plan and Include Client Statistics toolbar buttons selected.

2. Execute a query and order by a field on which there is no index (see Figure 24.11).

3. Click the Execution Plan tab. Notice that the execution plan includes a sort (see Figure 24.12). A sort is very inefficient when executing a query.

FIGURE 24.11
This query is ordered by LineTotal, for which there is no index.

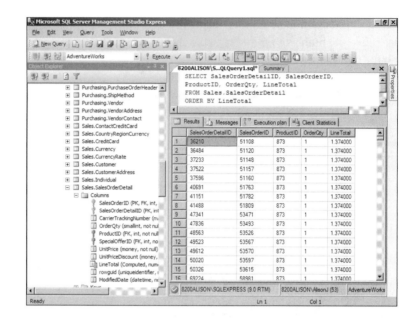

FIGURE 24.12
Notice that the execution plan for the query includes a sort.

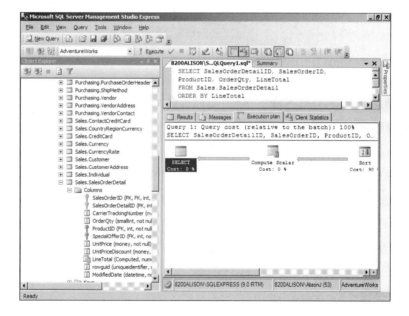

4. Click the Client Statistics tab and note the Total execution time so that you can compare it to the optimized query.

5. Create an index on the field by which you are ordering (see Figure 24.13) .

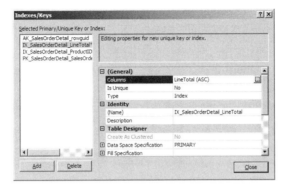

FIGURE 24.13
Create an index based on LineTotal.

6. Execute the query again.

7. Compare the Execution Plan tab. Notice that the execution plan no longer includes a sort and instead includes a bookmark lookup (see Figure 24.14).

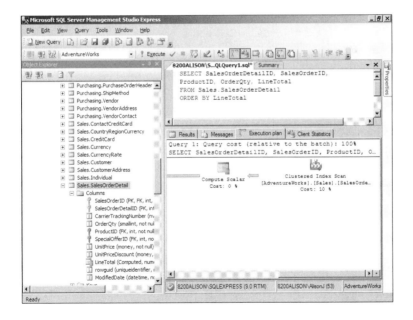

8. Compare the Client Statistics tab and note the Total execution time. It should be less than the one without an index.

Setting Query Options

SQL Server Management Studio Express provides you with a plethora of options that you can use to affect how your queries process. To access and modify these options, follow these steps:

1. Select Query Options from the Query Menu. The Query Options dialog appears (see Figure 24.15).

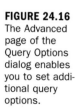
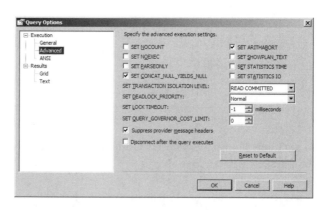

2. Using the General page, you can set options such as determining the maximum number of rows that SQL Server returns before stopping. This valuable setting ensures that you don't accidentally execute a query that returns millions of rows.

3. Using the Advanced page (see Figure 24.16), you can set additional options. An example is the SET NOCOUNT setting. When turned on, SQL Server refrains from returning the number of rows processed. This improves the performance of your queries.

FIGURE 24.16
The Advanced page of the Query Options dialog enables you to set additional query options.

4. The ANSI page (see Figure 24.17) enables you to set some of the SQL-92 standard query execution behavior, such as how SQL Server handles nulls.

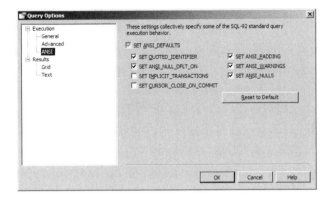

FIGURE 24.17
The ANSI page
of the Query
Options dialog
allows you to
set some of the
SQL-92 standard query execution behavior.

5. The Grid page (see Figure 24.18) of the Query Options dialog enables you to affect how SQL Server displays the output from the query.

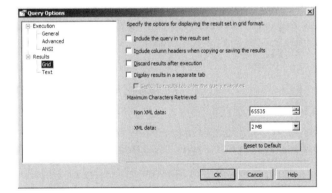

FIGURE 24.18
The Grid page
of the Query
Options dialog
enables you to
affect how SQL
Server displays
the output from
the query.

6. The Text page (see Figure 24.19) of the Query Options dialog enables you to set the options that apply when you opt to display the result set in text format, or to redirect it to an output file.

FIGURE 24.19
The Text page of the Query Options dialog enables you to set options that affect you when you display the result set as text.

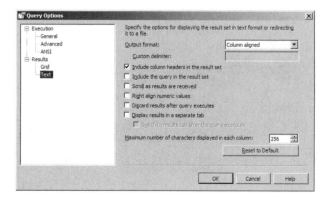

Summary

Learning how to create queries can be moderately difficult. Learning to create efficient queries is even more difficult. In this hour you learned how you can use SQL Server Management Studio Express to design and test the queries that you will include in your stored procedures, triggers, functions, and other objects that use T-SQL. You saw how you can use the tools built into Management Studio to display and analyze the estimated execution plan for a query. Finally, you learned how to add indexes so that queries can execute more efficiently, and how to set query options.

Q&A

Q. *Name the query analysis tool that shipped with SQL 2000, and compare it to what is available in SQL Server 2005 Express.*

A. SQL Server 2000 provided a tool called the Query Analyzer. This tool is now built into SQL Server Management Studio Express.

Q. *Explain why you will probably want to analyze the queries that you include in your stored procedures, functions, etc.*

A. Using the analysis tools built into SQL Server Management Studio Express, you can analyze your T-SQL statements to ensure that they execute as efficiently as possible. You can modify your queries at will, and observe the effect that those changes have on performance.

Workshop

Quiz

1. Name the tool on the toolbar that enables you to run the query that you type into the query window.

2. Name the tool on the toolbar that enables you to view the execution plan each time that you run a query.

3. Name the tool on the toolbar that enables you to view client statistics when you run your queries.

4. What is the most important thing that you can do to improve query execution?

5. By setting NOCOUNT to off, you are optimizing performance by ensuring the row count is not returned (true/false).

Quiz Answers

1. New Query.

2. Include Actual Execution Plan.

3. Include client statistics.

4. Add indexes.

5. False. By setting NOCOUNT to on, you are ensuring that the row count is not returned.

Activities

Build a query based on the Sales.SalesOrderDetail table. Display the SalesOrderID, OrderQty, UnitPrice, and LineTotal, ordering the data by LineTotal. Execute the query. Notice the number of rows affected on the Messages page. Indicate that you want to view both the execution plan and the client statistics. Run the query again. View the results in both the Execution Plan tab and the Client Statistics tab. Add an index based on LineTotal. Re-execute the query, noting the differences in the execution plan and client statistics. Finally, go into Query Options and click to set NOCOUNT on. Run your query again and notice that the number of rows affected no longer appears in the Messages pane.

APPENDIX A

Using the NorthWind Sample Database File

Many of the examples in this book utilize a sample database called NorthWind. You can download this database from `http://www.microsoft.com/downloads/details.aspx?FamilyID=06616212-0356-46A0-8DA2-EEBC53A68034&displaylang=en`. In this appendix you'll learn:

▶ What you need to about installing the sample file

▶ How to attach to the sample NorthWind database file

What You Need to Know About Installing the Sample Database Files

The download process will create a file called SQL2000SampleDb.msi. Here are the steps that you must take to install the NorthWind sample database:

1. Locate the SQL2000SampleDb.msi file in the location to which you downloaded it.

2. Double click the SQL2000SampleDb.msi file. This will launch the Setup Wizard.

3. Click Next to continue. The License Agreement appears.

4. Click "I Agree" and then click Next. The Choose Installation Options step of the wizard appears (see Figure A.1).

5. Click Next. The Confirm Installation step of the wizard appears.

6. Click Next to start the installation.

7. After the installation is complete, click Close to exit the wizard.

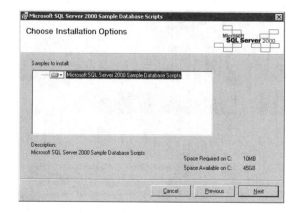

Attaching to the NorthWind Sample Database File

Once you have installed the sample files you must make SQL Server aware of them by using a process called "attaching to the database file." Here are the steps involved:

1. Open up Microsoft SQL Server Management Studio Express.

2. Right-click the Databases node and select Attach. The Attach Databases dialog appears (see Figure A.2).

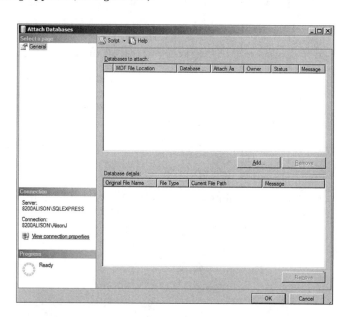

3. Click the Add command button. The Locate Database Files dialog appears (see Figure A.3).

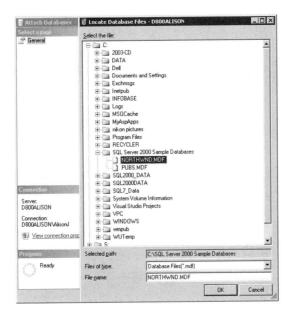

FIGURE A.3
The Locate Database Files dialog allows you to locate and select the database file to which you want to attach.

4. Locate the NorthWind database in the location to which the installation process copied the file. By default this location is c:\SQL Server 2000 Sample Databases.

5. Click to select the NorthWind database.

6. Click OK to close the dialog. You have returned to the Attach Databases dialog, which appears in Figure A.4. Note: If the log file is in the same location as the database file, there is no need to separately locate the log file.

7. Click OK to complete the process. The NorthWind database now appears in the list of databases available on the server (see Figure A.5).

FIGURE A.4
The Attach Databases dialog contains all of the information required to complete the attachment process.

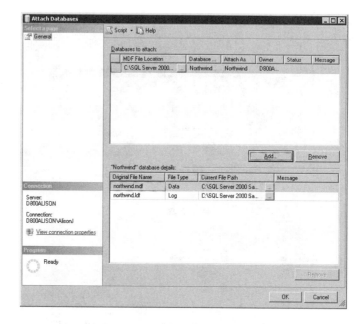

FIGURE A.5
After attaching to a database file, it appears as one of the files available under the Databases node of that server.

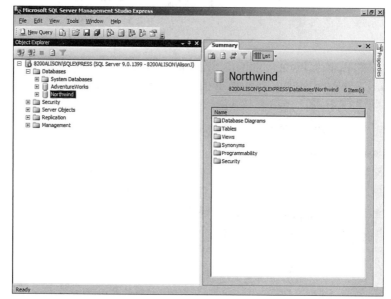

Index

Setting Next Statement button (Debug toolbar), 338

Step Into button (Debug toolbar), 334-335

Step Out button (Debug toolbar), 338

Step Over button (Debug toolbar), 337

Watch expressions, 341-344

executing until next breakpoint, 336

Column Permissions dialog (Permissions page), 383

columns (tables). *See also* fields (tables), 9

computed (tables), 70

identity (tables), 69

permissions, 382-384

Table and Column Specifications, foreign key table relationships, 88-89

Command objects (ADO.NET)

databases

data retrieval SQL statement example, 229-230

update SQL statement example, 232

methods, 229

properties, 228

single row/column retrieval SQL statement example, 230-231

COMMIT TRANSACTION statements, stored procedures, 209-210

Completing Microsoft SQL Server 2005 Setup step (SQL Server 2005 Express Edition installation), 34-35

Completing the Microsoft SQL Server Management Studio Express Setup step (SQL Server Management Studio Express installation), 37

composite keys, 11

computed columns (tables), 70

Connect to Server dialog (SQL Server Management Studio Express), 37

Connection objects (ADO.NET), 224

ConnectionString property usage example, 227-228

SQL Server Security SQL server connection example, 226-227

Windows NT Security SQL server connection example, 225-226

connection pooling, 226

connections options (SQL Server configurations), 393

Connections page (Server Properties dialog), 393

ConnectionString property, usage example (ADO.NET), 227-228

constraints (tables), 64-69

CONTROL permissions, 378

Convert function, views, 165

COUNT functions, 115

COUNT_BIG functions, 116

Credentials node, 47

D

DAO (Data Access Objects), data access development, 223

data access, development of, 223-224

data recovery, 396

data types

fields, tables, 62-64

user-defined (tables), 71-72

DataAdapter objects (ADO.NET), 235-236

Database Access tab (Login Properties dialog), 356

Database Creators (dbcreator) fixed-server roles, 357

Database Diagrams node

New Database Diagram dialog, 82-85

Remove from Diagram command, 86

Database node (SQL Server Management Studio Express), 43

Attach Databases dialog, 55

Database Role dialog, 363-364

Database Role Properties dialog, 361-362

Database User dialog, 370

database

attaching to existing databases, 55

creating, 49, 52-54

Master database, 44

Model database, 44-45

MSDB database, 45

TempDB database, 45

Database Properties dialog, 396

Database Role dialog (Database node), 363-364

Database Role Properties dialog (Database node), 361-362

database settings options (SQL Server configurations), 393

Database Settings page (Server Properties dialog), 393

Database User dialog

Database node, 370

Properties node, Securables page, 374-377

databases

backups, 396-397

basics of, 7

client-server databases, components of, 7

defining, 7

design masters, synchronization, 48

diagrams, basics of, 17

login access, granting, 355-356

databases